Gypsies, Roma and Travellers

A CONTEMPORARY ANALYSIS

Other books you may be interested in:

Young Refugees and Asylum Seekers: The Truth About Britain
By Declan Henry   ISBN 978-1-913063-97-9

Dilemmas and Decision Making in Social Work
By Abbi Jackson   ISBN 978-1-914171-20-8

Social Work and Covid-19: Lessons for Education and Practice
Edited by Denise Turner   ISBN 978-1-913453-61-9

Out of the Shadows: The Role of Social Workers in Disasters
Edited by Angie Bartoli, Maris Stratulis and Rebekah Pierre   ISBN 978-1-915080-07-3

The Anti-racist Social Worker: Stories of Activism by Social Care and Allied Health Professionals
Edited by Tanya Moore and Glory Simango   ISBN 978-1-914171-41-3

To order, or for details of our bulk discounts, please go to our website www.criticalpublishing.com or contact our distributor Ingram Publisher Services (IPS UK), 10 Thornbury Road, Plymouth PL6 7PP, telephone 01752 202301 or email IPSUK@ingramcontent.com

Gypsies, Roma and Travellers

A CONTEMPORARY ANALYSIS

Declan Henry

CRITICAL PUBLISHING

First published in 2022 by Critical Publishing Ltd

All rights reserved. No part of this publication may be reproduced, stored in a retrieval system, or transmitted in any form or by any means, electronic, mechanical, photocopying, recording or otherwise, without prior permission in writing from the publisher.

Copyright © 2022 Declan Henry

British Library Cataloguing in Publication Data
A CIP record for this book is available from the British Library

ISBN: 978-1-915080-04-2

This book is also available in the following e-book formats:
EPUB ISBN: 978-1-915080-05-9
Adobe e-book ISBN: 978-1-915080-06-6

The right of Declan Henry to be identified as the Author of this work has been asserted by him in accordance with the Copyright, Design and Patents Act 1988.

Cover design by Out of House Ltd
Text design by Greensplash
Project management by Newgen Publishing UK
Printed and bound in Great Britain by 4edge, Essex

Critical Publishing
3 Connaught Road
St Albans
AL3 5RX

www.criticalpublishing.com

Printed on FSC accredited paper

Disclaimer

The names of persons interviewed for this book have been changed, when requested. In some cases, other details have also been changed in order to protect identities and to ensure the confidentiality and anonymity of interviewees is maintained.

Dedicated to Adrian, Adam and Abigail

Contents

	About the author	*ix*
	Acknowledgements	*x*
	Foreword by Allison Hulmes	*xii*
	Introduction	1
Chapter 1	Context setting	3
Chapter 2	Romany Gypsies	25
Chapter 3	Roma	47
Chapter 4	Irish Travellers	71
Chapter 5	Health	91
Chapter 6	Education	103
Chapter 7	Religion	115
Chapter 8	Crime	131
Chapter 9	Discrimination	151
Chapter 10	LGBT issues	165
	Epilogue	*176*
	References and suggested reading	*181*
	Useful contacts	*185*
	Index	*192*

About the author

Declan Henry is a creative non-fiction writer and comes from a distinguished academic background. He studied at two of London's elite universities – Goldsmiths and King's College. He holds a Bachelor of Arts (Honours) degree in Education and Community Studies and a Master of Science degree in Mental Health Social Work. Declan is a registered social worker and is the author of eight books (including this book), two booklets and numerous published articles. He is the bronze winner of the 2017 Independent Publisher Book Award in the LGBT non-fiction list for his book *Trans Voices: Becoming Who You Are*. Declan has written on a wide range of diverse topics, including mental health, young refugees and asylum seekers, transgender people, Islam, suicide prevention and young offenders. He is also a reviewer for the *New York Journal of Books*. Declan was born in County Sligo in the Irish Republic and now lives in Kent. www.declanhenry.co.uk

Acknowledgements

There are a great number of people who I would like to say thank you to for helping me with my research for this book.

Firstly, I would like to pay tribute to all the GRT people who contributed their stories or had some verbal input into my research. Their resilience, enthusiasm and good humour made a lasting good impression upon me.

Secondly, I would like to single out the following professional people who spoke to me in a private capacity for their time and knowledge: Wanda Barnard, Rebecca Street, Gillie Heath, Lak Khaira, Sarah Irving, Izaak Botton, Andrew McCormack, Kiren Rehal, Daniel Baker, Thomas Acton, Caitriona Kelly and Priya Mendez.

Thirdly, I would like to extend thanks to the numerous professionals within GRT agencies in the UK who assisted me, including: Mattey Mitchell (Friends, Families & Travellers), Chris McDonagh (Friends, Families & Travellers), Mia Hasenson-Gross (Executive Director, René Cassin), Dr Carol Rogers (Buckinghamshire New University), Dr Lucie Fremlova (author and independent researcher), Greg Sproston (Traveller Movement), Aluna Lepadatu (Roma Luton Trust), Assen Slavchev (Roma Luton Trust), Dezider Horvath and Andrea Jackova (Romani Slovak Czech Community, Kent), Dr Anthony Drummond (Leeds Beckett University), Lynne Tammi (University of Dundee) and Claire Rice (GATE Herts).

Special thanks also to professionals within GRT agencies in Ireland who assisted me, including: Caoimhe McCabe (Pavee Point), Bernard Sweeney (TraVision), Grainne Fennell (Southside Travellers), Ellena Costello (Irish Chaplaincy), Joleen Kuyper (Roma worker at the Donegal Travellers Project), Siobhan McLoughlin, Ann Friel and Annie Mongan (Donegal Travellers Project), Oein De Bhairduin and Jacinta Brack (Irish Traveller Movement), Gerard Griffin (National Co-ordinator, Youthreach Ireland), Thomas McCann (Traveller Counselling Service), Chris McDonagh (Traveller Mediation Service), Vivienne Ivers (Galway Traveller Movement), Alice McDowell (Galway Misleór Festival) and Leona Collins (Offaly Travellers Movement).

Many thanks to my contacts in Eastern Europe, including Ion Bucur (European Roma Rights Centre, Moldova) and Juliet Ory in Romania.

I would also like to offer special appreciation to Trish Nolan, Irish vocalist and multi-instrumental artist, who allowed me to include a verse of her song 'Broken Lines' in the chapter on Irish Travellers. Much appreciation also to Robert Dawson, author of

Gypsy Traveller Folk Tales, who kindly allowed me to use my abbreviated version of his compilation of the folk story 'Four Tasks and Mother Hedgehog'.

Many thanks also to Allison Hulmes from the British Association of Social Workers (BASW), who has kindly written the foreword to the book for me.

Last but by no means least, let me say a big thank you to Di Page (Director at Critical Publishing) and her team for all their wonderful guidance and support.

Foreword

I was honoured to be asked to write the foreword to this important and much needed book by Declan Henry. I am especially pleased, as Declan is a social worker whose writing is clearly rooted in our international codes of ethics and social work values.

Any book that contains the powerful and raw words *'Gypsies and Travellers are Britain's internal refugees – shunned and abandoned by their country of birth... through racism, prejudice and poverty'* has got right to the heart of the lived and living experiences of Gypsy, Traveller and Roma people in the UK today. It is an honest book which delves into areas that have previously been viewed as 'off limits', and Declan Henry is able to do this because his approach is rooted in integrity.

It is a thoroughly researched book which is illuminated by direct testimony; I have, in fact, seldom read a book about the diverse communities which contains such a high degree of direct testimony, amplifying the richness, strengths and also the complexity which lie beneath the catch-all acronym GRT. This is a real skill; Declan has clearly created safe spaces, allowing the book to be filled by three-dimensional characters who leap up from the pages. This direct testimony is handled with empathy and respectful curiosity and gives unparalleled access to the real lives, feelings, perspectives, hopes and fears of Gypsies, Roma and Travellers – they are telling their own stories in much the same way as the oral tradition, which has been the primary means of communicating for centuries.

The testimonies also manage to capture some of the tensions between elders and younger generations when trying to protect ethnic identity and culture, while also wanting to access the same opportunities and choices as gorgers (people who are not Gypsies and Travellers). Declan has shed light on the impact this has on the health and well-being – particularly mental health – of all Gypsies and Travellers, irrespective of age or gender.

The book helpfully sets out to bust many of the myths and stereotypes – from the romanticised to the misunderstood – which only serve to perpetuate racism and discrimination. Declan roots this racism firmly at the door of structural and societal oppression and not at the feet of Gypsy, Traveller and Roma people. He challenges the reader to question their own internal biases and perspectives and helpfully includes lists of clear and unambiguous 'Truths' which we need to see spelt out in writing if we are to shift the stubborn, prejudicial mindsets which persist, even in some of those who espouse anti-racist views.

Declan Henry does not pull his punches or baulk from tackling the big concerns and taboos impacting on the lives of Gypsy, Traveller and Roma people – such as domestic abuse, suicide, criminal justice, shame and LGBT issues – and nor should he. We need to shine a light on what's happening, to challenge the stereotypes around these taboos and prevent this epidemic of grief and loss, which is often associated with these issues and threatens to overwhelm the communities.

The need for the general public, policy makers and professionals who support the communities to fully understand the distinct histories, cultural practices and challenges faced by Gypsy, Roma and Traveller people is vital. Declan sets out why this is important – it's important because the needs of each of the ethnic groups are distinct to them – so targeted health, education and social care services that are based around ethnicity data need to be disaggregated to reflect, capture, and then respond to, the distinct needs of each of the ethnic groups. As of 2022, ethnicity data is not disaggregated, and Roma people have only been able to self-identify since the 2021 census.

This book has an important role in helping the public, policy makers and those who directly support Gypsy, Roma and Traveller people. In Chapters 2–4, Declan clearly sets out the distinctions between each of the ethnic groups. He even drills further into the differences beneath the overarching descriptors of 'Gypsy, Roma and Traveller' to highlight that Roma can also be Jewish or Muslim, that Gypsies can be Romanichal or Kale and a multitude of other tribes or clans which are central to ethnic identity and cultural practices. The different ethnicities may share similar experiences of oppression and discrimination, but their origins, history, culture, values and norms are particular to each of the ethnic groups. How each of the ethnic groups is supported has to be nuanced and not a 'one-size-fits-all' approach which we too often see.

It's refreshing to see a book on Gypsy, Traveller and Roma people dealing with the experiences of LGBT Gypsy, Traveller and Roma people. Without taking an intersectional lens, we perpetuate the discrimination and suffering of LGBT people in our communities and deny them their fundamental human rights to exist as whole people. Experiences of guilt and shame already cast a long and damaging shadow within each of the communities and this is often rooted in the fundamental religious beliefs held by many community members and traditional attitudes around what constitutes a family. Being lesbian, gay, bisexual or transgender adds further layers to these experiences of guilt and shame that shouldn't be allowed to exist, and which often leads to rejection by family and community. We need to hear the stories of LGBT community members and understand how best to support them, in a way that they are in control of, because they have been taking control of their own grassroots movements for emancipation.

As community members, we also need to take ownership of the harm we visit on our children if we do not love, support and accept them in their entirety.

If you really want to understand who Gypsy, Traveller and Roma people are – to hear directly from them in all their richness and complexity – their experiences of oppression, disadvantage and persecution, but also the fierce determination to mobilise, organise and create change from within – then this book is necessary reading and one I will be recommending to all social workers and social work students.

After all, Gypsy, Traveller and Roma people have been negotiating a hostile world for over a thousand years and benefit from wisdom and knowledge that has been passed down through the generations. Despite multiple attempts at cultural and ethnic genocide, we are here to stay.

Allison Hulmes, Welsh Kale Gypsy
Co-founder member of the Gypsy, Roma and Traveller Social Work Association

Introduction

This is a documentary-style book based on dozens of interviews with Gypsies, Roma and Travellers (GRT) in the UK, Ireland and Romania. The voices of many ordinary GRT people are captured throughout the book, giving rise to first-hand accounts of their daily lives, desires and struggles. These are revealed in short and long vignettes, extended life stories and case studies. Oral storytelling and information sharing have been vital to many GRT communities. One of my aims in reaching out to as many GRT people as possible was to allow them to share their stories on a wide range of social issues that affect their lives and those of their families.

Interviews were carried out with staff members working in non-government organisations (NGOs), some of whom were GRT people, and others who shared the passion and determination to improve GRT people's quality of life. They did this by challenging racism and discrimination and campaigning for improvements on issues such as the current lack of appropriate accommodation for GRT people.

State research in GRT communities is limited and underfunded, but some NGOs have carried out their own research and many of their findings are cited in the book. But NGOs, like many others in the voluntary sector, have limited resources, and therefore the financing of research is limited. Often, anecdotal evidence is relied upon based on the professional opinions of NGO employees who comprise highly knowledgeable staff members that possess great expertise in GRT history, culture, lifestyles and customs.

Undoubtedly, the state needs to provide more research funding to determine what types of services would be beneficial in helping to fight racism, poverty and health and educational inequalities. This, in turn, may help shift the ingrained prejudice towards GRT people that society is reluctant to relinquish. As you will learn from this book, much work is needed for society to realise the existence of GRT people – to accept their unique ethnicities and appreciate their many gifts and skills.

I have compiled a comprehensive reference and suggested reading list (which can be found at the back of the book). This list contains references used in the text relevant to the key areas discussed in this book: accommodation, health, education, crime, discrimination and LGBT+ issues. There are other references and books listed that are useful for historical background information on the lives of GRT people.

Mixed among the voices of the interviews and the references and sources contained in the text are my own professional opinions and observations resulting from my 20-plus years' experience as a social worker.

I hope you enjoy the journey this book takes you on and you learn lots of new information about these extraordinary ethnic groups who are, undoubtedly, some of the most remarkable people alive on the planet today despite the racial inequalities and social injustices they routinely face.

Chapter 1 | Context setting

Introduction

Gypsies, Roma and Travellers are Britain's internal refugees – shunned and abandoned by their country of birth; not by war or means of torture but through racism, prejudice and poverty. There appears to be an inability for 'gorgers' (non-travelling people) to accept that Gypsies, Roma and Travellers (GRT) are ethnic groups first and communities second. They are never lifestyle choices that can simply be reversed through changes in statutory legislation.

At present there is a complete inequality between GRT people and the rest of society – a separation and often a complete lack of understanding, empathy and willingness to listen to their voices, their desires and their need to be able to live authentic lives in accordance with their beliefs, culture and heritage. Some of the GRT people I spoke to for this book believe they are at the beginning of a civil rights movement, which is probably at the point where black people were in America during the 1940s and 1950s. They have activists who are very vocal and hope that within the next ten years there will be a marked improvement in people's understanding and appreciation of GRT issues.

The biggest problem activists face is the low respect that society holds towards Gypsies, Roma and Travellers. Perceptions need changing. Biases need questioning. Discrimination needs challenging. One Romany Gypsy summed this up well when he said, '*We could be good friends. We could be good neighbours. We are good people.*'

Background information

The generic term Gypsies, Roma and Travellers (GRT) is used frequently throughout this book when referring to these different groups; however, at other times the distinctive identity and ethnicity of each community is fully recognised and acknowledged. The term GRT is routinely used by NGOs, policy makers and researchers to collectively describe ethnic groups with a history of nomadic lifestyles. While Roma and Romany Gypsies share a core root history, their journeys over centuries have differed enormously. Irish Travellers and Scottish Gypsy Travellers do not share Roma/Romany history and have their own cultural heritage roots.

In the UK, many people fail to differentiate between the various groups and often refer to them collectively as Travellers or Gypsies. While the groups sometimes have different origins and history, there is no mistaking that all of the groups have many similarities. They all face daily discrimination in education, employment and healthcare. All, at one point or other, will have hidden their ethnicity to avoid discrimination and prejudice. They have all experienced being stopped by the police solely because they are GRT. The groups will all have been on the receiving end of hate crime and hate speech. All GRT people whose identity is known will have been refused access to services, including pubs, cafes, shops, cinemas and nightclubs, because of their ethnicity.

***

It is estimated that as of 2022 there are approximately 300,000 GRT people now living in the UK (Travellers' Times, 2020) but there could be more, as some Gypsies and Travellers either don't participate in the census or fail to reveal their true ethnicity. Gypsies and Travellers are the most disliked and discriminated group of people in modern-day society. Nothing comes closer. They are communities who are reviled, persecuted, loathed, and sometimes feared, on a widespread scale – but who have survived against all odds but at great cost to their identity and reputation.

Several questions need asking. Have Gypsies, Roma and Travellers fought enough to protect their rights or has suppression of the prejudice become too overpowering – thus rendering them silent? Should their argument become louder with a 'Martin Luther King' figure in their community stepping forward and campaigning for equal rights and justice like black and Asian people have done on racism and discrimination? A force of change, a radicalisation, is needed to bring about acceptance and some level of respect and trust that has continuously eluded them.

While some middle-aged Travellers admit that life in a house is much more comfortable than in a caravan or mobile home, they acknowledge that the choice to live a travelling lifestyle has largely been taken away from them. The majority who now live in houses in the UK and Ireland have had to accept that these circumstances are a dilution of their culture and heritage. The direct effect of this has meant that younger generations of GRT people will never get to know what travelling life is really like. They have little knowledge, understanding or reality of what hardships their grandparents or ancestors endured with life on the road travelling from area to area. Although society readily discriminates against GRT people, they are often fondly associated with storytelling, singing, music and dancing, but most people are still ignorant of their roots and many still think that Gypsies are indigenous to the UK and Ireland.

Perhaps the image of fortune-telling and clairvoyance has created an air of mystery around Gypsies and Travellers, who have always been hard workers. Occupations have changed to suit the modern age, including tarmacking and landscaping. The sons and daughters of the travelling hawkers have become market stallholders, horse traders have become car mechanics and the rag-and-bone men have moved into recycling, with some owning large paper mills. Others are demolition or building contractors. Earning a living in bygone times included fortune-telling, harvesting and horse dealing, while others earned a living mending fences, digging ditches or laying hedges, as well as rat catching. But over the years they have adapted to new ways of making a living – and have sought jobs that do not require an education. Although some English Romany women have always been in the workforce, their main role historically to the current day has been to concentrate on looking after the home, children, cooking and doing housework.

Although times have changed, there are certain traditions and culture that have continued to play a part in both settled and travelling life. Great pride is taken in the ownership and exhibiting of traditional wagons and other horse-drawn vehicles, even if they are more likely to be transported to events these days by low-loader than pulled by horse. Production of hand-crafted goods – pots, pans and hand-crafted baskets – have plummeted but some of these can still be bought at horse fairs.

A brief history

Horne (2019) states that the origins of Gypsies can be traced back to Western India in the state of Rajasthan in the tenth century. Dissension among various groups living in Rajasthan ended in civil war breaking out, which resulted in a mass exodus of what later became known as the 'Gypsy Diaspora' which spread across the Middle East before mainly settling in Eastern Europe. During the departure from India, the Rajasthan exiles stopped in Greece in the port of Methone. Here it was noticed that they looked different because of their dark skin colour and the bright clothing they liked wearing. It was also noticed that the Rajasthani kept to themselves and rarely spoke or interacted with other groups. Because of these differences people became suspicious of them, resulting in disdain. They were soon made to feel unwelcome and eventually shunned, forcing them to relocate to the hills outside of Methone. Soon afterwards, local people started to refer to this new hillside community of people as 'Little Egypt' because they had mistakenly thought that the Rajasthani were Egyptians because of their dark skin.

Several hundred years passed before they first came to Britain and became known as Gypsies when their name was worn down from 'Egyptian' to 'Gipcyan' to Gypsy. They have been here since at least the sixteenth century and according to Bowers

(2016) the first recorded mention of Gypsies in England can be found in a document from 1514. Gypsies were made to feel unwelcome in Britain almost from the outset. Henry VIII disliked the increasing arrival of large numbers of nomadic people into the country, which was not helped by his advisers telling him about practices which included palm-readers and fortune-tellers.

The dislike of Gypsies was sealed further by the disclosure that most of them were Catholics after the Vatican had issued them with papal letters of protection, giving them safe passage across Europe into Britain. The king introduced legislation – the Egyptians Act (1530) – to make it illegal to be a Gypsy in identity and practice after it was claimed that Gypsies used methods to deceive people by fortune-telling as well as committing offences such as robbery. This legislation also enforced the law to forbid any more Gypsies entering Britain and giving them a mere 15 days' notice to leave. If they refused to do this all their property was confiscated. This was the first time they had to start concealing their identity to survive. It could be said that public hostility towards GRT people and their way of life has remained in place since the reign of Henry VIII. The Egyptian Act was in force for 24 years until 1554 by which time Mary I had ascended to the throne. The new queen amended the Act by allowing Gypsies to stay in Britain but only if they gave up travelling. Those who refused to do so faced hanging. However, the lives of many Gypsies had already been destroyed by that stage after being forced to become slaves when sold to slave colonies in the West Indies and the New World.

The slave trade was designed to clear out Gypsies who were considered by many to be strong and idle beggars, criminals, and dissolute and loose persons. As well as losing their freedom, they were also stripped of the chance at becoming equal human beings to all others – and this remained in place until the eighteenth century, which saw the monarchy losing its authority. Only then did Gypsies become freer and more visible in society with sporadic communities popping up in larger towns and cities in Britain again – although they still faced widespread discrimination and distrust.

Injustices continued and by the twentieth century barbarity in Europe saw the start of a three-year mandatory sterilisation of Gypsies in 1930. It was also made illegal for a German to marry a Gypsy. It was only after the Second World War that Britain started to recognise Gypsies as an endangered race of people and started protecting them from enforced slavery and exploitation. Indeed, they had become the last group of people who, up until that point, had not been exempt from such practices.

Many attempts have been made over the years to eradicate GRT people completely. Although Gypsies and Traveller communities have been recognised in UK law as ethnic groups by the Equality Act (2010) which protects them from discrimination, the government has struggled to accept the legal definition of what it is to be a Gypsy or Traveller. It recommended that GRT people had to travel for a specific amount of time each year before they could be officially regarded as GRT. If they did not travel or failed to travel within the expected specifications, they could not be regarded as belonging to the GRT community. This action assumes that belonging to the GRT community is dependent upon an action, rather than a genetic, biological or historical factor. While the effects of this requirement are still being borne out, its absurdity does not perturb the GRT communities who have survived discrimination and attempts of eradication for many centuries. However, new trespassing laws (outlined in Chapter 9) will interfere greatly in travelling and will seek to criminalise Gypsies and Travellers who park anywhere that is not on an authorised site irrespective of the circumstances. How can this be seen to value and respect the lifestyle of a recognised ethnicity?

DNA and identity

While Roma have remained steadfast in their rules of only marrying within their own community, Romany Gypsies and Travellers have sometimes married people from outside the community. The truth is that if a DNA test were carried out on members of the GRT communities it would indicate certain country ties, such as Italian, Greek, Mexican, French, Romanian, Lebanese, Dutch, Russian, Iranian, and so on. According to Hancock (2013) this would explain why most Romany Gypsies are considered 'white' despite their Indian origins.

My father was a Romany Gypsy, but my mother was a gorger but she grew up alongside Gypsy people and knew of our customs and traditions before she married my father. Gypsies are far more tolerant of gorgers than gorgers are towards Gypsies, mainly because Gypsies have a taboo name: A greyhound will always chase a rabbit. If you crossbreed with another dog, you will get a lurcher who will chase the rabbit. And even if you continue to crossbreed after that, the dog will continue to chase the rabbit. Do you know why? This is the Gypsy gene. It is a tribal feature stamped into their bloodline. So, any person with any bit of Gypsy in them will chase the rabbit. It is an inbuilt adrenaline. I am a realist who says things as they are. Most Romany Gypsies in Britain are of mixed heritage but most of them will not admit it. You must understand that Gypsies are a very proud race of people and want to claim their pride. Admitting that their DNA has become weakened, unlike Roma Gypsies, is not something they are willing to do. The denials are often astonishing. I have often heard crazy excuses like someone saying there was an Albino in their bloodline which was the reason for the blond hair and blue eyes. They feel that by lying like this, they can claim to be one hundred per cent Gypsy. So, the truth is most Gypsies in Britain are only half-Gypsy because of marriages with gorgers over the centuries. Those who deny this I am afraid are just shallow in their thinking.

Paul – Romany Gypsy

Marriage outside the GRT communities is acknowledged and is far less frowned upon today than it was 50 years ago. It is only in the last 20 to 30 years that Romany Gypsies and Irish Travellers have started to intermarry because before that there was a clash between the two different cultures with Romany Gypsies considering Irish Travellers troublemakers as well as being unhygienic in some of their practices. According to some Gypsies, mixed marriages do not break the blood bond or weaken the culture and heritage.

Gypsies and Irish Travellers mix better these days. Often in the past we were not encouraged to mix because of their public quarrelling and how Gypsies were tarred with the same brush as them, although we are very different. But nowadays we meet up with each other and integrate better at horse racing, horse shows and sales. We also do boxing and dog racing (Lurchers) together. We even marry each other these days – this would never have happened in my grandfather's time. Many Gypsy customs are like Indians, where our heritage was first formed. We like to be flash and show we have money. You see this at weddings where no expense is spared. Rich Gypsies like to drive in big four-wheel drives and live in big houses. I can always spot a Traveller's house. It will be big, garish and have a horseshoe displayed somewhere on its exterior!

Richard – Romany Gypsy

Living arrangements

1. The following are the main types of accommodation that GRT people inhabit in the UK:

    » Roma live in settled accommodation which is either privately rented or social housing.

    » Romany Gypsies and Travellers tend to mainly live also in 'bricks and mortar' housing and are often settled together, but still retaining a strong commitment to Gypsy/Traveller culture and traditions.

    » Other Gypsies and Travellers live permanently in authorised sites in caravans or mobile homes, on sites provided by the council, or on private sites.

2. At least 10 per cent of Gypsies and Travellers still prefer to live nomadically and move regularly around the country from site to site (Travellers' Times, 2020). They stay in unauthorised sites or by the side of the road and/or elsewhere where they can park for short periods (currently under threat with new trespassing laws – see Chapter 9).

3. Some Gypsies and Travellers live in settled accommodation during winter or school term-time but like to travel during the summer months when they

stay in unauthorised sites or elsewhere (also under threat with the new trespassing laws – see Chapter 9).

The Traveller Movement (2021) estimates that around 60,000 to 70,000 families still live in caravans in the UK. A fifth of these live on unauthorised sites, a fifth on their own legal sites and the remainder on local authority sites. Ninety per cent of planning applications from the GRT community are declined in contrast to 20 per cent in the general population. Although those living on sites settle better than previously and move around far less, some still travel a few months of the year before returning to their permanent base on a site; such is their desire to live a nomadic lifestyle. Those who still travel have recognised that it is harder to live like this than in the time of their parents and grandparents. Society has changed and many Gypsies have changed too. Although the inherent desire remains for the Gypsy lifestyle, more Gypsies and Travellers have settled because of work. There are fewer authorised sites and more bureaucracy. Many feel the need to be settled in houses and have permanent addresses as they have their own registered companies (roofing, building, landscaping). Previously, they would have travelled up and down the country and would have done casual work wherever they went. Times have changed and more men have recognised that stability is required to make a decent living and provide for their families. It is harder on children at school if their parents travel widely and it's also harder in terms of accessing healthcare, including registering with a GP, if the person doesn't have a stable address.

There are 250+ registered Traveller sites in Britain with few spare spaces available. There are long waiting lists for pitches on sites. In addition to this, there is a national shortage of housing for members of the GRT communities. It is estimated that there are around 1.1 million households on local authority housing waiting lists – some GRT people believe that it would be easier to get a home if they weren't from their backgrounds (Rice, 2021). However, some people specifically want to live on sites and not in houses – they feel best connected to their heritage this way and because a whole community lives on a site and tends to look after each other.

The government must do more to identify land for the Gypsy and Traveller communities to live on. There needs to be a statutory duty on local authorities to meet the assessed need for Gypsy and Traveller communities and sites.

There has been continuous failure on the part of the government to identify enough land for families to live on – yet the Home Secretary has created laws to imprison, fine and remove the homes of families living on roadside camps for the 'crime' of having nowhere else to go, as outlined in the Police, Crime, Sentencing and Courts Act 2022. This Act was the result of calls to criminalise trespassing, which has not been helped by some Travellers who have created a bad reputation for the wider community by leaving temporary encampment areas (car parks, fields and other green spaces) full of rubbish. Incidents of human waste deposited in ponds and lakes, and old cars and scrap items being abandoned, fuel this unwanted reputation.

Classification and language

It is recommended that you should always ask the person what they identify as rather than making assumptions, especially if it is unclear whether someone is a Gypsy or a Traveller. Terms such as 'pikey' are highly offensive. Even the name 'Gypsy' is sometimes a contentious word. While most Romany Gypsies use it to self-identity, others find it offensive, particularly Roma, who have a stern dislike of the word and find it insulting. Irish Travellers, who identify themselves as 'Travellers', never use the term Gypsy when identifying themselves because they have their own separate history, culture and language, although some exceptions might occur if someone has dual ethnicity and are half-Gypsy and half-Traveller.

Romanes (also referred as Rummaness, Romany and Romani) is the language of Romany Gypsies and Roma but consists of numerous dialects that have been formed over centuries, which has prevented it from remaining one pure single-stranded language. Its origins are in the ancient Sanskrit language, which shares certain similarities with Urdu, Hindi and Gujarati. Romanes has developed and evolved over many centuries, borrowing words from other languages as its people migrated from India. Across Europe, there is a wide diversity of Romani dialects. For example, in countries like Slovakia, the Czech Republic and Russia, Romanes is Slavic based and in countries like Romania, Bulgaria and Moldova it is Latin based. It is used as a secondary language in most cases because there is not one solid, pure version of Romanes that all Roma can speak.

Most Romany Gypsies in Britain speak Poggadi Jib, which is a mixture of Romanes and English that uses mostly English grammar. Some elders speak Romanes fluently, but fewer young Romany Gypsies learn the language; most just use words and certain terms in their vocabulary that they have learned from their parents and grandparents. 'Ladge' is one of the terms; it just means 'shame', but is maybe used a bit more frequently in the everyday than its English equivalent because of the sense of shame that many Roma and Romany people are made to face in their daily lives through rejection, humiliation and prejudice towards them. Another is a phrase, '*Rom Romensa thai Gadjo Gadgensa*', which means to be 'A Romany among Romanies and a non-Romany among non-Romanies', used to describe the concealment of a person's ethnic identity, which again is often a regular occurrence for both Roma and Romany.

The Romanes language is primarily a spoken language and therefore isn't a standardised language with a dictionary; hence spelling of words is sometimes left open to interpretation and personal choice. Here is a list of words that some readers may be familiar with after hearing them spoken from time to time:

- *chore* – steal;
- *mush* – a man;
- *burrow mush* – big man;
- *bar* – pound (£1);
- *kushti* – nice;
- *gavver* – police officer;
- *pani* – water;
- *gorger* – non-Gypsy;
- *rom* – man;
- *romni* – Romany woman;
- *rai* – lord;
- *kenna* – house;
- *kher* – home;
- *divas* – day;
- *rahti* – night;
- *dik* – look;
- *dik akai* – look here;
- *luuva* – money;
- *wonga* – coal;
- *tuud* – milk;
- *gatta* – finish;
- *mahto* – drunk;
- *juuk* – dog.

Illiteracy is very high across all age groups in GRT communities. Some people mistakenly think that younger people have better literacy skills than their parents and grandparents but this is not the case. Admittedly, they might have social media accounts but this is mainly for visual purposes. Language skills are also poorer than in other ethnic groups and mainstream society, with GRT people relying heavily on colloquial language.

Falsehoods

Society is saturated with fallacies about the GRT community with suppositions freely dispensed and believed before being passed on. There has also been a hankering after handsome Gypsy men, who for some people have held mystery and allure. Keet-Black (2013, p 5) states:

The image of a Gypsy as a carefree, swarthy, dark-haired nomad wandering aimlessly round the country in a brightly painted caravan has been perpetuated by generations of artists and writers who have chosen to portray romantic fiction rather than the often-stark reality.

Other myths and misconceptions held by society include the following.

- » *The similarities in lifestyle and occupations of the different groups have blurred the distinction for the casual observer, resulting in the misconception that all Travellers are Gypsies.* They are not, and vice versa, not all Gypsies are Travellers.
- » *Gypsies and Travellers do not have to send their children to school.* They have a legal right to be educated along with all other children. Parents have the same legal rights to educate their children as every other parent.
- » *Gypsies and Travellers do not pay taxes.* All Gypsies and Travellers living on a local authority or privately owned sites pay council tax, rent, gas, electricity, and all other charges measured in the same way as for other houses.
- » *Gypsies and Travellers are lazy and do not work.* The truth is they have a very strong work ethic and have continuously sought employment through history. Many own their own businesses and are self-employed.
- » *Gypsies and Travellers subsidise their living through crime.* All of those on social welfare are means tested like any other member of the population. As in all communities, a minority get involved in crime but it's unfair and inaccurate to say that this is the majority because that is not true.
- » *Gypsies and Travellers invade other people's land and cannot be removed.* They have a right to lead a nomadic lifestyle but there are not enough authorised sites for them, resulting in many having to set up home wherever they can.

- *There is a myth about Gypsies suggesting they appear out of nowhere when you go to sleep at night.* The truth is that Gypsies used to travel (and some still do) all day long from early in the morning before arriving at their destination in the early hours of the next morning. This meant that when locals woke up, they saw the Gypsies had arrived and wondered how they had got there.
- *All Gypsies and Travellers live in caravans.* Most Gypsies across the world now reside in houses. Being nomadic is more common in Western Europe, where some Gypsies still live in caravans.
- *Gypsies and Travellers are dirty.* The truth is that Gypsy culture is built upon strict codes of cleanliness learnt over centuries of life on the road with strict guidelines still in place to the current time.
- *Much of today's crime is GRT related.* The truth is that a lot of crime does occur in the areas where GRT people reside, but this is not directly related to them – rather this is the result of residing in deprived neighbourhoods as opposed to GRT people committing all the crime.
- *Women are promiscuous by the way they sometimes dress.* There is a high level of good morals in the GRT community around sex before marriage and faithfulness, coupled with a low divorce rate.
- *Traveller accommodation lowers nearby house prices.* Independent research has shown that there are no price reductions in house prices adjacent to Traveller accommodation.
- *The age-old myth that Gypsies are endowed with special supernatural powers, including the ability to curse and see the future.* There is no validity or truth to this and it mainly relates to superstitions of the past or mere folklore.
- *Ask the ordinary Irish person and they still have the view that Travellers live at the side of a road or in a caravan site.* The majority of Travellers in both Ireland and Northern Ireland live in standard housing accommodation. Around 10 per cent live in unauthorised roadside/sites (Anonymous, 2019).
- *It is widely considered that Roma (and sometimes Romany Gypsies) come mainly from Romania.* 'Romanian' refers to people from the country of Romania and does not relate to Roma/Romany; although there are sizeable Roma populations in Romania, other Eastern Europe countries, for example Bulgaria and Moldavia, have similar numbers.

More people need to be proud of their heritage and culture and not to deny or try to disguise it. Gypsies have always been shunned as a people. When you look back at history, you see that people had their tongues cut out for saying there were Gypsies. People were hanged in the fifteenth century in this country for who they were. We have had to look after each other and although we still do to a certain degree, many of our customs and traditions are dying out. There is less of an appreciation of what went before us, and the struggles people had to endure. Older people value the culture more. I know Gypsies who have moved into houses but still cook meals outdoors and when practical they even light fires outside because they were so used to this way of life. Up until 20 years ago, it was traditional when a baby was born, everyone from the local community would visit the baby's home and put money in the cot. These days people prefer to buy presents instead.

Jay – Romany Gypsy

***

The comment

A community outreach worker with experience of working with GRT people made this comment to me during my research:

They want to be treated like everybody else... but they don't want to behave like everybody else.

When first reflecting upon this comment, it may be easy to assume that GRT people do things that are bad or illegal but expect respect nonetheless despite wrongdoing. But the main point to garner from this is that they are seldom treated like everyone else, irrespective of wrongdoing or any other factor. Their existence alone causes even the kindest and nicest person to wrongly think they are dirty and 'scum' and the lowest class of humanity because the media has conditioned society to this way of thinking by buying into the negative portrayal of GRT people in the tabloid press, along with the negative attitudes already ingrained in society. Unfortunately, the actions of one person or one family in a GRT community have made people think that this is representative of the entire community. The media rarely speak about racism towards GRT people and never highlight anything positive about the respective communities.

NGOs in both the UK and Ireland have expressed their disquiet about politicians in both countries who freely espouse their prejudice about GRT people by publicly announcing that they should be punished, criminalised and eradicated because of their nomadic lifestyles which they consider anti-social in order to appease voters who already hold prejudiced views towards them. There is no hate crime in Ireland that prevents comments like this being made and while the UK may cite the Race Relations Act (1976) and the Equality Act (2010) as barriers from things like this occurring, the truth is that legislation has failed to protect GRT communities from entrenched racism, prejudice and discrimination.

So please re-read the statement: *They want to be treated like everybody else... but they don't want to behave like everybody else.* Are you now able to view it from a different perspective?

The insult

The following description was cited in the *Encyclopaedia Britannica* in 1954 (cited in Travellers' Times, 2020, p 20):

The mental age of the average adult Gypsy is thought to be about that of a child of ten. Gypsies have never accomplished anything of significance in writing, painting, musical composition, science, or social organisation. Quarrelsome, quick to anger or laughter, they are unthinkingly but not deliberately cruel. Loving bright colours, they are ostentatious and boastful, but lack bravery.

Little has changed in the general belief that GRT people are inferior human beings to the rest of society. This is both wrong and insulting and everybody in a position of authority needs to challenge this type of blatant discrimination and prejudice. Liddle (2013, p 7) wrote an opinion piece in *The Spectator* magazine describing Gypsy, Roma and Travellers as *'lazy, criminal, and unintelligent'*. He claimed that usage of the terms 'gyppo' and 'pikey' were a *'useful means of lumping them all together'*, which is a prime example of the racism endured by GRT people.

Truths

The following list, compiled from discussion with NGOs in both the UK and Ireland, contains many truths about GRT people which are needed to address the many falsehoods and misconceptions that persistently lurk in the mindsets of people – sometimes without individuals knowing that their views are wrong, outdated and discriminatory.

- » Romany Gypsies, Irish Travellers and Roma are legally recognised as ethnic groups and protected from discrimination by the Race Relations Act (1976, amended 2000) and the Human Rights Act (1998).
- » Gypsies, Roma and Travellers should be seen as ethnic groups rather than 'lifestyles'. All the different GRT groups in the UK have a shared language or dialect and some shared cultural practices, most will identify as an ethnic

group, and all individuals from all groups are legally recognised as ethnic minorities under the Equality Act (2010).

» Romany Gypsies have been recognised in law since 1988 and Irish Travellers have had legal recognition as an ethnic group since 2000. Both groups are covered and protected by the Race Relations Act (1976) and its Amendment Act (2000).

» 80 per cent of GRT people in England and Wales live in houses, flats or maisonettes, which means that only 20 per cent of Gypsy or Irish Travellers live in caravans or other mobile or temporary structures.

» Although Gypsy and Traveller people have been present in England since at least the sixteenth century, Roma migrants from Eastern and Central Europe have tended to arrive much more recently, from 2004 onwards, although small numbers have always migrated to the UK.

» The vast majority of Gypsy and Traveller caravans (80 per cent) are on authorised sites that have planning permission.

» Gypsies and Travellers place great value on family bonds and networks. There is an emphasis on a strong family unit coupled with sense of loyalty to each other. Consanguine marriage (marriage between individuals who are closely related) is still widely practised. Great value is placed on children within families.

» Christianity remains the main religion to the GRT community with 95 per cent of Gypsies still identifying as Christians (the remaining 5 per cent are Muslim and mostly found in Russia and Belarus). Eighty per cent of UK Romany Gypsies and Travellers identify as Christian.

» Every borough in the UK has a duty to provide legal sites for GRT communities, showing mixed results in various parts of the country. Some authorities do not view it as a priority, which pushes some GRT people into living in unauthorised sites and/or illegally by the roadside or other public area.

» The number of young Traveller men under the age of 30 who die each year by suicide is six to seven times the national average in the general population.

» There is a disproportionate number of GRT prisoners in the UK – as many as 5 per cent of the population.

- » There is a strong cultural tradition (and expectancy) of travelling to family and cultural events such as funerals, weddings, family illness or Gypsy and Traveller fairs.
- » Nomadism is a shared heritage of Gypsies and Travellers and not a present reality. Not all Gypsies and Irish Travellers 'travel' – or may only 'travel' to traditional cultural events like the Appleby Horse Fair.
- » Many Gypsies, Roma and Travellers face daily prejudice based on negative stereotyping and misunderstanding. This is because people generalise from the anti-social actions of a few and project that onto the whole population. Prejudice against them is longstanding.
- » Historical persecution has seen every EU country having had anti-Gypsy laws at one point or other. In the sixteenth century a law was passed in England that allowed the state to imprison, execute or banish anyone that was perceived to be a Gypsy.
- » Gypsies and some Traveller ethnicities have been recognised in UK law as being ethnic groups protected against discrimination by the Equality Act (2010) under groups with 'protected characteristics'.
- » The 2011 census was the first time that the census collected information about Gypsy and Traveller people. The 2021 census was the first time there was a box for 'Roma' to tick to correctly identify themselves.

We hold on to our values. We like the old-fashioned ways and don't want them to fizzle out. We like the outdoor life and don't feel the cold. We are natural nomads. Although I live in a house, the urge to buy a cruiser and travel around the country is always there. The feeling of being able to cook and eat some grub outdoors is enticing – a good rabbit stew would be lovely. Most Travellers would like to have a bit of land and some rent land and others buy it. That way you can have horses which are what a great many people want to have.

Oliver – Irish Traveller

Who am I?

The thought on many GRT minds is 'Who am I?' in terms of identifying their place in the world. This affects younger generations the most given the fast-moving changes in their communities over the past 30–50 years. They have not lived through many of the key changes but have felt the fall-out from them through their parents and grandparents. The need to conceal identity as a means of self-preservation along with other factors will be explored throughout this book, including staggeringly high statistics in mental health and the introduction of a drug culture in Gypsies and Travellers in the past decade. Failure in state systems of education and health and policies that seem determined to rid society of GRT culture and lifestyles have also attacked the psyche of GRT people, who have often been powerless to do anything to stop the prejudice inflicted upon them.

When you are with a Gypsy – be a Gypsy, and when you are with a gorger – be a gorger. I would say 75 per cent of Gypsies downplay who they are. Some find this harder than others, especially if you have dark skin and there are other obvious clues including accents. I read somewhere once that Gypsies can never really hide who they are because of the way they act, look, walk, talk, live, smell, sound, drink, write, eat, dress, smoke, dance and make love. When I was young, I remember my mother putting on a posh voice when she took me to the GP surgery. She felt the need to pretend so that we wouldn't get treated differently to everyone else. But pretending all the time erodes self-worth even when it is done to exist peacefully.

Denis – Romany Gypsy

GRT communities tend to be insular, whereby lots of people know each other, socialise together and see life within their communities as their only way of life. Everything is seen from within the viewpoints of their community simply because they have never seen or done anything differently. But changes have begun to take root in younger generations. Although they adopt some of the customs and traditions of their community and family, they see people outside their community living life differently and want to try out new things. Some young GRT people are developing liberal attitudes, are better educated and have better vocabularies. This new mentality clashes with the traditions and values of their parents and grandparents. Older generations didn't understand racism, while younger generations have truly woken up to this reality. There is a better capacity for debate among them but they are more sensitive than their forebears. Older generations are more resilient, insular and immune to criticism, while many of their children and grandchildren have lost this resilience.

Some of the younger people worry about what other people say about them. They think about it constantly to the point of obsession. They look at 'Love Island' on telly and want to be in touch with the modern world and be glamorous. They don't want to be seen as people who travel around in motor homes. This is a thing of the past to them and they have no real interest in it.

Naomi – Romany Gypsy

Personal responsibility

Many people question why GRT people don't take greater personal responsibility for their poor reputation in society. But others consider this an unfair question. The question ought to be what do you think becomes of a community exposed to such poor treatment. It's very difficult for a community to take personal responsibility when a system has failed that community through under-investment. This disadvantage has existed for generation upon generation and the horizon looks like it will continue to exist for many more generations to come. Thankfully there are pockets within society who stick up for GRT people and have denounced comments made by politicians running for office when they have attacked Travellers and made derogatory comments about them as a vote appeaser.

GRT communities are not equality based. It is not a level playing field and discrimination and prejudice seems to be a universal experience for all GRT people irrespective of wherever they live. GRT people deserve to be full participants in society. Thankfully NGOs and advocacy groups, most of which are GRT led, lobby government over legislation and are making their voices heard. They have produced reports that are educational as well as campaigning for change. But when it comes to change, I'm afraid we are still a long way from massive changes taking place including a shift in the way the needs of GRT people are prioritised, but our lobbying will continue until the needs of our communities are respected and implemented. But seeing the day when this happens often seems more of a wish than anticipation.

Pavee Point – Dublin-based NGO

Other GRT communities

Although this book deals mainly with Romany (British) Gypsies, Roma and Irish Travellers, it is worth stating that there are several other groups within the GRT communities. Travellers are divided into two groups – those that are ethnic Travellers such as Romany Gypsies and Irish Travellers and those who travel extensively for purely economic reasons such as Show People and Circus People.

Welsh Travellers and Romany

Welsh Travellers are descendants of families who migrated in the seventeenth and eighteenth centuries from the southwest of England. They quickly became well known for wood carvings, as wagon builders, horse dealers and fishermen. They were known to be excellent musicians, and many were skilled harpists and fiddlers. These days, most reside in houses, but they still retain their traditions and customs whenever possible. Welsh Romani have been living in Wales since the sixteenth century. Some families speak 'Kale', which is a variety of the Romanes. Welsh law considers Welsh Romany to be an ethnic minority group.

Scottish Gypsy Travellers

Gypsy Traveller is the official term adopted in Scotland for Scottish Travellers which has been used since the early 2000s. Scottish Gypsy Travellers are also known as

Nawkens or Nachins. Their origins lie as Travelling Scottish metal workers, which can be traced back as early as the twelfth century, but the bulk was formed after war and land clearances during the eighteenth and nineteenth centuries which led to evicted and dispossessed people taking to a nomadic way of life. The customs and beliefs of Scottish Gypsies and Travellers tend to be like those of Irish Travellers and English Romany Gypsies. They were established as an ethnic minority group in Britain in 2008.

Scottish Gypsy Travellers have been known to exist since the break-up of the clans in 1745, although some historians state that indigenous nomads existed in Scotland before this time. There are few Romany or Roma Gypsies living in Scotland and the reason for this is mainly because there is little employment to be found. However, a small group known as 'Border Gypsies' live close to the Scottish/English border, which consists of Scottish Gypsy Travellers who have married Romany Gypsies.

There are hardly any differences in cultural practices between Scottish Gypsy Travellers and Irish Travellers. Both communities place great emphasis on cleanliness and family values, and members of both communities marry young. Scotland is like Ireland in that it is a Celtic country and is mostly rural and agricultural. But Scotland is unlike Ireland in the sense that Scottish Travellers are free to roam the countryside in their caravans without facing strict legal restrictions. There are more stopping places made available to them. They are also 'tolerated' more and encounter less discrimination from settled people. Likewise, there is less media sensationalism in its reporting of Scottish Travellers. Mental health is very taboo among Scottish Gypsy Travellers and, like Irish Travellers, the suicide rate among young men is very high. There is also a cultural inclination to be fearful of going to doctors. Female Scottish Gypsy Travellers tend to remain at school longer than boys but more often than not rarely exceed beyond the second year at secondary school. One of the biggest concerns raised about the educational system in Scotland for Scottish Gypsy Travellers is that it entails either attending school in person or not being able to receive any alternative option. It is felt that a more pragmatic stance is needed, including making educational outreach work available in Gypsy Traveller sites.

Scottish Gypsy Travellers and Irish Travellers sometimes clash over land and issues with stopping places. This is mainly clan feuding as opposed to xenophobia on the part of Scottish Gypsy Travellers and consists mainly of small-scale skirmishes. Both groups are in the main friendly towards each other and some marry into each other's community. Employment in Scotland for the Travelling communities is scarce and this too has been known to raise tensions between both communities when competing for jobs.

Accommodation for Travellers in Scotland is a prime issue, including a shortage of both transit sites and local authority accommodation. Gypsy Travellers are usually placed at the bottom of the accommodation waiting list and when it comes to their turn are often offered temporary accommodation with shared kitchens and toilets, which impacts greatly on their cultural practices around hygiene and washing clothes and cooking utensils.

New Travellers (New Age Travellers)

New Travellers consist of people who come from a wide range of cultural and social backgrounds that have taken up a nomadic and bohemian lifestyle in the past 50-plus years, including hippie movements and free-festival movements of the 1960s and 1970s. They are known for desiring an alternative lifestyle and like to travel rather than reside in one place. Few New Age parents believe in traditional education for their children and usually choose to educate them at home themselves. New Age Travellers are known to like travelling to music festivals and other large gatherings, which led to new legislation being introduced in 1994 (Criminal Justice and Public Order Act) preventing large convoys gathering for music festivals and setting up tents. In fact, this new legislation criminalised unauthorised camping for all Travellers. These days, members of this community tend to call themselves simply Travellers with some finding the term 'New Age' or 'New' offensive.

Barge Travellers/Boatpeople/Liveaboard Boaters

Barge Travellers are like New Age Travellers but live on the UK's 2200 miles of canals. Barge Travellers form a distinct group in the canal network, and many are former New Age Travellers, although this way of life first developed in the eighteenth century. These days, there are fewer Barge Travellers than in previous decades and this way of living is far more popular in countries like the Netherlands, where living and working on the waterways is a lifestyle choice. Liveaboard Boaters live on narrowboats, barges or river cruisers, whether on a home mooring, a winter mooring or continuously cruising on a canal or in a marina.

In addition to ethnic Gypsies and Travellers, there are other communities in Britain who as of 2022 are not recognised under equality law because they are termed as economical. This means that not everybody who lives a nomadic lifestyle is protected under equality law. Examples include the following.

Showmen

Showmen, also referred to as 'Fair Grounders', are occupational or cultural Travellers as opposed to 'ethnic' Travellers. They share many cultural traits with ethnic

Travellers. They are a cultural minority who have owned and operated funfairs for many generations and their identity is connected to their family businesses. Their rides and attractions can be seen at funfairs throughout the summer months. They are fewer in number these days owing to the popularity of theme parks. Due to travelling about, the average British Show People have a mix of English, Scottish, Welsh and/or Irish heritage in their DNA. Many of them are partial Romany and partial Irish Traveller heritage, but despite this Show People developed as a group separately to both Irish Travellers and Romany Gypsy Travellers, and their roots, cultures, traditions and identities remain separate and distinct. Due to its being an insular community, most marriages are from within the community. They have their own language called Paylaree (a combination of Romanes and slang). Showmen usually have winter quarters where the family settles to repair the machinery before the next travelling season.

Circus People

The origins of the first circus in Britain can be traced back to 1768. Circus People tend to have many similarities to Show People/Fair Grounders, but circuses tend to be owned and run by individual families who take great pride in their traditions, which are passed down through family generations. Although circuses are still a common sight in Britain, there have been fewer in recent decades. Attitudes to performing animals have changed and many circuses no longer have animals in their shows. These days acts are made up from performers from abroad drafted in to make up a repertoire for the yearly circuit.

Conclusion

The above sections have provided a snapshot picture of the vast landscape and indeed complexities of GRT communities. As you will have seen, there are many myths and misconceptions – many handed down through the generations with little thought of what might be true or what might have changed over the years. Things have changed, and radically so, in the past 50 to 60 years. Are you one of those people who did not know that Gypsies originated in India? What about Roma? Did you think they are just strange people who have emigrated from Romania? Perhaps your knowledge of Travellers also needs updating.

In the chapters that follow, the reader will be taken through a closer viewing of Romany, Roma and Irish Travellers. Individual contributions from members of these communities are included, providing you with a first-hand account of different views and opinions in an ever-increasing world of change in the lifestyles of these communities. Although many changes have occurred, external negative perceptions remain difficult to shift. Discrimination and low levels of respect towards these disadvantaged and largely socially disregarded people are still in place like they were centuries ago. State laws that promote anti-trespassing have become 'ethnic cleansing' tools that desire to eradicate Gypsies and Travellers; however, centuries of resilience and will-power have firmly cemented GRT people's survival.

Chapter 2 | Romany Gypsies

Introduction

This chapter is designed to give readers a better understanding of what life is like for Romany Gypsies in current-day Britain. Unfortunately, many people in the general public see Romany Gypsies as threatening and malicious. Bowers (2016) summed it up by saying that no other ethnic groups in Britain have aroused as much curiosity, romance, hatred and fear as Gypsies, who are often misunderstood, maligned and exoticised because most people's perceptions of Britain's Gypsies are based on a mixture of romanticism, prejudice and ignorance.

Keet-Black (2013) states that Gypsies were first identified in York in the sixteenth century and, even then, they were the topic of ridicule when described as being unlike other people because they were physically different, especially by the way they dressed in flamboyant brightly coloured clothing. Life in Britain 500 years ago was difficult for most people unless you belonged to the upper classes but even back then life was more difficult for Gypsies than any other group of people as they lived on the fringes of society and had few friends or contacts outside their community. This meant that they were often unemployed and to survive and escape persecution, they constantly moved about the country, coupled with a terse relationship with settled people who disliked and distrusted them. Given that many of the problems faced by Gypsies then are still occurring today surely shows the deep level of prejudice, hatred, distrust and outright racism that has become so embedded in people's psyche against a community they know little about.

Romany life

Fraser (1995) states that Romany Gypsies (or Romanichal, or Romani Chals, which they also sometimes are termed) have been coming to Britain since 1514 after migrating from continental Europe, where they had lived since the Roma migration from India in the tenth century. However, it is worth noting that there were already indigenous nomadic people in Britain when the Romany Gypsies first arrived, such as Scottish and Welsh Travellers, which indicates that there were other indigenous cultures who also preferred a nomadic lifestyle.

Different nomadic cultures, ethnicities from various communities, including Romany Gypsies, have merged through marriage in Britain over the years. While this has shown assimilation, it has resulted nevertheless in a dilution of pure Romany culture and DNA, as already mentioned in the opening chapter of this book. This contrasts with Roma and Irish Travellers who have managed to stay closer to their origins than perhaps Romany Gypsies had wished or indeed intended. Steve, who identifies as a Romany Gypsy, explained how he feels about being of mixed ethnicity:

I don't have many gorger friends. I keep to myself. Most Travellers stick to themselves because we feel if we associate with too many of them that we will lose our culture and heritage. In my opinion, it doesn't matter whether you are black, white, rainbow coloured, Irish Gypsy or English Traveller, Romany – whatever. We were all put on this planet to live a handsome life. My mother was a jam-and-bread eater [non-Traveller], and my father is an English Traveller. I have often been called a weedo [slang term for a white or light skinned person] – or a half-breed — or a wannabe Gypsy. But I ignore the haters and get on with my life.

Steve – Romany Gypsy

Victor – a proud Gypsy

Gypsies are made to feel inferior to settled people with many hiding their ethnicity as a result, but equally there are those who are openly proud of who they are.

I am a proud Gypsy man. It is in my blood. Anybody can buy a caravan and travel but that does not make them a Gypsy. It is something you must be born into. For me, it is who I am, and it is important to me to hold my head high. I am also proud of my language, which sadly the younger generation fail to appreciate. I was brought up in a house where it was important to learn the language. As a young child, I remember my grandmother in her trailer and when my brothers and I went to visit her, she would open her cupboard and tell us the Romany names for all the items inside. This was a great way to be introduced to the language. It made me proud that we had our own language that was distinct to us Gypsies. There needs to be a revival in our community of the language, particularly among the young generation who have little or no knowledge of even basic words. But we are not big on education in our community and really must break the cycle. There are still few who complete secondary school. I did not go and neither did my children. We can all read but spelling can sometimes be a problem. Look at how well black and Asian people have done. They have only been coming here to this country in the last 70 years, but they value education. Unfortunately, with us there is still the mindset that boys leave school at 12 or 13 and go and work with their fathers and that girls leave school at this age too and stay at home and help their mothers with the housework. Until such time that we have educated Gypsies in powerful positions in this country, little will change. But that would take at least another generation or two for that to happen.

I asked several Romany Gypsies to tell me what they considered to be good attributes of their community. They offered the following points.

- » Gypsies are very family orientated. Mothers would do anything for their children.
- » Once you gain the trust of a Gypsy, they treat you as one of their 'family'. They are fiercely loyal.
- » Gypsies are close knit, connected and share among themselves.
- » Gypsy women like to look feminine. They love bright-coloured clothing and dresses and like wearing costume jewellery, including big earrings.
- » Gypsies love animals – horses, dogs and ferrets.
- » If you are a guest in their home, they will make you welcome and comfortable and offer hospitality.
- » They are very clean people. There is a saying '*ask any Travelling woman what her favourite perfume is, and she will tell you bleach*'.
- » Gypsies have great community spirit and 'pull' together in times of need – whether it be for weddings or funerals. One person will pay for one thing and another person for something else.
- » They are incredibly resilient and recover faster than anyone else if they are down and out.
- » Gypsies have a great work ethic and are hardworking and proud.
- » They are great adapters and throughout history have always had to adapt to new situations.

Ricky's story

There is good and bad in every community. I was brought up to have traditional values and to respect people. My father always said, 'show me your manners and I will show you mine'. We look after each other in the community. If somebody messes with one of us, they mess with us all. Once anyone crosses us, they are out. Loyalty is expected. My parents always gave me good advice, guidance and support. I know the difference between right and wrong. My father told me to never hit a woman. I was brought up to be honest and was never a kid who went to shops and stole. School was okay for me, but some kids expected me to be tough because of my background, which meant I was often challenged into fights. It was a case of other lads thinking that if they beat me in a fight, this would be good for their ego.

I would say that 70 per cent of English Gypsies are still traditionalists with good morals living honest lives. They will not see their families go without. But there is the other 30 per cent who get involved in thieving, violence and other criminal activities and end up in prison. Gypsies try their best to look after their families and carve out an honest living. Historically, they have not been afraid of going out and looking for work such as scrap metal dealing, fruit picking and the like. Many families work together and build up business together in construction and patio paving. There is an honour in the family name, so you work hard to achieve. My grandfather's motto, which he passed down to my father and which my father passed down to me, was that as a family you are working for the 'one pot', which means that everything you work for is yours and will be your children's one day too.

But times are changing now. It is very different to my grandfather's time when he lived in a wagon. Granddad always said his horse was a companion who pulled his wagon and that his dog was a friend who helped him put food on the table after they went out shooting pheasants. Most Gypsies now live in houses but we are still keen horse people. Even to this day children are encouraged to ride horses from an early age. Gypsies still marry second cousins although several marry outside the community because this is now less frowned upon. If the person has a head on them and has good morals, they are accepted. There is more emphasis on marrying someone decent, because as my father told my sister, if you don't marry a bum and be left with their baby, you can marry whoever you like. Abortion is still frowned upon, especially in church-going families. Nobody wants social services to get involved because it damages the family reputation. Nobody wants to be seen as someone who cannot take care of their children. People do not get married as young as they used to or have as many children as before. In my grandfather's time, he was married and had three children by the time he was 22. This applies equally to men and women. Sex outside marriage was not a big deal in my family. Whenever I told my dad I fancied a girl, he would joke with me and say 'Go – you get in there boy!' Customs have always been important to Gypsies. We are very clean people and often remark about non-Gypsies and their hygiene practices around animals. For us animals are not allowed near your living quarters so therefore dogs are never allowed inside. We do not like cats because they lick themselves and it is thought they spread germs this way. Family gatherings are still large in number whether this is weddings, funerals or baptisms. We put aside differences at these events and there is never any conflict although sometimes people who have had disagreements tend to avoid each other. Funerals are big affairs. Gypsies are usually buried together in a section of a cemetery which is favoured by the community.

Changing times

I spoke to Gypsy men in their fifties and sixties who told me that when they were young, they used to travel all around the country doing seasonal work where they did fruit picking – strawberries, plums and apples – and potato picking. They joked about making many farmers rich because of their hard work. They were cheap labour, often only earning a few 'shillings' a day, but reminisced with great fondness about this way of life which is now almost obsolete. Back in the sixties, seventies and eighties, they said it was the norm to travel around in a 'tourer' (trailer) doing odd jobs and looking for casual work. Historically, Gypsies did not like regular jobs. They preferred their independence and liked to be doing odd jobs here and there, because, at their own admission, they are weak at time-keeping and regular commitment.

Back in their childhood days they worked six days a week in all types of weather. One Gypsy recalled how he used to chop wood and go around and knock on people's doors selling it. No Gypsy goes in search of seasonal work anymore. This old way of life has largely vanished in the past 30 years and with it some of the Romany Gypsy culture, which means fewer and fewer Gypsies travel around the country. Many say that the beginning of the end of true Gypsy life was when the wheels of the horse-drawn wagons stopped turning, although afterwards different modes of transport like caravans replaced the wagons. They would light fires with dry wood and cook outside and while eating would talk and laugh and listen to old stories from the past in a high-spirited manner.

The majority of Romany Gypsies in the UK now reside in houses but while around 30 per cent still reside in mobile homes, trailers and chalets, many of these are on authorised council sites resulting in less of a transient lifestyle (Horne, 2019). Those living on sites still try hard to keep the culture and many find work doing block paving and landscape gardening. But the general trend these days is for Gypsies to be self-employed, whether they live in a house or in a trailer, whereby they work within a 20–30-mile radius of where they live. Long-distance travelling looking for work is a thing of the past.

Many older Gypsies feel the younger generation in their community have no understanding of this lifestyle because they have not been brought up in the traditional culture. The men I spoke to joked that many young people would be afraid of their designer clothes smelling of smoke if they sat near a fire. The older Gypsies shook their heads when speaking about the younger generation of Gypsies who they said are only interested in big shops, fashion, soaps on television, magazines and earning quick, easy money. Many they said are Gypsy in name only because they have no lived experience of what it really was like to be a Gypsy like they experienced in their younger lives. They felt the actions of the young generation do not live up to being a Gypsy because their appreciation of the culture is limited due to wanting an easy life.

One of the men who told me about his earlier life was Alan. From a young age and for the past 40 years, Alan has travelled around the country doing fairground work involving fun and coaster rides. He started doing it with his father and later with his sons. But his business ended when coronavirus forced the country into lockdown. Although Alan loved his work and the freedom it provided him, he was mindful of how difficult it was to make a living having to get the public to part with their money. When the work ended, his sons went off and found other jobs, including delivery work and tarmacking, while Alan started buying and selling horses. Alan loves doing what he describes as 'Romany things'. So much so that when he got married, he arranged for a horse-drawn caravan for him and his wife to tour around Cumbria lakes and moors. He lives in a bungalow now but is looking to buy some local land to develop into a Traveller site where 12 families could live. However, he is wary of his local council, who might object to planning permission because he fears they might prefer to build a row of shops on it.

Alan thinks the traditional Gypsy lifestyle is dying out except for what he calls the 'hard-core' Gypsies, who find it hard to settle and continue to travel around various parts of the country, remaining in places only for short intervals. The nomad lives of past generations are quickly becoming such a thing of the past that when some younger Gypsies hear their parents and grandparents talk about their bygone struggles on the road, they receive similar reactions to those they might expect if they were discussing pre-historic times. But the reality is they are often only discussing what everyday lifestyles from 20–30 years ago were like.

More and more from his community live in houses these days than ever before in history, and he acknowledges that this has brought changes – some for the better, including children staying on in school and becoming better educated. Alan thinks young people have far better options these days than his generation, who had to go out and survive for a living. He added that people are not getting married as young these days, and young people usually now pick their partners. They wait until they have some money and a place of their own before marriage. More and more younger female Gypsies go to college or have jobs these days.

But young people today come with a lack of awareness of the struggles of those who came before them, with Alan claiming that young Gypsies in their late teens and early twenties know nothing about their families being squatters, being moved on by the police or being at loggerheads with council officials over rights to Traveller sites. He laughed when he described young Gypsies these days wanting an easy, comfortable life with a regular job and income. Alan states that most of the younger men are into well-toned bodies and are, hence, frequent gym-goers. But Alan is not of the opinion that young people have everything and believes that his generation was more outgoing and more outspoken. He feels his generation worked hard and were grateful for the simple pleasures in life. It was unimaginable at the time that designer clothing would one day exist.

Romany Gypsies tend to abide by the Gypsy code, which means protecting our own people, feeding our children and doing what we must do to survive without any outside influences. Even if that means going hunting rabbits for dinner; we will always do our best to keep our traditions and culture alive. We are guarded because all our lives we have been made to be seen in a bad light, which has meant prejudice in the media, prejudice at school and prejudice from the police. Some Romany Gypsies face worse discrimination than others. It depends where you live. Some people accept us, and others treat us like outcasts. Do I feel bitter about my early life experiences – the name calling and the put-downs? Well, it made me a stronger person and has made me realise that being a Romany Gypsy is who I am. We do not pretend that it is a fairy-tale lifestyle. We don't lord it over anyone. We just want a decent life and to raise our children.

Danny

Horse fairs

But despite the growing number of profound changes in Gypsy lifestyles over the past two decades, annual horse fairs remain steadfast in the community – for example, the Appleby Horse Fair in the town of Appleby-in-Westmorland in Cumbria where thousands of Gypsies and Travellers visit each summer. This is more than just a horse fair but an annual gathering – a summit almost – where lifelong friends and their families gather for an annual get-together and catch up on news and family happenings. The horse fair is held each year in June and has taken place since the reign of James II, who granted a Royal charter in 1685 allowing a horse fair to take place close to the River Eden. Appleby attracts about 10,000 Gypsies and Travellers, about 1000 caravans, several hundred horse-drawn vehicles and about 30,000 visitors. It is billed as the biggest traditional Gypsy fair in Europe. The horses are washed in the local river and trotted up and down the streets. There is a market selling a variety of goods – some traditional to the Gypsy Travelling community – and a range of other horse-related products. It is almost obligatory for every Gypsy in the country to attend this annual fair because people risk missing out on an enjoyable experience.

Gypsy men love meeting up with other Gypsy men. They have a mutual respect for each other because we are cut from the same cloth. Although I now live in a house, I still have a caravan. I know many other Gypsies who have the same and like myself spend a certain amount of the year travelling around the country. April to September are the prime months for travelling because this takes in all the various horse fairs and races including Epsom, Cambridge and Doncaster. Admittedly, there is a bit of drinking and gambling at the races because Gypsies love that type of thing. Once I used to travel six or seven months of the year myself, but as I get older the amount of time I spend on the road is now less because it is a hassle finding sites with all the red tape etc.

Wallace

Several other smaller horse fairs take place all around the country each year, including fairs in Leicestershire and Kent. Well-known events include the Gypsy Horse Fair at Stow-on-the-Wold in the Cotswolds, which attracts hundreds of sightseers twice a year. Gypsies gather from all over England. This is a great gathering where hundreds of horses are paraded and sold in one day. Another well-known fair is the Danny Cooper New Forest Drive, which is the biggest in England. This is a traditional family event which has been running in August of each year since the late 1990s. This event sees hundreds of riders from the Gypsy community make their way across Hampshire's New Forest. Many do these rides to raise money for charity. As well as raising money for charity, the event is also an opportunity for people to buy and sell horses. The journey takes them onto Balmer Lawn in Brockenhurst and ends back at the Coopers' home in Totton, where they have a party with music, singers and a DJ. Another positive factor about this event is that it attracts many young Gypsies and their friends who have a very enjoyable time participating in an event that brings them closer to their cultural roots. Another big annual attraction is St Boswells Horse Fair in the Scottish Borders, which attracts Travelling communities from across the UK and Ireland. The fair has been in existence for over 400 years and is held in July each year.

John's story

I never hide my identity any more but when I was young, I used to get the hump sometimes at work where I would hear people use the word 'pikey' but as my father often said, 'you sometimes have to dance with the devil for a pound'. So,

I kept my mouth shut because I knew what might happen if I said something. I once told a client that I was a Gypsy and they never used me again. We are despised because people get poisoned by what they see on television. Our lives are not like what you see on the telly. We do not all drive flash cars and those that do may have worked and saved hard for it, but the public perception is that if a Gypsy drives around in an expensive car, they have stolen it. Some Gypsies and Travellers have low overheads in the sense that if they live in caravans or trailers, they do not have mortgages, and those with good jobs buy good things including expensive cars.

Members of the Gypsy and Traveller communities do lots of charity work that goes unrecognised. I once did a bike ride from London to Paris in support of the Great Ormond Street Hospital. I know many people who give food to food banks. But every charitable thing we do is questioned with some people thinking that if we do any type of fundraising, that we are going to steal the money. Can you imagine if black people, Muslims or Jews were treated with this level of suspicion and hate? But people get away with it because it is not illegal to call a Gypsy or Traveller a 'pikey'. I support the campaign Black Lives Matter, but I also think that every life matters and that Gypsies' lives matter. I try not to get bitter about it and just want to get on with my life, but I cannot stop thinking that it has been like this for a very long time. Did you know that there were lots of Gypsies murdered in the Second World War? But then, after all, people forget that Gypsies have been hunted down like dogs since the thirteenth century.

The thing about living in a caravan is that you have more freedom. When you live in a house, you have more luxury. My father grew up in a wagon in Great Yarmouth, but I have had far less experience of life on the move. There is far less of this nowadays. Years ago, it was necessary for work reasons, but most people have more settled work these days. People in the past had to carve out a living like fruit picking whereby they would spend half the year travelling around the country before remaining settled in one spot for the remainder of the year. My father used to say to us as children 'The world will not bow down to you'. Although things have got easier, there are still those who discriminate against us because of our accents. They instantly detect a twang in our voices and automatically negativity comes to the surface in the way they think about us. Some outright object to employing us. So yes, there is a big divide in our communities, which stems back to school. I remember even when I was at primary school it was always the Gypsy boy who got expelled if a fight broke out among a group of lads, even when a gorger boy would wee into a water gun and spray it at us. We were seen as the bad ones and that has stuck throughout the decades – throughout the centuries to the current day. You only must look at films like Snatch to see how acceptable it is for Gypsies to be called dirty rotten pikeys. If any other group of people were depicted in this manner, there would be an outcry. But when this is said against Gypsies and Travellers, there is no outcry – only silence and acceptance.

My father taught me old-fashioned values – to respect elders and women. I live by these morals. I cannot understand why any man would hit any woman. I know some Gypsy women are fiery but that is never an excuse. My father often said, 'Never put your hands on a woman'. Why would you hit a woman you love?

Health in the Gypsy and Traveller communities is improving. A prime reason, I think, that people died prematurely in the past was because they did not eat particularly good diets and ate fatty, oily fry-ups. The quality of life for those of my grandfather's generation for example was completely different to my parents or the current generation. Men in the past slept under their wagons – never inside. They worked long hours doing hard labouring jobs. Nobody does that type of 'slavery' any more.

I'm not playing a victim here because to be honest it doesn't affect my life all that much. I am like others in the sense that I have accepted it and I leave people to have their opinions. But the people who hate us and discriminate against us are the same ones who have never spoken to one of us in their life because of fear. If they were to get over that fear and speak to us, they would realise that we are not bad people – well most of us anyway – and they could ask us questions and learn about our culture and heritage if they tried. But they have fixed opinions and are not willing for these to shift. This is helped greatly by the media who promote any negativity at any opportunity. Take for example, if there is a mess left after the Appleby Horse Fair, that will be on the front pages of the tabloids who bad-mouth us – but when the same happens at Glastonbury there is nothing said.

Fights do break out in the Gypsy and Traveller communities usually because of broken promises. A Traveller's word is his bond and when he breaks this, tensions and family feuds take place. It is deeply frowned upon to break an agreement and do a roll back. An example of this is when somebody agrees to buy something and then changes their mind, particularly if they deny making a promise or deal in the first place.

Many of the younger Gypsies in Britain have turned half a back on their community partly because of their fear of discrimination. They want to fit in. They want to live in houses and have steady jobs and do not want others to know about their background. But my motto is that in life no matter where you are going, you should never forget where you have come from. This comes at a cost and sadly a

> lot of young people in our community do not have direction in the sense they have little or no knowledge of their culture. Few speak Romanese, which is declining in the sense that there are only around 20–25 per cent of Romany Gypsies living in Britain who speak the language, with the remainder knowing only a few words. Unless it is spoken and kept alive, it will die out completely.

Children's Services

Prejudice, stereotypical images and an overt presence of discrimination about Romany and Traveller children has sometimes led to social workers and other professionals thinking GRT children automatically suffer some form of abuse or neglect. The definitions of abuse and neglect are stated in the *Working Together to Safeguard Children Policy* as outlined in Allen and Riding (2018, pp 30–1).

- » Abuse can be physical, sexual or emotional and can be defined as a form of maltreatment of a child by inflicting harm on them or failing to protect the child from harm. Children may be abused by an adult or adults, or another child or children.
- » Neglect can be defined as a persistent failure to meet a child's basic physical and/or psychological needs, which is likely to result in serious damage to the child's development and health. This can include not providing them with adequate food, clothing and shelter; not protecting them from physical or emotional harm or danger; not providing adequate supervision; and not accessing healthcare for them when needed.

It is important to understand that Gypsies (Romany and Roma) and Travellers are two distinct ethnic groups. They share experiences of oppression and discrimination in key areas – but society wrongly labels them together and refers to them as 'Travellers' without being able to differentiate their cultural heritage and roots. This has been drip-fed from stories in the press and media that portray Gypsies as violent, thieves and liars. Mistaken assumptions often lead to professionals losing sight of the needs and indeed the views of these children, by placing their own personal values and considerations above those of the best interests of the child or children in question. Allen and Hulmes (2021) refer to this as aversive racism, which overlooks cultural differences in child-rearing practices because some social workers unknowingly have prejudicial views of GRT people that won't be obviously apparent in their manner, but subconsciously at least will possess negative feelings, thoughts, opinions and beliefs about them. Therefore, it is questionable whether social workers treat GRT children the same way as they treat non-GRT children because their knowledge base of GRT culture and lifestyle is limited. Unfortunately, an over-involvement of social workers working with families who have experienced a history of institutionalised prejudice and mistreatment has resulted in children being taken into care unnecessarily, leading to the cultural needs of children often being left unmet. It is virtually impossible to get a foster or adoptive parent who can meet the child's cultural needs. There are no GRT adoptive or foster parents in the UK. Social workers have no government guidelines about how to work with GRT families who move between local authorities.

It has also been noticed by GRT members of the British Association of Social Workers (BASW) that GRT children are often removed from families without adhering to policies that consider the cultural traits of a community. It is often common on Traveller sites for children to sleep in one trailer by themselves while parents sleep next door in another trailer as this is part of their customs. Ordinarily, before settled children are placed in care, social workers explore other family members (grandparents, aunts and uncles) who would be willing to provide respite or be in a position to offer longer-term care in order to keep the child within the broader kinship family unit. This is seldom, if ever, considered for GRT children, so ingrained is the prejudiced view that relatives will collude with the parents of the child and will either be untruthful or withhold information from services.

While there is often little evidence of this, risk is taken out of context and, in the process, the child or children in the middle of this are harmed. Removal is considered in the first instance when in fact this is the worst possible outcome for the children involved unless there is evidence that the children in question are being subjected to abuse and neglect that cannot or has not been addressed in a Child Protection Plan. Police involvement in social care situations with GRT families is also used when not needed but is borne out of a fear of what social workers (and other professionals) think or assume (including perceived violence) will be the case for GRT people, who they think will turn involvement from social care into an unnecessarily hostile environment type of scenario.

Some of the main presenting issues that Children's Services encounter are poverty, overcrowding, properties in poor state of repair and upkeep, large families, unknown people staying with families, large numbers of dogs and other animals, children sleeping on bare mattresses and no lightshades. If care proceedings are instigated, consideration will need to have been given to other alternatives like suitable family members where the child(ren) can stay otherwise children risk being placed with families who do not have a Romany or Traveller heritage. There isn't reliable data to confirm the exact numbers of GRT children in local authority care, but it is estimated that two-thirds of Romany and Traveller children who have been assessed by Children's Services were not considered to be at risk of significant harm.

Referrals to Children's Services come in mainly from schools, the police, the Probation Service and mental health services. Social workers carry out a Child and Family Assessment on each child referred and open to their services. Assessments concentrate on three main areas.

- » The child's development needs – including whether they are suffering, or likely to suffer, significant harm.
- » Parents' or carers' capacity to respond to those needs.
- » Impact and influence of the wider family, community and environmental circumstances.

A children's social work team in the southeast of England provided me with some examples of GRT cases that were subject to Child and Family Assessments.

Example 1

A Romany Gypsy girl aged 17 dated a Romany Gypsy boy of the same age. They had sex. Both families of the girl and boy talked them into getting married. They married and the girl went to live with her husband's family. Within weeks, he started becoming violent towards her – often pulling her hair and kicking her. She was deeply shocked because she married with the notion that everything was lovely and romantic between them. The girl reported the abuse to the police after she received a bad beating. What further compounded the matter was that the boy's family watched the beatings as this was normal behaviour to them. Instead, they expressed surprise at her unwillingness to conform to the life that they expected her to live. She wanted to still go out with friends and get her nails done but her husband's parents expected her to stay in and do the housework. The marriage lasted three months before the girl returned to live with her parents.

Example 2

Bill suffered from PTSD and was under the local community mental health team who noticed that his children were struggling with his moods when he took it out on them. At first, he was hostile towards the social worker who went around carrying out an assessment. At one point he got very aggressive and defensive but calmed down when the social worker explained to him that they were there to help him. Trust slowly built and after that he opened up and was very cooperative with services. In fact, he became so accepting that help was being offered to him and his family that he warmed sufficiently to the social worker by making offers of tea during the visit. One day the social worker had a flat tyre and Bill even offered to fix it, such was the extent of the rapport that had developed between them.

Example 3

The Probation Service did an unannounced visit to the address that their client had given them and during the visit they discovered that a female and a young child were living in the house and that previous reference to them had not been made. What made it particularly alarming was that the offender had a long criminal record for violence including carrying knives. Upon further investigation it was discovered that the offender had deceived services about the occupants of the house and that the woman and her child were relatives. Excuses were made that the woman and child had only recently moved in, but further checks did not substantiate this information. The offender was given a final warning for his deceptive behaviour and was asked to move to different accommodation. This also resulted in the child being assigned a social worker after being considered a Child in Need.

Social work is about social justice, human rights and anti-oppressive, anti-racist and anti-discriminatory practices. But social workers may fall victim to anti-Gypsy and Traveller media stereotypes that have been ingrained in many people's psyches. This clashes with social work values and amounts to overt racism and while this may be unintentional, it results in misunderstandings and discrimination, prejudices and bad practice.

The ability to have honest, respectful conversations about 'white privilege' and what this means to white ethnicities outside the BAME (Black, Asian and Minority Ethnic) triangle is an important part of social work practice.

GRT professionals within British Association of Social Workers (BASW) believe that every social worker should undertake specific GRT training and be culturally competent in the issues affecting GRT people – or otherwise, they should not be allowed to work in these communities. It is so important to understand the cultural identity, nuances and lifestyles factors in these respective communities. The fact that this is mainly missing from social work training needs urgent attention and while some small changes are being made, it is not enough, hence the chronic lack of knowledge and understanding that exists about GRT people among social workers.

Children coming out of care have been known to experience great difficulties with their cultural identity, having been cut off from it after they became looked-after children. Their culture had been removed from them when they entered the system. Untrained foster carers will be equally ignorant on GRT culture, and may hold prejudiced stereotyped views of GRT people garnered through the media. Young Gypsies coming out of care often have a feeling of not belonging anywhere and have been known to want to live outdoors and therefore start travelling. It is concerning that the new anti-trespassing laws prevent this from occurring, which in turn risks an increase in mental health issues including suicide and substance misuse issues.

Victoria's story

When I was growing up, nobody used to call us Gypsies. But one day my father said we must stop being referred to as 'Travellers' because this is what gorgers always call us. Now when people ask, I tell them I am a Romany Gypsy.

My husband hides his identity at work because he fears that if anything goes missing, they will accuse him of stealing. He has often had to keep quiet when colleagues make comments about 'Gypos'. He won't let me tag him on Facebook in case anybody at work finds out about his background.

Women can be quiet and stay in the background, but I'm loud and express my feelings. I make decisions by myself, but I never argue with my husband over important things. I accept his choices; however, I'm aware I can persuade his decisions too. As my mother used to say, 'The man is the head of the family, and the wife is the neck'.

Before lockdown, I wanted to go to dance classes, but my husband didn't think this was a good idea for women with children. I think he was fearful of me mixing with gorger women, especially as a few I was friendly with were regular pub-goers. Maybe my husband thought they would lead me astray. Anyway, I respected his wishes and didn't go to the classes. Not many of the gorger women understand how we like to respect our husbands and want to look after them. They think we are doormats, but we're not.

Domestic violence does take place in Travelling communities, but it is not as bad as folk make out and no greater than in the gorger world. The suicide rate amongst Traveller men, though, is very high as increasing rules in society make it harder for Traveller men to be Traveller men. Many consider society is against us and compare the way we are discriminated against as the genocide of our culture. Traveller men lash out because they feel helpless, especially when their identity is under pressure. It eats away at their self-confidence, self-image and self-esteem. What people don't understand is that we respect our families and that if a couple experience difficulties the wife is still more likely to stay with her husband because she doesn't want her children to grow up fatherless. Our divorce rates are still low in comparison to gorger communities. I guess we stick to the saying that we made our bed, so we must lie in it.

> *When we were young, nobody was openly gay in our community but that has steadily crept up over the last decade. I get annoyed when some deny there are any gay Travellers because if they opened their eyes more, they would see that there is even a Gay Pride march that Travelling communities participate in annually. But many people are still uncomfortable with it. Some of the older generation think being gay is a mental illness. I have three sons and if any of them told me they were gay, I would love and respect them, but I would be worried about the judgement they would receive. I know things are changing but they are not changing enough.*
>
> *Our way of life is under threat. There are not enough Traveller sites available now, which is why nearly three-quarters of the Travelling community currently reside in houses. Those living in a house will never experience life on the road like their parents and grandparents, but this does not mean they cannot be real Travellers with hearts containing our traditions, culture and values. There is so much bickering and belittling amongst Gypsies and Travellers these days. Every day you see someone telling someone else that they are not a proper Traveller because of XYZ. You just need to read Facebook posts to see people accusing house-dwellers of not being a proper Traveller or insulting an Irish Traveller by saying they are inferior to Romany Gypsies.*
>
> *My children are still very young. Recently I had to tell my daughter, who is three, that she is a Gypsy because there is nothing about our lifestyle to make this obvious. I want to teach her about our culture, heritage and history. I want all my children to be proud of who they are because I remember being bullied at school and called horrible names. This never got to me because I always knew how special it was to be born a Gypsy and that gorger children would never understand. Our communities must readjust and realise our culture is so rich and that this can never be taken away from us just because we must modify our lives when living in bricks and mortar.*

Bruce's story

Some years ago, when I worked in a youth offending team, I met Bruce who was sent to me on a youth referral order after being sentenced for a minor offence. Now aged 17 it was nice to meet him again in his home along with his mother, who I also knew from my previous involvement. When I knew him the first time, we had not directly discussed his cultural background. I only knew that he was from a 'Travelling' background, his parents were separated and that he was a middle child with an older and younger sister.

Like many social workers, I hadn't received any training in GRT culture and therefore was completely ignorant of his culture and heritage. Our meeting again came about after a colleague of mine was introduced to Bruce through another Romany Gypsy client who was Bruce's friend. My colleague told me that he had met Bruce, who enjoyed talking about his background, telling stories and explaining things about his culture that he had learned from his grandfather.

I sought official permission to speak to Bruce after he agreed to meet me. I instantly noticed that he had grown into a tall, handsome young man and, as before, the family home was immaculately clean inside. Over tea in the kitchen, Bruce filled me in on his life since we had last seen each other. He was now mainly working with his grandfather doing some scrap metal work as well as helping in his father's gym. He was into physical fitness himself and trained at his father's gym several times a week. Long term, Bruce is interested in getting a job in the construction industry and was looking into doing his CSCS (Construction Skills Certification Scheme) card, which is a health and safety pass that is compulsory for getting work on building sites.

Bruce spent a lot of time with his maternal grandparents growing up and was very close to them. Bruce's grandfather had travelled extensively growing up and relayed stories to Bruce about the nomadic upbringing he had, which was something that neither Bruce nor his mother had directly experienced. His grandfather owns some land and often takes Bruce out rabbit snaring and fishing, and they also have made several trips together to the Appleby Horse Fair over the years.

Josephine (Bruce's mother) also contributed to the discussion at times and added the following during the conversation:

Things are changing. Travellers are now mixing with more people because the bad reputation image has weakened.

My daughter's boyfriend is a gorger and they have just had a baby. Bruce's girlfriend is a gorger too and none of this bothers me if they are happy, that's all I care about.

More Traveller women have jobs these days. I have worked myself for the past two years in a residential home for elderly people.

Men want to better themselves and are very money orientated. They always have on the front of their minds the need to have a job to provide for their wives and children. Travellers are not a lazy culture – men can never sit down.

Bruce expressed himself well and came across as a mature young man beyond his age. He told me that in Romany Gypsies family values are passed down, which to him means some respect to others, being kind, not being greedy, not being racist as well as treating people well and having an ability to help each other.

Like many other young men, Bruce loved his mother's home cooking. I asked him about his favourite meal. He introduced me to a meal called 'Joe Grey', which he said he loved. This meal, which is a traditional Gypsy recipe, consists of *6 sausages, 6 rashers of bacon, 4 large tomatoes or a tin of tomatoes, 4 large potatoes which are sliced, 1 onion and 3 stock cubes.* A Joe Grey is served as a runny stew, with crusty bread and butter. Bruce said hardly a week passed by when he didn't have a Joe Grey for dinner.

The other topic we discussed was blood sports, including fighting chickens. Cock fighting is a bloody and cruel sport whereby pit cockerels are made to fight each other until death, with some contests lasting just seconds while spectators place bets. It has been illegal for almost 200 years. If caught, organisers can receive a short prison sentence, but this isn't a deterrent because the fights are usually held in private. Sometimes sharp metal spurs are attached to the birds' legs before fights to increase the chance of injury and up the stakes. The surviving birds are often left to suffer from the horrific injuries sustained, rather than receiving any professional veterinary treatment. Bruce had attended several cock fights with his grandfather and was keeping an open mind about whether the 'sport' was morally wrong. He also spoke about his love of dogs. He liked the Saluki and Whippet breeds favoured by Romany Gypsies. Bruce's dream was to one day own a house in the country along with some land where he would be able to have his own horses and dogs.

Case study – **Wayne**

A new group of Travellers had come to the village. I listened to a woman question out loud what havoc they would cause without knowing that I was a Gypsy myself. She then went on to ask, 'Don't they steal children?' I kept my lips zipped. Maybe that sort of thing happened 300 years ago. But honestly, where do they hear about these things? They must read it in a book or something.

We used to settle in a village five or six months every year when I was a young boy. My mother used to go to the nearest school and get us enrolled. You could always count on one teacher who would introduce us to the class 'Now, listen everyone – this is Wayne who comes from a Gypsy and Travelling background and he is going to be with us for a while'. I used to say to myself 'Thank you very much dear for doing that', while everybody around me would stare as if I were a leper. This type of singling out meant that I was not seen as a person. I felt looked down upon before I even had opened my mouth. As a child, you take that to heart. You feel the dagger looks while you are made to think, 'I'm not in love with any of you either'. But my mother had other ideas and used to always tell us to never be nasty to gorger children. She told us they were innocent and asked us to always share sweets and things with them. The thing about being a Gypsy is that I can spot one off a mile away. We can easily detect each other by our language. Say a few words and you will get a response. I know ten generations of my family. My father and I never stop talking about our ancestors. So, when I meet another Gypsy, I ask them, or they ask me 'Who are you one of?' (What family are you from?) So whatever family name they say, I will know someone from their family tree. There are wannabe Gypsies in the sense that someone will come up to one and say, 'My grandfather was a Gypsy', without having a clue who they were or where they came from. It is as if they romanticise about such things. Of course, some might be telling the truth but have never bothered digging too much into their ancestry, but others will be talking rubbish!

Case study – **Tina**

'Mixed minority' is the way my children describe themselves as their father is Jamaican. My parents were English Romany Gypsies. My mother was considered a 'posh' Gypsy because she came from a Show People family. My father was less posh! He did manual jobs including metal scrapping, potato picking and demolition work. But they were childhood sweethearts.

My first husband was mixed race. My brother was livid at me for marrying outside the community. My father less so and joked with me by saying 'You're darker than him'. My children conceal who they are. They don't trust easily and usually wait to get to know someone before telling them their background.

I come from a family of eight children and had the best – most privileged – childhood imaginable. As a child, I was free to roam the fields, free to swim in the rivers and ride bare horse. My older brothers and sisters looked after me as it was their job to help raise the younger children. School was awful for me. I was a child who wanted to learn but because of my dyslexia was made to sit at the back of the class. The secrecy will remain with me forever. My sisters used to tell me to not tell anyone about our Romany background because of fear that we would get picked on. I stopped going when I was 14. It was my choice, but I made up for it later in life and have done NVQ qualifications as well as becoming a foster parent.

Most women have a good life. Husbands look after their wives. They don't go short of food or nice clothes. But if a man tells his wife not to do something, you don't cross the line by challenging him. But being a Gypsy is a hard life. Facebook is the death of us with all the moaning. People have no respect for us and will constantly write nasty comments like 'Oh the Gypsies are in town'. Is it any wonder people fear us? Likewise, the GRT communities have several Facebook pages that are anti-gorger and offer a defiant and aggressive response to questions. They interpret anything said or mentioned as a slur against them when often it is clearly not the case. I do know that gorgers don't respect that Gypsies fought in the World Wars. They pay homage to Gurkha soldiers but not to Travelling men who fought bravely.

The GRT world will be different in 50 years' time – for Romany Gypsies in Britain, you will have a much-diluted version of Gypsy culture and heritage. All the good is being sucked out of it. Drug culture is becoming worrying. Culture is dying out slowly because the younger generation have all been born in houses and don't want to know about the lives of their parents and grandparents. They are not interested in oral storytelling. They are not interested in the Romani language. They'll tell you that they speak it, but they don't. They have made up their own version of it and it's now more a slang dialect than anything else.

Conclusion

Some Romany elders believe that in 20 years' time, their community will see many young Gypsies bearing the 'name' only because the Romany way of life has radically changed in past decades. Many of the old customs and traditions are dying out given that the majority of Romany have now given up travelling. Some elders feel that young people have far less respect for their culture, where morals and decency are no longer respected and many possess the sole ambition of getting rich quick by whatever means. However, they acknowledge that some middle-aged Romany men are doing well and hold down respectable jobs in roofing, guttering and block paving. They are registered with agencies that endorse their reputation as proven reliable tradesmen.

The older Romany lament the bygone days of travelling and are adamant they will never lose touch with their roots. Although most are settled in houses, they still crave to travel and were it practical or affordable, they would still like to spend a portion of the year travelling to various places around the country in their caravans. Indeed, there are many different perspectives to be obtained in Romany families ranging from those of grandparents down to their grandchildren. Remnants of the past filled with history, traditions and customs meet the current generation of Romany who no longer have the same level of vested interest that their forebears had in their past. Therefore, often the struggles of the past have become history and 'stories' as opposed to shared lived experiences. While the young listen to these stories, they are satisfied that the past of their parents and grandparents is not their present lifestyle.

Chapter 3 | Roma

Introduction

Many myths exist about the GRT communities, as mentioned in the list in Chapter 1, but what is missing from that list is a prime myth that exists about Roma people. A common misconception is that Roma are true, authentic Gypsies who are superior to Romany Gypsies and indeed Travellers. It is still widely believed that Roma live exclusively in Romania, travel around in expensive ornate wagons and enjoy a bohemian lifestyle. Of course, this is not true. Roma in Eastern Europe mainly live in rundown accommodation, whether this is in urban or rural areas. Their nomadic way of life was surrendered without choice under communist rule. Exclusion, racism, discrimination and disadvantage permeate every aspect of their daily lives. The vicious cycle of poverty, lack of education, unemployment, health problems and destitute lifestyles is common in Roma across Eastern and indeed Western Europe. This chapter covers my research in Romania as well as looking at the lives of Roma in other Eastern European countries. It also looks at what life was like when new Roma arrivals came to the UK and what life is currently like for those in both the UK and Ireland.

Roma background

The word Roma is used as a catch-all term for European 'Gypsies' who have the same origins as Romany Gypsies and who share the same linguistic heritage with Britain's long-established Romany Gypsy community. There are about 12 million Roma worldwide. They are traditionally travelling people who, like Romany Gypsies, originated in Northern India but now live worldwide – about 1 million live in the United States and roughly 800,000 in Brazil but the largest majority live in Europe – mainly in Eastern Europe but also in certain Western European countries like Spain, Germany, Italy and Greece (European Union Agency for Fundamental Rights, 2020).

Roma are essentially Romany Gypsies from continental Europe and make up one of Europe's largest (Indo-Aryan) ethnic minority groups. Unlike Romany Gypsies in Britain, Roma stopped living nomadic lives generations ago. The term 'Roma' accurately distinguishes between European Roma and UK Romany Gypsies.

Roma left the Indian subcontinent nearly a thousand years ago and began to move westwards along the Silk Roads in search of trading opportunities – and ever since then they have faced continuous marginalisation. They are also still doing the lowest-paid manual jobs in both Britain and Europe. Roma communities have been the biggest victims of both poverty and xenophobia in Europe for centuries.

Roma groups first arrived in medieval Europe in the 1100s. In some countries, such as Romania and Bulgaria, they now make up 12 per cent of the population. Turkey has an estimated number of 2.75 million with large numbers also in Russia, Slovakia, Hungary, Serbia, Spain and France (European Union Agency for Fundamental Rights, 2020). Roma in Europe are also known as Tziganes, Zigeuners and Gitanos and are divided into many distinct groups known by a variety of names which relate to various occupations. For example, Romanian Roma consist of approximately 40 different clan groups including Caldari (tinsmiths and coppersmiths), Fieraru (blacksmiths), Ursari (bear trainers), Grastari (horse dealers) and Lautari (musicians). Similar clans exist in all other Eastern and Western European countries.

Sinti Roma

The Sinti in Central Europe, who are the largest group of Roma in Europe, mostly live in Germany and are closely related to the group in France known as Manouche. Other small groups of Sinti live in Austria, Switzerland, Italy, Netherlands, Serbia and Croatia. Sinti have lived in Germany for well over 600 years. Sinti Roma bore the terrible fate in the Second World War of being sent to concentration camps. Even before the war, they were persecuted, resulting in some Sinti being forcibly sterilised under the Law for the Prevention of Hereditarily Diseased Offspring. Others were barred from entering the country after the head of the SS issued a decree in 1938 entitled 'The Fight against the Gypsy Menace'. Support from many non-Nazis was strong because of the prejudice they had for Sinti, who they stereotyped and blamed for crime and anti-social behaviour. Nazis too deliberately sought them out, resulting in their fate being paralleled in many ways to that of Jewish people because they were considered an inferior race. Before the start of the war, German police deported over 5000 Sinti from Austria to Lodz, a ghetto used for housing Jews. Sinti were placed in a segregated section. The conditions were horrific – many died of typhus within months as a result of starvation and lack of medicines. Those who survived were transferred to the killing centre at Chelmno where they, along with thousands of Jews, were poisoned by gas. Shaw (2015) states that up to half a million Sinti and other Roma were murdered during the Holocaust and the Second World War. Despite this inhumanity, torture and death, Roma were forgotten after the war and many had to fight hard to get recognition and compensation for their persecution.

Repeat of history

Irrespective of wherever Roma have lived, they have always historically faced discrimination and persecution. They have been referred to as Gypsies, which they consider a derogatory word. Few people know the true history of Roma, how they were originally a Hindi people from Northern India, or know anything about their travels, persecution and survival. As Roma people have an Indian origin, they are sometimes drawn towards Asian people whose language is also rooted in Sanskrit such as Urdu, Punjabi and Hindi. Roma people may express themselves very loudly because people from oral cultures speak directly with spontaneous expressions. This involves face-to-face speaking with good eye contact seen as honesty. They often like working with their hands (preferred in those from nomadic cultures). Oral cultures have the highest respect for the spoken word before the written. Roma culture places emphasis on understanding body language and eye contact. Memories of those from oral cultures are more practised, being in constant use. The spoken word is revered and remembered. Plain, loud and direct speaking is normal. A good loud discussion or argument is enjoyed. It is acceptable for children to interrupt conversations and for several to talk at once with the most persistent and loudest winning the day. Emotions are expressed openly and immediately, and confidence is respected and encouraged in children.

Quarmby (2014) explains that due to Roma often having a visibly non-white appearance and distinct linguistic differences, they often face an added layer of discrimination from wider society, which can compound the prejudice they may face. Shortly after arriving in Europe, Roma were made slaves in Romania (which continued until the nineteenth century). In countries like Switzerland and Denmark, Roma were put to death throughout the medieval era. Many countries like Germany, Italy and Portugal ordered their expulsion. History is sprinkled with savage acts of cruelty – Roma children abducted from their parents, women having their ears cut off, Roma people branded with hot irons. To force assimilation, the use of their native language was forbidden in some countries. Some countries forbade natives to marry any Roma person. In the post-war era, Roma people remained an oppressed group, especially in the Soviet Union. Sterilisation, via injection, in some Eastern European countries like the Czech Republic remained up until 2002 in the hope of getting rid of the Roma gene to limit their population. In Italy, up until recently, even those born there were being denied housing on the grounds that people living in cheap metal containers in isolated Roma camps were deemed to be in permanent housing.

Aggravated anti-Gypsy prejudice remains to this day throughout Eastern European countries including Romania, the Czech Republic, Moldava and Bulgaria, Serbia, and

Montenegro where Roma are regularly subjected to widespread racism, discrimination and human rights violations. They have been repeatedly pushed to the margins of society. Nobody advocates for the promotion of social inclusion of Roma into society. Instead, anti-Gypsyism is the norm with no public outcry against injustices and a total failure of the state to protect them and their rights. Both politicians and the media have always had a propensity to highlight problems caused to others by Roma rather than acknowledging or reporting the difficulties and hardships imposed on them by society.

There has also been little improvement in societal attitudes towards Roma in Western Europe. In recent years about 10,000 Roma were expelled from France after their camps were destroyed. Most of the Roma had lived in illegal shanty towns within the city of Paris on abandoned train lines. Politicians publicly branded them as foreigners who 'cannot integrate' into the French way of life. There were various attacks on them organised and orchestrated by locals, who themselves were often from poor and immigrant backgrounds. The attacks were initially provoked by a racist rumour detailing the age-old myth of Gypsies stealing children, as Wayne alluded to in the case study in Chapter 2. In several European countries, adults still scold children with expressions such as '*If you don't behave, Gypsies will come and take you away*'. Literature is full of such tales, including Victor Hugo's classic 1831 novel *Notre-Dame de Paris*, where one of its central characters, La Esmeralda, was a child who was abducted and raised by Gypsies.

Roma in Romania

Romania has one of the largest numbers of Roma in the world. My research took me to Bucharest to view a neighbourhood considered by many to be one of the most deprived parts of Eastern Europe. Ferentari is a makeshift 'ghetto' settlement about five kilometres from the centre of Bucharest. This is home to a large majority of Roma, where living conditions are considered close to those of sub-Saharan Africa in terms of illiteracy, infant mortality and malnutrition. Ferentari is seen as Romania's desire to separate Roma from the rest of the population. This is viewed by many as institutional racism whereby the state and society believe that Roma are less human and less valued than other citizens despite Roma people having lived in Romania for several hundred years. On the one hand they are left to 'rot' in Ferentari, whose geographical area covers approximately one square mile of rundown blocks of flats known for its severe social problems including extreme poverty, mass unemployment, low levels of education and high drug usage. On the other hand, Roma have little choice but to stay in this area because they cannot afford to go elsewhere. This is coupled with the fact that despite the terrible environment, it is 'home', where their families have lived for many generations.

Many Roma people will have spent their entire lives in Ferentari. They are technically living there illegally in abandoned and disused state property. The high-rise blocks are usually studio flats where many families live in one large room. Overcrowding is the norm. The studios have no kitchens, meaning that cooking provisions are improvised. There are no individual bathrooms either, with each family having to share a bathroom at the end of the hallway on each floor. My research in Bucharest led me to discover that the sanitary conditions in these rundown housing estates are practically non-existent because the sewerage system does not cover the entire area. Rubbish can often be seen packed high on the streets because many of the people are unregistered and therefore don't pay taxes. In return this means that the residents of certain areas in Ferentari are not entitled to amenities such as having their rubbish collected. The stench on the streets, particularly in summertime, is unbearable. This has resulted in tuberculosis being ten times more prevalent than in the rest of Romania. Roma in Ferentari have a life expectancy that is 20–25 years shorter than that of the general population. Adults suffer heart conditions, cancer and lung diseases, while children often suffer from respiratory diseases and infections and parasitic diseases because of overcrowding, poor nutrition, poverty and disease. Many families don't have a fridge and the meat and food go off. They often buy the cheapest food available as well as buying food that is out of date. Clean water is also a rare commodity. The crime rate in Ferentari is very high with around 18,000 crimes committed each year including 350-plus murders, robberies and violent crime. This is completely disproportionate to other parts of Bucharest and Romania where crime is relatively low.

There is less help given to Roma people these days from NGOs since Romania became a member of the European Union (EU) in 2007, which saw a reduction in funding. The Roma have been accused of becoming too accustomed to help from NGOs, which includes food and clothes that make them dependent on outside help and therefore unable to secure their own rights. But you must question the fairness of this accusation given the extreme poverty that is a daily lived experience for many people. There is even less foreign aid coming from countries like America, who also believe that the EU have a responsibility to Romania and its citizens – but fail to understand the exclusion of Roma from Romanian society in this dialogue. If becoming part of the EU has benefitted Romania, sadly it has not contributed to changing the lives of Roma living in Ferentari in terms of better living conditions, employment or improved healthcare facilities. In fact, since Romania joined the EU, hundreds of thousands of Roma have flooded European cities, complaining of racism and poverty in their home countries.

Despite the negative things that are said about Ferentari regarding its poverty and violence, there is some positivity on the horizon although this is taking place on a gradient as opposed to fast sweeping changes. While the area has improved in the last five to ten years, it remains mainly an underclass area but there are parts of it becoming more and more working class. In the process, the gap between Ferentari and its neighbouring areas is blending more into one. In the process, more working-class people are moving into the boundary of Ferentari working as taxi drivers, mechanics and cleaners. Buildings are being renovated, supermarkets are being built and restaurants are being opened and some Roma people are finding employment in the area. Regeneration and redevelopment are in progress, which is starting to make Ferentari look more like a regular neighbourhood in Bucharest. Provided proper investment is given to improve the accommodation blocks that house many Roma people, many lives will be changed for the better in the sense that they will have become better integrated into Romanian society and part of the working class. Romanians consider that the bad reputation Ferentari has is caused by the Roma population living there, but it is completely unfair to use them as scapegoats. In any area or community where poverty and deprivation has become the norm, the ethnic origin of its inhabitants can hardly be nominated as the sole cause of its problems.

Roma in other European countries

Just like in Romania, Roma communities in other parts of Eastern and Western Europe are regarded as the continent's largest and most marginalised ethnic minority. Daily 'existence' for many is marked by poor housing, high rates of unemployment or low incomes, poor education provision, as well as low literacy rates and poor health. In Eastern European countries, the nomadic days of Roma people came to an end under communist rule. These days they all live sedentary lives, unlike some in Western European countries where a small degree of nomadic or semi-nomadic lifestyles still exist.

The number of Roma households living in dilapidated houses or in poor neighbourhoods is more than three times higher than in the case of non-Roma households. Amnesty International (2010) note the existence of significant differences between the living conditions of Roma in different localities and even regions. They add that even in countries like Bulgaria that offer urban housing to Roma, 70 per cent live in segregated neighbourhoods. Roma households in villages are characterised by tendencies to overcrowding because the number of people per room is relatively high. In Eastern Europe, there is limited access to social housing, resulting in Roma having little or no chance of receiving this provision.

Forced evictions from informal settlements where Roma had no choice but to live owing to being excluded from social housing schemes often take place in countries like Bulgaria, Romania, Slovakia and Serbia. They get moved instead to camps with no heating, water or sanitation – often making people homeless in the process with no proper place to live. Nobody in authority believes or advocates their rights to adequate housing. Roma people have been condemned to a life of constant insecurity, wandering from one makeshift camp to another. Like Roma living in Italy, they are also sometimes placed into metal containers as homes, which are poorly insulated and damp inside and placed near sewage or industrial waste land.

Segregation in education is widespread in countries including Hungary, Romania, Bulgaria, Slovakia, Croatia, Bosnia and Herzegovina, Moldova, Ukraine, the Czech Republic, Serbia, Slovenia and Macedonia. Here Roma children are placed in separate classes to other students. A 'white flight' phenomenon exists whereby parents remove their children from school if their children are mixed with Roma or if there is an overrepresentation of Roma children in a particular school. This has seen an increase of Roma children being placed in 'special' or practical schools for children with mild mental disabilities. Roma parents are made to believe that by going to these special types of schools, it protects their children from prejudice and discrimination from teachers and other pupils – but this is a fallacy. Instead, children receive a reduced curriculum and this results in few going on to mainstream secondary school.

The way of life of the Roma is largely influenced by their traditions and socio-cultural norms. The roles in Roma families are clearly distributed and imply a paternalistic character, the men being responsible for the socio-economic welfare of the family, and the women for the household and the education of the children. Early marriages are one of the main reasons for dropping out of school, especially for girls.

According to experts, the main impediment on the labour market in the case of Roma is the lack of necessary training and qualifications. At the same time, it cannot be denied that there are situations in which employers refuse to accept a Roma person holding a position in the company, due to stereotypes. Many refuse to acknowledge this openly, citing reasons that relate to insufficient level of education or experience, or lack of other professional skills. Roma in European countries routinely face prejudice, and this is the cause of widespread social inequality and human rights abuses. Indigenous Eastern Europeans keep themselves apart from Roma, who they refer to as 'The Blacks'. They are called 'cioara', meaning crow in Romanian, because of their dark complexion. Job opportunities are few, resulting in high rates of unemployment for Roma. It is estimated that 90 per cent of Roma are unemployed in Eastern European countries, resulting in men mainly going to work in neighbouring countries such as Italy, Austria, France and Germany. However, some Roma families in countries like Romania and Moldova migrate each year to Russia and Ukraine to do seasonal work. Moldova is the poorest country in Europe but has seen an increase of Roma people building houses in the north of the country from the money saved from their overseas employment.

Young Roma people continuously face inequalities because of poverty, absenteeism in the education system and the marriage of adolescent girls before adulthood. Child marriage and school dropouts are closely linked, especially for Roma girls. Such marriages expose girls to the dangers of pregnancy and early childbirth, as well as to a high risk of violence.

Roma girls are disproportionately disadvantaged from the perspective of education: only 63 per cent of young Roma women aged 16–24 years have an education, compared with 99 per cent of young non-Roma women of that age. According to the United Children's Fund (UNICEF) data, only half of Roma children in the Republic of Moldova go to school. In comparison, 90 per cent of children of other nationalities attend school.

(Banari, 2020, p 26)

This is not exclusive to Moldova but is also true of Roma communities in other Eastern European countries. Child marriages have always been part of Roma culture, designed to ensure that marriage to someone outside the community does not take place. This is particularly common in the Kalderash clans in Russia, Bulgaria, Romania and Hungary. It is very common for Roma parents to sell off children as young as ten years old. Parents arrange their daughter's marriage and the groom's family are expected to pay a hefty dowry for the bride as part of the agreement. The bride usually moves into the home of her future husband and is expected to help his mother do the household chores. The 'couple' keep separate bedrooms and do not get married and consummate their union until the age of 14 or 15.

Controversial bride markets among the Kalderash clan still exist in Bulgaria, where each year in the town of Stara Zagora in the centre region of the country thousands of young virgins parade themselves in front of older boys and young men who bid for them along with their families. Young girls take weeks to prepare for the market – deciding what dress to wear, how to style their hair, how to make themselves look a little older to heighten the chances of a better bid. This may appear degrading to the outside world, but these young girls take great pride in this and have grown up believing that their main role in life is to marry a good man and serve him as best they can. To the Roma people, a custom like this bride market is one way of holding on to their traditions and identity in an ever-increasing changing world.

In traditional communities, the Roma woman wears a long, multi-layered and richly coloured skirt, large earrings, long, braided hair and sometimes a flower in her hair. Roma tradition says that a woman's legs should not be visible. In fact, the entire lower part of a woman's body is considered impure. Violation of this principle is very serious, so long skirts should always be worn. Symbol of luck, red is the favourite colour in the traditional dress of Roma women. Roma women have preserved their own style; only married women have the obligation to wear a scarf. In some areas, women are well known for their tradition of wearing gold money, in hair or sewn on clothes. Men do not have a specific dress to wear; they often wear wide-brimmed hats, long moustaches, pants, a vest and a shirt. On holidays, they are fans of brightly-coloured costumes.

Ion Bucur – European Roma Rights Centre

In some Eastern European countries (like Slovakia), Roma attend different churches to indigenous people, who perceive themselves as 'white' and Roma as 'black'. The Roma population in Eastern Europe are predominantly Christian-Orthodox while some are Catholics and a small minority in Russia are Muslim. However, Roma in all countries are also adherents of other religious cults and denominations like Jehovah's Witnesses, Adventists and Baptists. Roma join these religious groups because of certain benefits they receive in return – money, food, clothes, school materials and furniture. Roma households will contain religious memorabilia. Roma perceive 'Gadje' (non-Roma) society as unsafe and immoral inhabited by paedophiles and drug dealers. They believe there is little respect for marriage, family or children.

The history of Roma persecution and ethnic cleansing means there is reluctance in declaring their identity. Roma may say they are Czech or Slovak or Romanian until they feel safe to say Roma. A previous Slovak Prime Minister promised to *'actively effect the irresponsible growth of the Romani population'*. Many Roma have fled Slovakia over the past 20 years to seek asylum in neighbouring Western countries and since 2005 whole families have been coming to Britain. Roma continue to encounter openly racist and discriminatory attitudes in both Eastern and Western Europe that are widely accepted in society at large – even in political quarters where those seeking election promise harder policies to crack down on 'Gypsy crime' and 'Gypsy beggars'.

Roma are distrusting of the police because in Eastern Europe, ethnic information was used by the police to hand families to the Nazis and most Roma families today remember relatives who died in the Holocaust – which the Roma call *Porrajmos*, meaning great suffering or great devouring. Roma were particularly targeted by the Nazis during the Second World War. A supplementary decree to the Nuremberg Laws was given by Hitler in 1935, which classified Romani people as *'enemies of the race-based state'*, thereby placing them in the same category as Jewish people and, as such, the fate of Roma in Europe at the time was parallel to that of the Jews in the Jewish Holocaust. Research on the numbers who perished in gas chambers at Auschwitz varies from several hundred thousand to 1.5 million people. Many were tortured before their deaths, including some being placed in pressure chambers, testing drugs on them, freezing them, attempting to change their eye colour by injecting chemicals into children's eyes, as well as various amputations and other brutal surgeries as mere experiments totally ignoring the pain and suffering endured. West Germany formally recognised in 1982 that it had committed genocide against the Romani people. Some countries have set aside a day of commemoration to mark the occasion; for example, Poland has officially adopted 2 August as a day to remember the Romani genocide.

Roma arrivals to the UK in the 2000s

Roma have only started coming to live in Britain in large numbers since the mid-2000s after various accession countries joined the EU, including Romania, Bulgaria, Estonia, Latvia, Lithuania, Czech Republic, Slovakia, Poland, Hungary, Slovenia and Croatia. The first groups arrived on coaches and sometimes arrived with no spare clothes or any possessions. But nevertheless, they began to settle and form new communities across major towns and cities in the UK. This section explores the early days of Roma in Britain during this transition, which was often challenging for the new arrivals and workers involved.

Wanda, who worked as a youth worker in a southeastern town outside London, provided me with her recollections of those early days:

One day a young man walked into the church, looked around and then walked out. I followed him and found out that he was Roma from Slovakia. This led to a youth club getting formed in the church hall every Friday night where up to 80 young Slovakians – both boys and girls aged from 10–18 – would meet. Discrimination was soon discovered between Roma and non-GRT Slovakians after some youth workers were employed but left shortly afterwards citing the reason that they did not want to work with this group of young people. Eventually, some council youth workers stepped in and joined the Slovakian group with other local young people from Cambodia, India, French African and White British. The result was not good. The Slovakian group did not mix with the other young people and were territorial about their space. Arguments were frequent about choices in music and activities. Intimidation was also noticed between the Roma boys and White English girls whereby the boys had to be ticked off for taking pictures of the girls without their consent. Eventually the two groups had to be separated. Damage was also commonplace from young people from breaking doors to swinging on curtain rails to sticking pool cues through the ceiling to urinating in wastepaper bins. Despite this, the church in question persevered for ten years but a decision to terminate the youth club at the church came when a group of young Roma barged their way into the kitchen one night and told a group of elderly people to f*** o**; however, by this time several complaints had been lodged and it has been long since noticed that the building was in chaos every time they entered it. After the group nights were stopped, the police tried to negotiate their return after they noticed an increase of young people on the town streets every Friday night, but it was too late.

Despite the negativity of this experience, Wanda retains a lot of affection for Roma and recognises that they came to Britain not having a clue about boundaries, respect and discipline. She said it would be fair to say they were ill-disciplined because they did not understand the context of discipline as it had never been taught to them in their community. They were continuously eating sunflower seeds and spitting out the pips all over the place. Smoking at a young age seems very accepted in Roma culture. Among themselves, they referred to good Roma and bad Roma. The Roma people from Sobrante were known to experience extreme poverty, while those from the city of Kocscie had better living conditions.

Arriving in Britain was their first time to live in a culture so vastly different to their own. Here were young people who came from extreme poverty and had lived such difficult lives in Europe and they had arrived in a country that places great emphasis on boundaries. Here they were in a new country tasked with going to school for the first time in their lives. Many of the schools in the areas quickly excluded them because of their behaviour, while others would not offer them a place. That is not to say that some of the older Roma did not try to curtail behaviour that became over-boisterous among the younger ones. In fact, some of them showed a sense of responsibility and were encouraging their younger peers to become interested in the rich Roma culture that exists in music, poetry and storytelling. They also loved singing and playing the piano accordion. They were taken on residential trips and to the theatre, which were things they had never experienced before.

The young people were not usually promiscuous and often boys and girls became couples from a young age and would remain in a relationship until they later married with some holding off from having sex until then. However, boys tend to be sexually active from the age of 14 but many marry young. Young girls wear sexualised clothing from a young age. Gender roles in Roma are both historical and deeply entrenched. Males are seen as breadwinners, while women are expected to stay at home to cook and clean. During my visits to Roma households, it was the norm for males to do the talking, while women retreated. They are a guarded community after years of oppression and misrepresentation. These were people who had previously lived in countries in ghettoes and when they arrived here, at first they might have thought that they would get treated the same.

It was only after living here for a few years that they started to form a sense of belonging – and had become aware that the levels of oppression they endured back home were not on the same level here.

Roma face a lot of racism in the UK with some analysts questioning whether they contributed to Brexit happening, particularly in some areas of the country where people did not understand their lifestyle and culture and were against the migration of Eastern Europeans into the country. Many saw them as a predominately non-English-speaking group in their community who displayed anti-social behaviour and who lacked respect and cleanliness which indigenous citizens found unacceptable. There is still a lack of understanding of the Roma/Gypsy lifestyle and an unrealistic and unfair attitude of expecting other cultures to change to 'fit in' with British values and customs. Perhaps this eroded over time, and they have become more westernised – particularly young people who have formed their own friendship network of people outside their family and community after adapting to a British way of thinking. Wanda finished by saying that when she occasionally meets some of the former young Roma in the street who had attended the youth club, they always greet her in a friendly manner and stop for a chat. Many are now married and have their own families. She was pleased to say that most had learned English, had jobs and seemed to have integrated well. She said they were happy to talk about themselves – life in general – and were always friendly and fondly reminisced about the days they attended the youth club.

***

Some community outreach workers shared with me their experiences of working with Roma after their arrival in the UK. Roma communities were and remain closed where individuals have had bad experiences speaking to professionals, police or the press, resulting in them being tricked or misrepresented. Language too is also a barrier as many older people do not speak English. The views of the outreach workers bring clarity from many different avenues of day-to-day dealings with them.

Roma communities are very close knit, secretive and guarded. They are a hard-to-reach group and have huge trust issues with professionals, police and the outside world. They use the word 'Gadje' when referring to a non-Roma person. They believe that social services only come to take children away into care. Roma live in cramped living conditions not helped by them generally tending to be hoarders. They are very family orientated and sometimes marry their first cousins. They have big families coupled with lots of relatives coming to stay for sometimes lengthy periods of time. Sometimes there is no space left vacant including people sleeping in living rooms and hallways. Hygiene is often an issue and goes against the grain of Gypsies being considered clean people. Roma people do not think anything about walking around with dirty feet with dirt baked on them or wearing the same clothes for a week without changing. Many Roma have denial issues and will not self-identify as Roma. They keep their culture hidden because of having received heavy beatings from the police in Europe and therefore do not identify themselves in case it would count against them. They are not very literate – with children often reading for parents. Men 'work' but may claim benefits. Jobs include scrapping or basic maintenance unskilled jobs available for men and usually cleaning for women. Many work (cash-in-hand) and claim benefits. English Gypsies think they are 'superior' to them, resulting in Roma Gypsies working for them. There are high rates of domestic violence and few role models. Young males aged 12/13 can be seen to boss their older sisters and mothers. Older boys have been known to engage in underage sex with girls in a forceful way – bordering on rape. Many men have a negative view of women both in their own community and non-GRT women. There are high numbers of Roma in the criminal justice system. Catholicism is much a part of their community. Even those who came with nothing might have a picture of the Virgin Mary in their pocket or purse.

William – Community outreach worker

Roma at a glance

Life for Roma in the UK is considerably better than in their countries of origin. Key changes in lifestyles as experienced include the following.

- » They have been made to feel better accepted by society with many feeling they have the law on their side.
- » They are better off financially through social housing, benefits and social care.
- » There is less discrimination in employment than in their countries of origin.
- » They are better aware of the necessity and value of education and the laws that surround this.

Some views of professionals who work with Roma in the UK:

- » Once trust is in place, they will trust you despite fear having played a big part in their past.
- » They are very family orientated and will protect and care for extended family members.
- » They are extremely resilient and try their best to manage with what they have.
- » They are well known for their love of poetry, singing, euro pop, line dancing and musical heritage.

Lane et al (2014) point out that Roma are prone to exploitation because of their experiences of persecution, racist attacks, bullying and frequent incidents of rape in their countries of origin. Across Eastern Europe, Roma are significantly over-represented as victims of trafficking because of the extensive and endemic social exclusion which renders women and children particularly vulnerable because many of them are not registered with state authorities. Young men are also prone to trafficking and exploitation and while those who come to England are more likely to be in employment and less likely to be drawing benefits, they remain at high risk of exploitation. Most have no qualifications and few speak English, which often means ending up in low-paid jobs on temporary contracts that have been organised by recruitment agencies or gang-masters.

There is a lot of economic abuse in the Roma community. It has a dark underbelly and is hierarchical amounting to adult exploitation and modern-day slavery. Really, the abuse is shocking. You will always be able to find a 'Boss' (as Roma refer to him) who is a richer, more influential member of the community. This is someone who steps in and takes charge of those deemed vulnerable and who are unable to speak English. The Boss will help someone find a job but will demand a monthly retainer for doing so. They will help find jobs for Roma like picking and packing, farm work and factory work. They will arrange for 'clients' to be picked up by a van and taken to their place of work where many Roma work 12-hour shifts, seven days a week for something in the region of 50 pounds a week. The Boss will also help find accommodation, which is usually poor in quality. A lot of Roma live in very poor housing – usually private multi-occupancy. It is not uncommon to find 10, 15 or 20 people living in the one house rented out by rogue landlords. I knew of one such place where there was a garage next door where its workers were allowed into the house to share the toilet with the residents. So, while the Boss will find accommodation for the worker, they shouldn't expect luxury but what they should expect is to be charged a high rent for living in squalor. The Boss will help open a bank account for people for a fee, complete any paperwork for someone who can't read or write for another fee. People seem to be made to rely on the Boss for help with a myriad other things including applying for benefits, registering at a doctor, finding a school. The Boss is listened to and respected, especially by those who are illiterate. This is looked up to, revered and sometimes feared – because he is seen as bigger, stronger and somebody with influence.

Judy – Community outreach worker

Domestic violence is considered by outreach workers to be very high in Roma communities and seen as a way of life – something that is 'normal' and tolerated within marriages. Roma women received minimal education and lived suppressed lives before coming to live in Britain. It is likely that some Roma children have undiagnosed mental health issues. Many also have learning disabilities and health conditions (infections). Many Roma lived in profound poverty when first arriving in the UK with some living in damp basement flats because they had not lived in an area long enough to make them eligible for council housing.

Interactions between the Roma population and public services have often been problematic and there have been examples of them experiencing difficulties accessing education and GP services. There have also been issues with the criminal justice system.

Some community outreach workers I spoke with told me that a lot of them fail to understand law and justice and operate by the same behaviour they used in their own countries – not realising that the laws and boundaries are different in the UK. However, Roma have acknowledged that police treat them better here than in their home countries and that they do not get beaten here when in police custody.

Roma people speak two languages, Romani and the language of their home country. Roma tend to live in concentrated groups in certain parts of the UK, including London and the southeast and southwest, East and West Midlands and northeast and west. They tend to live in fixed housing but are often prone to living in poor-quality rented accommodation and being vulnerable to exploitation by landlords. Roma people are unlikely to complain either because they do not understand how to enforce their rights or because they fear retaliatory eviction. Romanian Roma are becoming the fastest growing group of rough sleepers in Greater London. Roma are routinely being paid far below the National Living Wage. They are the least integrated into the general population and rarely reveal their Roma identity; when questioned where they come from, they will usually state their country of origin – Poland, Romania or Slovakia. Roma tend not to mix with Romany Gypsies and are reluctant to accept them into their culture. There are also language barriers – dialects – accents and pronunciation of words which are different. Roma tend to turn to each other for friendship and help as opposed to going to outsiders outside their community.

The men in our community see women as baby makers, which is not the way I want to live. They treat women like property and doormats. They see women as sex objects and men in the community are very selfish and self-serving. We are not respected until we have children and children are a must when you get married. There are many good qualities in the community. Family is everything – we look out for each other. When my father died so many people did so much for my family. We protect our children from bad people. Most parents spoil our children; we would give anything to make our children happy. Women are not supposed to work but still sometimes do. Men still control finances in the family. The roles have changed much over the past 50 years, but poverty is still a real thing in our community. Roma people are very suspicious of outsiders. We get told not to trust outsiders; some of the community scams people which disgusts me. A lot of young people do not finish school because they want to make money but many of the younger ones are finishing school because of legal repercussions but some still drop out to work because of family pressure to make money. Good things about us are our history, our culture, our language, and the way we have adapted throughout time. The way we have been able to bounce back from adversity. Many of us have skills and are logical thinkers; we are actors, musicians, dancers and so much more and people don't even realise it.

Kelly

Roma life in Britain today

The quality of life is better in Britain for most Roma than in their countries of origin. Accommodation for some might not be great but it is still better than places like Ferentari. Assen, a Roma from Bulgaria, who works as a community outreach worker, smiled when he told me, *'It is better to be poor in a rich country than to be poor in a poor country'* before adding, *'there is more security here'*. The economic prospects are terrible for Roma in their home countries. The benefit system in Bulgaria and Romania offers little money – as little as £25 a month, resulting in many Roma struggling to survive.

Education can be a big problem for Roma in Britain. Many can't speak English and may also be illiterate in the language of their country of origin. Other Roma only speak their native Romani but do not speak the language of the country of origin. Some Roma parents struggle to understand the education system as they are used to children starting school aged 7 and some children miss school due to visits to their home countries.

Employment is also a big problem for Roma in Britain. Many are on temporary zero-hour contracts working in jobs including Amazon, picking and packing, bread and meat factories and dairies. Roma people usually work two to three days a week, but many rely on benefits as a secure income. In order to get a National Insurance number many register as 'self-employed' but are in fact unemployed at the time, although a few do later become self-employed after setting up gardening, scrap metal and construction businesses.

Many Roma still retain strong links to their home countries. Many find the rules in the UK to be rigid, strict and slow. This has resulted in some Roma returning to their country of origin for medical treatment if the medical issue is serious and they are unprepared to wait for NHS services. Medical care in places like Romania costs a fraction of the price of private healthcare in Britain and it is quick. Others go home often because of strong family links – they miss home or have family still living there and some own properties in their countries of origin.

Some Roma will have travelled to the UK with their National ID card and need to return 'home' to get birth certificates and apply for passports, which takes time. Following Brexit, many Roma failed to apply to the Home Office for proof of settled status, which carries ramifications in key areas, particularly when applying for benefits and/or seeking employment and when looking for accommodation. Even those who applied may not have provided sufficient proof, which delays them getting a positive response. Those who receive settled status are issued with a monthly code where they need to log on to confirm their status. This proves to be a difficult process for those with literacy problems or those who lack computer skills.

Roma love their culture and are generally a close-knit community. They look after each other and there is a great sense of solidarity in helping each other. Men often do a weekly 'lottery' among themselves. An example of this is when ten men who are employed each contribute £100 before the lucky draw winner receives the cash prize of £1000. Those who work and have some spare money like to treat themselves to their favourite dinner for a special occasion. This usually consists of a wild game stew with onions, swedes, cabbage and tomatoes, seasoned with ground black pepper and hot chili peppers, and washed down with either beer or Calarasi brandy.

There are no mass gatherings for Roma like the Appleby Horse Fair for Romany Gypsies although impromptu gatherings can be called if a well-known pastor from Romania is over for a prayer meeting at one of the churches. Activist groups may include the acronym 'GRT' in policies and discussions, but the reality is that Roma and Romany Gypsies in the UK seldom mix or have anything in common in their day-to-day lives. Romany Gypsies have been settled here for a long time and are well established in British culture and way of life. The challenges are not the same and they often do not face some of the issues affecting Roma.

Some Roma find it difficult to express feelings when it comes to sensitive issues around mental health or in anything to do with sex or abortion. They have a naturally reserved attitude around contentious issues and struggle to comfortably share their vulnerabilities. Roma tend to dislike discussing homosexuality and refuse to openly discuss it because of their religious backgrounds, which are either Orthodox or Pentecostal. Few Roma come out as being gay because it is seen as being another extra layer of discrimination and they have suffered much persecution; therefore, they don't divulge personal information easily or just reveal part of the problem if they have no option but to seek help.

Some Roma are very traditional and family orientated and keep within their own community, while others are more influenced by British culture and will integrate better; however, Roma are used to exclusion in society. They expect it and many have accepted it as a normal part of their lives. There is still a lot of emphasis on Roma stereotypes in British life – an example is Roma women wearing traditional long dresses and head scarves entering shops and being almost guaranteed to get followed by security guards. Facebook stories about Roma are often discriminatory in tone.

Child protection issues

Roma parents are often terrified of social workers taking their children into care because that is mainly how they perceive social work practices to operate. Children's Services receive many referrals concerning Roma families when it is believed that children are neglected in overcrowded accommodation and/or missing education or presenting as tired and lacking in concentration while in class. It is likely that some of these referrals will result from a lack of awareness of Roma culture.

Imagine a father who is working long hours. His wife becomes pregnant and must attend various medical appointments, which means she sometimes leaves her 11-year-old daughter to look after two younger children without knowing that this is against the law. A neighbour notices the children being left alone and reports it to Children's Services. The mother speaks poor English and becomes very worried when social workers come to the house so she shouts and swears at them terrified that her children will get taken away. While issues are identified that need correction, the solution and help offered rarely results in children being taken into care.

Luton Roma Trust – NGO

Fear of authority figures remains high in the Roma community and it is not uncommon for some parents to lie, not through malice or as a cover-up for neglect or abuse but to placate social workers. It is not uncommon for some Roma families to switch accommodation which they think is of better quality to 'impress' social workers, only exacerbating them not being believed when their deceit is discovered. But with the help of an interpreter, parents calm down when things are explained to them. Slapping or smacking children is acceptable in Eastern European countries but some Roma are unaware that slapping a child can cause injury and be construed as common assault or that continuous smacking makes children resentful and angry and damages parental/offspring relationships. This can lead to children growing up thinking that hitting a child is acceptable. Sometimes Roma parents need educating on what is acceptable and legal behaviour in Britain. Unfortunately, newcomers to Britain often don't speak the language and therefore miss out on receiving important information. Roma communities and NGOs do their best at educating them about cultural matters, as well as advising on support services that are available.

***

Donna's story

Roma are diverse. There is a caste system in Roma like in India where some families believe their breeding is superior to that of others. So many differences in the different groups, different dialects and different customs. In Russia did you know that a Roma man won't let a woman go upstairs while he is in the house because it is the custom that a woman can never be higher above a man – even in the house in this way. Family live together in traditional families – grandparents, parents and their children, and aunts, uncles and cousins. Roma love big families – and love children (they believe that social workers will go to hell for taking their children away). More modern families – children are moving out after they get married and live by themselves. One thing they have in common though is they are all hot-blooded people who like having loud arguments. Over centuries, they have all adapted to the Eastern/Western European countries in which they were raised, and it is here that they have learned many of their experiences. There are many differences between different groups and clans, and this varies from those living in rural village settlements, towns and cities from these countries. Outsiders try to understand Roma, but they never understand.

Life in the UK is bigger, and society is more accepting. Nobody knows we are Roma. They treat me as an immigrant. But they don't think that I am strange, a bad person, a Gypsy like they do back in my country. People are friendly to me. I have more freedom. There is everything available to us in this country. We are treated as human beings. Education is free here and you get lots of support from the school. If a child is absent, the school rings the parents. This would never happen back home. Education is so important because many of the parents are illiterate.

Opportunities are open to all Roma living in Britain that far exceeds that back in their home countries. Britain is multi-cultural and therefore the attention Roma garners in other European countries is not as intense here. Roma need to realise though that they have the chances open to them here to change their lives. Many charities and NGOs have become a soft touch and instead of making people become independent and self-sufficient, they repeatedly help people who become reliant on their services. It's one thing asking for help with an unpaid bill or having problems with council tax or rent arrears – but to continuously make the same mistakes and then return asking for help for a second, third and fourth time is not good. It's no good them blaming the government or organisations for not helping them. The benefits system has made life too easy. The ideology is wrong as it makes them dependent. Some like an easy life. They are lazy bastards, and some are nasty crafty people who commit benefit fraud. They are happy to sit at home all day, smoke and watch telly. They are happy to do nothing. But the point to remember is that the opportunities are there for every single one of them to change and improve their lives. I know that many of them who first came here hadn't been to school and had no qualifications. Most of them had never worked in their lives. They need to stop thinking the way they did in their own countries before they came here. This is the time for new, fresh opportunities. Why did they come here otherwise? Back home, they didn't have these opportunities, but they have no excuses now. We need to see progress with the younger generation who were born here, have been to school and can speak English. They need to stop falling into the benefits trap. Where are Roma plumbers, Roma mechanics, Roma electricians? There aren't any. No skilled based. But the problem is their parents because a lot carry on and do what their parents did – nothing. Parents and what they say to their children needs to be looked at – how they are motivated and guided. But a lot of Roma come from very poor backgrounds, no education and have limited vocabulary. So, is it any wonder that some young people also look at their friends who are also influenced by their parents and end up doing nothing? That is the mentality, and this won't stop if they are given too many benefits. They will never learn. This stuckness must stop. It's a horrible life but they can't imagine ever having anything better as it's beyond their mentality to realise and understand this and it is beyond [the] *Western world mentality in understanding the Roma way of thinking.*

Unfortunately, some of them are attracted to drugs, gambling and prostitution. They like to pretend they are big gangsters but there are only small crimes in the Roma population and it is no larger than in any other group/community. But reporting about Roma crime is always highlighted by giving the public the impression that it is commonplace. Drugs are everywhere and are often inexpensive. Young people get drawn into this trap but no more so than in other communities. With drugs there is more drug running as opposed to heavy dealing with young people used as pawns for larger criminals. Some Romanian and Bulgarian Roma have given a bad reputation to other Roma – begging, burglaries and drugs. Trafficking and modern-day slavery occurs within Roma circles – in countries like Romania, it is not unusual for parents who live in poor villages to sell their daughters in the belief that they will get taken to Britain where they will earn money etc.

If we are treated equal, we can produce and succeed. There are Roma who ask themselves 'Why should I be of lower status?' But life is very hard for Roma in countries like Romania, Moldovia, Slovakia and Bulgaria. Roma are very artistic and talented in the arts. They are good at music, dancing and lyrics. It's in their body and is hereditary. Music binds all Roma together, such is the extent of their love of it. They are very good at playing musical instruments. They learn by listening like they did with Romanes – no alphabet, nothing written – only oral. Roma are very good at languages. They are very good at business – even those who have had little education. Their skills are rooted in their ability to survive. Many do well for themselves despite the odds – and become doctors, lawyers, actors and musicians.

Roma segregation in the UK is often caused by fear – fear of the system, discrimination and not knowing the culture. Roma communities often stick together. Many who are segregated are aged in their forties. They just associate with their families and other Roma families. Many don't speak English. But the picture is different for young people born in Britain – they are educated, speak good English, are more outgoing and have friends from outside their community. They also have a better ability in getting employment.

Romany Gypsies see us Roma as guests here. Their attitude is 'We were born here, and we are citizens – you are immigrants'. Our shared history is forgotten. Roma have been settled for well over 50 years since the communist regime forbade it. Just a handful of Roma still travel – some French Roma but this is only for seasonal travelling. Roma and Romany Gypsies have little in common with language because everyone speaks different dialects and use different words and have different pronunciations.

Roma in Ireland

Roma individuals and families have been coming to Ireland since the 1990s after the fall of communism when Eastern Europe opened its borders. Those living in Ireland have come from Romania, Hungary, Slovakia, Poland and the Czech Republic. All of them needed help accessing basic services because few spoke English. They had no understanding of schooling and were illiterate in their own language. Suspicion and dislike greeted them, and this has followed them since, culminating these days in social media postings which speak negatively of Romanian Gypsies living in local communities. To this day, if a Roma person is found guilty of an offence, details of their sentencing is posted and shared. *Big Issue* sellers are often met with racist abuse on the streets and told to go back to where they came from.

Large clusters of Roma are grouped together in housing estates, many in Donegal and bordering counties to Northern Ireland. The system at times appears to be set up against them. Many find it problematic accessing social housing if they haven't been part of the Pay Related Social Insurance scheme (equivalent to UK National Insurance payments) for a year. Instead, they wade their way through the difficulties faced in obtaining Housing Assistant Payments (equivalent to UK housing benefit) to access the privately rented housing market. A lot of Roma struggle to find a landlord without a good reference. Some fall into arrears and face eviction. Others are fearful of complaining about overdue repairs and live instead in poor conditions.

Unemployment rates for Roma in Ireland are very high. In 2022, Ireland is seeing the third generation of Roma since they first started arriving in the 1990s. Roma in Ireland are generally EU citizens. Many are now Irish citizens and now there are many second- and third-generation Roma who were born in Ireland. Even those born in Ireland and who now have children of their own have found it hard to break the cycle of poverty and unemployment. Leaving school early is a key reason along with racial discrimination. It is claimed that some prospective employers will not even interview anybody with a Roma surname. As a result, there is an over-reliance on claiming social welfare benefits, while some manage to sit their Safe Pass test which allows them to apply for work in the construction industry. Others find work in shops and cafes, but overall unemployment rates remain high.

It is noted that there is an incredible level of resilience and life skills present in Roma people. Their survival skills alone are remarkable. Despite the obstacles and racism they face, the Roma that have come to Ireland have settled and many appear happy. While the first generation who came to Ireland in the mid-nineties were unable to read and write or speak English, they have navigated their way and found a place they can call home. Young Roma children these days often speak three or four languages, including Romani, an Eastern European language, and English. They are also taught Gaelic in school.

Racist attacks on Roma people in Northern Ireland is part of a growing trend of discrimination against Roma people across Europe. In 2009 around 20 families of Roma people from Romania were forced to flee their homes in Belfast after coming under sustained attacks lasting several nights. Crowds gathered outside homes shouting racist slogans, smashing windows and kicking in doors (Anonymous, 2019). Roma compared these attacks to similar ones inflicted on them in Europe, including in the Czech Republic, Hungary, Italy, Romania, Serbia and Slovakia. While many people in Northern Ireland condoned these appalling racist attacks and urged the police to catch the perpetrators, no arrests were made, which highlighted that these attacks against members of the GRT communities are acceptable in Irish society, as they often are in other parts of the world. In Eastern and sometimes Western Europe, Roma are often victims of forced evictions, racist attacks and police ill-treatment, and are denied their rights to housing, employment, healthcare and education. This raises the question of whether Roma in Ireland are given the protection they require to enjoy safe and secure lives.

Roma keep outsiders at bay and stick together by themselves where they find solidarity, acceptance and understanding. They take a long time to trust because of the persecution they have endured; however, Roma young people and children tend to make friends more easily than their parents' or grandparents' generations. Roma have retained ownership of their culture and strongly identify with it. They pass down traditions from generation to generation. Females who retain traditional values will wear long skirts and headscarves as it is very important to them. They style their hair according to their marital status with different styles for those who are unmarried, married or widowed. Even if a woman or a girl does not adhere to traditional dress values and wears more contemporary clothing, they tend to maintain Roma hair styling customs. Roma music (mainly consisting of violin, cimbalom and brass) and songs about love and loss, together with dancing among the old and the young, feature heavily in their lifestyle as they feel this helps them maintain a link to their roots.

Conclusion

The lives of Roma living in the UK and Ireland are better than in Eastern and Western European countries because their quality of life is better – but there are still high levels of racism and discrimination towards this community everywhere they live. Although attitudes of acceptance may be higher in the UK because Roma's ethnicity and backgrounds are often hidden, incidents of hate and aggression are still commonplace for those whose ethnicity is more obvious. Roma are a much-persecuted minority and until there is a concerted effort from state bodies in Eastern and Western Europe along with the UK to end ingrained racism and prejudice, nothing will change. Roma have become scapegoats who are routinely negatively stereotyped with hardly anyone saying anything positive about them. Yet, their traditions and customs have many positive traits, including their fierce loyalty towards family and their ability to adapt and survive, but little will change until Roma people find a voice among them to openly challenge prejudice. I remember walking down a side street in Ferentari and stopping to listen to an old man playing a harmonica in a back garden. It was a lovely sound to hear and a reminder that despite the squalor, poverty and crime in the surrounding streets, there is a goodness that exists among the Roma that is easily overlooked or has been made redundant through prolonged criticism and pessimism.

Chapter 4 | Irish Travellers

Introduction

I grew up in Ireland where the word 'tinker' (or 'Tincéir' in Gaelic) was routinely used when referring to Travellers. Those who tended to be less discriminatory later referred to them as 'itinerants' but the prejudice remained the same. The relationship between Travellers and most of the population has been marked by hostility, prejudice and discrimination. Growing up in Ireland never brought me into direct contact with Travellers as I didn't go to school with them and was never taught anything about them. Their culture simply never got a mention. The only time I saw them was at the side of the road in some local towns. Small children would often play in the middle of the road, oblivious to traffic or danger, which often meant passing cars would have to slow down or stop when passing their caravans and tents. My ignorance of Travellers was profound, like many other people's, resulting in complete unknowingness about their origins, culture and heritage. Instead, their identity was discarded and completely devalued. It was not until later in life that I came to realise how cruel Ireland has been to them (and continues to be) when Travellers are as much inherently Irish as their settled counterparts.

Origins

Irish Travellers are a small indigenous ethnic minority nomadic group that has been part of Ireland for centuries with its own separate heritage, culture and language. An Irish Traveller presence can be traced back to twelfth-century Ireland, with migration to Great Britain first starting in the early nineteenth century. According to Anonymous (2019) there are around 40,000 Travellers in the Republic and around 5000 in Northern Ireland. Mac Laughlin (1995, p 14) states:

Irish Travellers are quite distinct from Gypsies and Romanies. It is well established that the latter entered Europe from India, whereas Gypsies are thought to be of strictly Celtic origin. Unlike Gypsies and Romanies, Irish Travellers are an endogenous, as opposed to an exogenous, social group and they have a far narrower geographical range than their European counterparts. Aside from small groups of Travellers of Irish descent in Europe and the United States, they are almost totally confined to Ireland and Britain.

Differences between Travellers and Romany Gypsies

Sometimes Irish Travellers are referred to as Gypsies, but they are not related to Romany or Roma Gypsies. Historically, few Romany Gypsies crossed the Irish Sea from mainland Britain, but some did settle in the larger urban cities at the turn of the twentieth century. Nomadic life for Romany Gypsies in Ireland never took off – most kept to urban areas in Leinster or around Dublin. There was often confusion between Romany Gypsies and Irish Travellers despite the fact that they dressed differently, with the Gypsies often favouring brightly coloured clothing, particularly in comparison to Irish female Travellers who tended to wear long dark dresses, an apron with side pockets and a woollen shawl. Traveller men wore wellington boots turned down and peak caps. While the older ones spoke with either British or Welsh accents, their offspring often spoke with Irish accents. During the 1950s, anyone seen driving an ornate wagon was considered a Gypsy. But harsh winter conditions living in a tent meant that 'wealthier' Travellers upgraded to horse-drawn caravans. Marriages between the two groups were common. They would meet at horse fairs – monthly markets and fairs in country towns. Another difference was religion. Travellers were Catholic, and Romany Gypsies were mainly Church of Ireland (Anglican). However, some marriages between the two groups took place.

Background history

'Irish Traveller' is a state-imposed term. The Traveller community instead refer to themselves instead as 'Pavee' or 'Mincéir', which are words from Shelta (otherwise called Cant or Gammon), the Irish Traveller language. There have been Travellers in Ireland since pre-Celtic times before Oliver Cromwell's invasion (1649–53). Very little research is available but what is known from historical records is that Irish Travellers have roots in Ireland which can be traced back several hundred years. They share ancestors with the rest of the population. Being nomadic was very common in Gaelic medieval Ireland for hundreds of years before British rule took root. A common myth is that Irish Travellers came into being after the Irish Potato Famine in 1845 after they were evicted from the land by British troops. This is false information but often used to devalue the lifestyle and culture of Irish Travellers.

Irish Travellers are historically known for their traditional craft in tin-smithing. They are also known as Na Lucht Siúil (The Walking People) for their nomadic lifestyle – moving place to place selling handmade items or animals. Male and female

Travellers worked and traded alongside settled people, mainly working for farmers or doing odd jobs.

Irish Travellers were very important in the history of traditional Irish music – fiddle playing and uilleann pipes. As well as having a passion for playing musical instruments, they also were known for singing and storytelling – often sharing their talents from town to town across the country.

The first official piece of policy for Irish Travellers did not come into existence until 1963. Travellers were referred to as 'itinerants' in this policy, which sought to find solutions to the integration, assimilation and settlement of Travellers with the rest of the population. However, this was perceived as a strategy to persuade Travellers to settle and stop their nomadic lifestyles because their traditional ways were a problem to society. In the years that followed and throughout the 1970s, little by little they were forced to move off roadsides and camp sites into either council accommodation or council-run camp sites. It was not until 1980 that the first Travellers' rights group was formed that campaigned for better recognition of Traveller culture, although it was not until 1995 that the Irish government first engaged with Traveller groups and organisations to look at key areas like healthcare, education and accommodation for Travellers.

The Equal Status Act (2000) made it illegal to discriminate against Travellers. However, this was quickly overshadowed by the 2002 Housing Miscellaneous Provisions Act (Trespass Act), which made it illegal for Travellers to camp on traditional lands. This had a devastating effect on the Travelling community, forcing most of them to stop summer travelling. It also affected their livelihoods in terms of horse keeping and scrap metal trading. The changing face of Irish Travellers had well and truly borne fruit, making them become more invisible in society as opposed to becoming integrated.

It was not until 2017, after almost a 40-year battle, that the Irish government granted recognition to Travellers as a distinct ethnic group with their own unique history, language, culture and identity. This has paved the way for them to reclaim their history after years of exclusion, discrimination and being 'outsiders' in their own country.

As explained earlier, Travellers mainly lived in the Irish countryside up until the 1960s when they moved closer to towns and cities after work dried up on farms and door-to-door selling of goods became less popular. There were two main types of Irish Travellers – they were either commercial nomads (selling tinsmith goods, china and flowers) or pastoral nomads (doing agricultural work although they themselves might have owned their own horses and other animals), but both categories travelled from area to area and often bartered their services in exchange for money or food items including milk, butter and vegetables, as well as asking for clothes. They moved around because it was the only way to generate customers because it proved difficult selling the same thing. Whole families were involved in the process – men, women and children all played their part, including trading at markets or door-to-door hawking. Other Travellers were singers, storytellers and fortune-tellers. Travellers tended to belong and operate as individual family units, and until urban life became imposed on them, they tended to avoid living alongside other members of their community. Ingrained discrimination against Travellers has always seen them as belonging to the lower echelons of society. Up until the 1960s, though, Travellers were better assimilated among the general population, but urban life meant large gatherings of them in one place soon cemented the public's opinion of them being seen as a problem in society – which remains unaltered despite the many changes that have taken place in Ireland over the last 50 years. A massive stereotype exists in Ireland that portrays them as deviant people. They have always been seen by society as racially inferior but anti-Traveller exclusion is currently at its highest point with many people considering them uncivilised and not having a place in modern Ireland.

We used to spend the winter in Dundalk but every springtime we would head off in our caravan to Galway to the Ballinasloe Horse Fair visiting relatives in Louth and Offaly on our way. We would spend seven months away before returning to Dundalk. My family lived in a caravan after my father sold his wagon in 1969. We still had lots of horses though because my father loved them. They either grazed at the side of the road, or he got permission from local farmers to graze them in nearby fields where we lived. It was a hard life. We had no toilet, so you had to do your business behind a tree. But my mother had a big steel bath where she used to wash us in although me and my brothers often went and washed in the river. Despite our lack of materialistic things, we were happy, maybe because we did not know that there was another side to life. It was only in 1976 when I reached 18 that we moved into a house. Although we missed aspects of the simplistic life we had known, a new dawn emerged and gradually we became accustomed to newfound luxuries. Now we had a permanent roof over our heads and food in our bellies. What more could anybody want? We were poor but everybody else was the same. But we were smiling, and, in some ways, we gradually used to poke fun at Traveller children who still lived in caravans with remarks like 'Look at the dirt of them' knowing that they did not have a toilet or bath like us. Living at the side of the road was never legal. The guards would come and shift people along. But people became more knowledgeable of the law – and discovered that before that the guards could not come and ask people to move without having obtained an eviction notice from the court in the first instance.

Tom

Irish Travellers at a glance

The following statistics have been obtained from the Donegal Travellers Group's (2021) *Strategic Plan 2021–2026*.

- » Irish Travellers have an average of five children compared to a national average of three children.
- » 31 per cent of Travellers reported cost as a factor in eating healthily.
- » 13 per cent of Traveller children complete secondary school compared to 92 per cent in the settled community.
- » Over two-thirds (67 per cent) have parents who only completed primary school.
- » Very few Travellers are aged 65 or over compared with the national average:
  - » 42 per cent are aged under 15, compared to 15 per cent nationally;
  - » 63 per cent are aged under 25, compared to 35 per cent nationally;
  - » 3 per cent are aged 65 and over, compared to 11 per cent nationally.

Further statistics obtained from the Housing Executive Belfast's (2020) *Irish Traveller Accommodation Strategy 2020–2025* include the following.

- » Travellers are much less likely to own their own home (bricks and mortar) – about 20 per cent in comparison to 70 per cent of non-Travellers, although those who live in caravans, mobile homes and chalets tend to own them.
- » Only 12 per cent still live in caravans or mobile homes – they are less likely to have central heating, piped water and sewerage facilities. Irrespective of what type of accommodation, overcrowding (84 per cent in caravans etc and 53 per cent in houses) always seems to be a big problem and a major contributor to health problems.

Irish Travellers often face the same problems as Romany Gypsies and Roma owing to a gross shortage of culturally appropriate housing which should include:

- » grouped social housing;
- » serviced sites (piped water and sanitation);
- » transit sites;
- » private sites (operated by Travellers).

Addressing the need for suitable, sustainable accommodation is long overdue. Overcrowding is beyond crisis point with large families forced to live together, even on sites with families who they may have longstanding grievances against.

While the government has delegated responsibility for providing Traveller-specific accommodation to local authorities, this obligation is not being met. The national government needs to do more to ensure that local authorities are acting in a coordinated fashion to meet the need for Traveller-specific accommodation.

(Watson et al, 2017, p xi)

There is a shortage of political will to change the lives of Travellers. Those fighting in the corners of Travellers are mainly NGOs with Travellers themselves within these organisations campaigning for better quality and culturally appropriate accommodation that promotes inclusion, a sense of belonging and security. Many feel the state never grants anything out of the goodness of their heart to Travellers. It must be hard fought. Change is coming from Travellers – they have been fighting for years. The collective voice is getting stronger against those in power who seek to alienate Traveller culture.

Current lifestyles and traditions

Travellers sum up their way of life as *'having a sense of freedom in life, being prepared to live in new places and trying new things'*. It is a hard life and many still struggle with daily life. Many of the older Irish Travellers did not know their date of birth because many Travellers in those days were not registered at birth. Many never went to school. There is still only a life expectancy of 65 years of age (Anonymous, 2019). Male Irish Travellers have always been known as rough men and fighting men. Publicans usually must know them well before they get served in a pub. Even those allowed in pubs may be asked to leave after two or three drinks. Travellers have very broad accents (and mannerisms). They say 'De ya' instead of 'Do you' and 'You know I mean?' instead of 'Do you know what I mean?' Family name is so important to these close-knit communities; having a close family helps people get through tough times. Marriages predominantly take place within the wider family circle. Two-thirds of Irish Travellers are related with up to one-third being first cousins.

Most Travellers live in houses these days with electricity, heating and water, but their employment opportunities are limited because of deeply entrenched discrimination in the workplace that is embedded in society. Eighty per cent of Irish Travellers are unemployed (compared to 12 per cent of the general population) or do cash-in-hand jobs whenever they can find ad hoc work (Anonymous, 2019). Many have fallen into the benefits trap of staying put to claim benefits, often resulting in impoverished lifestyles. Those who work are mainly self-employed as scrap metal dealers, selling clothes and bed ware, gardening work (tree surgeons) or building work, mainly doing roof repairs and block pavements.

I grew up in rural Limerick in the 1960s where there were many big families living on the side of the road. I remember asking a Traveller woman once how many children she had, and she replied '21 that lived'. Travellers are warm hearted and generous – decent people – wild decent people. I rented out houses to many of them. Once you gain their trust, deep friendships begin. I remember a tenant asking me into a house to watch a video of bare-knuckle fighting, which was something they would never show to someone outside their community unless you had gained their trust. Then there was the man who couldn't afford to pay me the rent. He came to my office one Monday morning and asked if he could sing for me instead as means of payment. I thought at first he was joking but he was serious about the offer and before my face recovered from the shock, he burst into singing at the top of his voice some verses of 'Danny Boy':

O Danny Boy, the pipes, the pipes are calling
From glen to glen and down the mountainside
The summer's gone and all the roses falling
'Tis you, 'tis you must go and I must bide.

You could rent to one person and never have a problem and then rent to a member of the same family and encounter all sorts of difficulties ranging from anti-social and intimidating behaviour to breaking fixtures and fittings, taking doors off hinges or to letting animals including young foals to roam wild inside.

Gerard – Irish landlord

Eleven per cent of Irish Travellers in Ireland are street homeless and 3000 still live by the roadside in various parts of Ireland without sanitation or running water (Anonymous, 2019). Living at the side of the roadside has never been legal with the Gardai (police) coming and shifting people along. But Travellers became more knowledgeable of the law – and discovered that the Gardai could not come and ask people to move without having obtained an eviction notice from the court in the first instance. Very few live by the side of the road now and hardly anybody lives in a tent. The Miscellaneous Provisions Act (2002) makes trespassing a criminal offence whereby Travellers who live on the roadside while they await accommodation and have nowhere else to go become criminalised. Some Travellers own their own land; those living in Traveller-specific accommodation such as caravans, trailers and chalets often live on sites that are inadequate in the provision of standard services and facilities, including electricity, water, heating, drainage, sanitation and waste disposal.

Mary's story

Big changes have occurred in the last 20–30 years. Everyone lives in a house nowadays. They do not have enough communication with other Travellers. It was a hard life in my younger days, but we shared things. I slept in a tent – no telly, no phone, no light. Heat came from a fire outside. But I was kept busy with chores including baking bread. I did not have much schooling. We travelled around too much and would often only spend a week in one spot. I can't read nor write. I find it hard using a phone, but I am good at memorising stuff. When I was young, I used to go to a nun who helped me prepare for my Holy Communion and confirmation.

Times have changed so much, especially for young Travellers. Young ones these days would not be able to cope with that type of life. The life I had would be a rare sight these days. Nowadays young people love partying, clubbing and drinking. They are stuck all the time on their phones or on Facebook. We led a much simpler life when I was young. We loved playing cards. We also played horseshoes and would scream with delight if one of us was able to throw the horseshoes around the stake on the ground. Not many people live on the sides of the road. So where would you get a space to pull in with your caravan? Sure, they prevent it left, right and centre. Some put up big stones to stop anybody stopping. It is rare to see anyone living on the roadsides in Ireland these days.

There were 12 of us in my family. I have nine children of my own now and 18 grandchildren. None of my own children have lived on the side of the road or on a site. They were all born and raised in houses. My sons have their own construction business. Even though I now have lived in a house for the past 40 years, I still miss living in an open space. My daughters and their children come with me to a camp site in Wicklow every summer. I love the outdoors but with the younger generation the novelty of sleeping in a tent soon wears off and after a few days they start missing home. Then they moan about missing the washing machine or having enough water to wash themselves or they complain about not being able to cook properly outdoors but I love cooking outside. You can't beat a dinner of bacon and cabbage and boiled potatoes in their jackets. I love to bake griddle bread as well.

Nine years ago, I was invited to go to New York and speak to the United Nations on poverty. I have volunteered with Southside Travellers in Dublin for 33 years and have given advice on housing and entitlements to a great number of people. Many in our community live in poverty – terrible standard of social housing that is overcrowded. Many of the properties are in poor state of disrepair. Many Travellers in Ireland are unemployed and have little money to survive on, especially those with large families. Life is a terrible struggle for inner city families. They live in cramped and overcrowded houses. There is no space outside for children to play so they are cooped up all the time. Some are forbidden to have dogs in their houses. Some services claim to be afraid to go to the homes or sites of Travellers – even the Meals on Wheels service for the sick and elderly because they fear that they will get attacked or robbed although this type of thing rarely occurs.

***

The quality of life for Travellers in Ireland is still low, with the gap wider between the Traveller community and other citizens. Up until the 1980s, Travellers had little or no rights – including no cultural rights. They were not recognised as an ethnic group and their language was devalued. A more enlightened approach developed, and although laws were passed aimed at combating prejudice, there is still much inequality to overcome because Travellers are rarely given a chance to participate in any meaningful decision-making policies about themselves. Only when this happens will a reversal take place whereby instead of being portrayed as a problem, the question would switch to addressing the problems faced by the Traveller community. Many Travellers who live in houses refer to themselves as 'Settled Travellers' – a term coined by the media to imply this is a good thing and that such Travellers have assimilated to the 'norms' of society by doing so. This, too, is discriminatory, but it is also a very mistaken concept. The truth is a Traveller remains a Traveller irrespective of their accommodation. You only need to ask if a non-Traveller would become a Traveller if they went to live in a mobile home and went on journeys around the country. The obvious answer is 'no' because Travellers come with their own unique shared history, family, ancestry, viewpoints and opinions, and cultural rules.

Adulthood is defined differently in the Travelling community. Someone aged 40 is considered old. Young people aged 16 are considered adults, and girls tend to marry young. These are often arranged marriages in a culture that still grapples with its own sexist culture and toxic masculinity. Few Travellers marry outside the community, and those who do are mainly men. However, domestic abuse is not deemed higher than in the general population. There is a mental health crisis within the community, which is seven times the national average. A lot of Travellers turn to alcohol and substance misuse to quench their internal emotional struggles.

The language spoken by Travellers is widely known as Cant or to its native speakers in Ireland as De Gammon, and to the linguistic community as Shelta. The language is a variation of Irish Gaelic but borrows and adapts words from old and new forms of English and Irish and follows an unwritten tradition. It is often described as a slang and secretive language used to prevent outsiders from understanding conversations between Travellers. Primarily a mixed language, it stems from a community of Travelling people in Ireland who were predominantly Irish speaking and is based heavily on Hiberno-English (or Irish English). It is a set of English dialects natively spoken within the island of Ireland (including both the Republic of Ireland and Northern Ireland). Usage of the language has declined in the past 50 years, resulting in few Travellers being able to fully speak it. Attempts to revive it among social media groups have resulted in little success.

Although the media have moved on from calling Travellers 'itinerants', most people won't have met a Traveller and therefore depend on media reporting for information. Negative stereotypes in media tend to portray Travellers as dirty, vile and violent. The media usually concentrates on just a few key areas: crime, accommodation and discrimination. The truth is that there are rich and poor Travellers, there are those who are disabled or able-bodied, those who are big into politics and those who are interested in economics, and those in the film and music industry, but rarely does the media reflect this diversity in the way it represents Travellers.

Watson et al (2017) refer to reports in the media that stated that one in five Irish people would deny citizenship to Travellers if they got the chance. Prejudice also runs deep with a large percentage of Irish people stating they would never buy a house next to a Traveller and would be horrified if a Traveller rented or bought a house next to them. However, there are some good pieces of work being done to reduce discrimination and educate people about Traveller culture. The Galway Misleór Festival in conjunction with the Galway Traveller Movement was created in 2019 to showcase the rich cultural heritage of nomadic culture, bringing together singers, musicians, storytellers and poets from all over Ireland, Europe and America to deliver performances to several hundred people who attend the annual three-day festival. The festival has been hailed as a powerful connection between Travellers and settled people in the sense that it has been transformative in the way it breaks down barriers.

On the one hand, it could be seen as being hypocritical that settled people are appreciating the talent of the 'nomadic' performers given that most people would not ordinarily talk or associate with a Traveller – but on the other hand, the festival provides the space for this to happen because there are so few opportunities for settled people to come into contact with Travellers. Here people from all types of backgrounds come together and despite their personal differences bond over their shared interest in the arts. The festival believes in giving validity to the performers involved by recognising their skills and talents and the necessity to give them the credit they deserve from a wider audience than would otherwise occur.

Introduction to colonialism

Some Irish Travellers believe that Ireland is still influenced by English imperialism despite independence since 1922. This viewpoint is formed by the ongoing ostracism of Travellers by Irish society.

One shouldn't be proud to be Irish, but one should be proud to be a Traveller. One shouldn't be proud to be Irish the way the Irish people have treated our families and our grandparents. Ireland is still using old English colonial systems, institutions, acts and laws, education system etc. Ireland is England and the only real Irish left in it are Irish Travellers.

Max

Irish Travellers still have remnants of old Gael culture – their community comprises clans who were brave and resilient. They still retain a stronghold over clanship, after 1500 years of Irish history that could easily have been destroyed by colonial rule which attempted to strip Ireland of its people and language. There remains great pride and honour in a family name enabling the clan spirit to become akin to something seen in the film *Braveheart*. Role models for Travellers are mainly found in their family tree/ancestors, such is the pride that comes with a family name.

There is also a residue of the ancient Irish Brehon Law to be found in Traveller culture, which was first set down in the seventh century and remained until the early seventeenth century when the English conquest of Ireland was completed. Ireland is still recovering from the English imperial colonial system that considered the Irish to be wild, primitive and violent people. The 'wild' Irish today are Travellers. They are the main target of suppression in the country that is repeating its own history without even knowing it.

In the most recent centuries, conflict in Ireland has seen fighting between the Irish and the English and the Catholics and Protestants. Politics may have changed since 1922 when Ireland became a free state from the remainder of the United Kingdom, but many practices remain the same. Many Travellers believe there are still traces of the old colonialist and imperialist system that was designed to separate and segregate people in its own land. Today's conflict in Ireland is between settled people and Travellers. Segregation exists, whether it is children being made to sit at the back of a class or setting aside certain days for Travellers claiming benefits to sign on at the dole office. Many have been systematically forced, because of the country's high levels of prejudice and hatred towards Travellers, to leave the country with most emigrating to Britain.

Irish Travellers today are battling an identity crisis, and many are going through psychological torture because of their exclusion. They are being made to feel cut off from the settled world and must deal with hostility and rejection on a frequent basis. This renders life to constantly battling negativity and developing internal oppression.

Joseph

Despite the first official piece of policy for Irish Travellers coming into effect in 1963, life has got progressively worse for its people. Inequalities in health, education and housing have not improved and coupled with this is the stripping away of Traveller identity and culture, hence the resulting deep-rooted psychological issues as they endure feelings of loss of culture and identity. Some young Travellers do not understand the concept of suffering or what their families and ancestors endured. Some feel shame about something they do not truly understand – which is not helped by society believing them to be a nasty, violent, horrible criminal group of people. Others feel they are rejects while being told to conform and assimilate, which further contributes to their trauma. Most feel that their history is being taken away from them, leaving young Travellers more confused than ever before about their worth in life – hence the high suicide rate (six to seven times the national average among young Travellers), which will be expanded upon in Chapter 5.

The education system has systematically failed Travellers by never addressing their ethnicity and culture in the curriculum. This would ensure that they felt valued and respected. Instead, young people are expected to view somebody else's world that makes them feel alien in their own country. Whether it's intentional or not, at present it reeks of unfairness and causes misery and psychological suffering to children, who deserve better treatment.

Child protection issues

Irish Traveller children are six times more likely to be taken into care than children in the general population (Watson et al, 2017). The issues that attract attention from Children's Services are like those cited for Romany and Roma children who encounter social care, including poverty, overcrowding and neglect. Social workers have been accused of not treating Traveller families as equal in comparison to non-Travellers. Children are often placed in care as a first option without other options being explored or tested in the first instance. Extended family members of children considered at risk of significant harm are rarely considered as suitable carers or are viewed with suspicion of not being truthful or fears prevail that if care arrangements are made with them that they will get broken. Critics of Children's Services highlight the complete lack of suitable foster carers where the importance of the culture and identity of Traveller children are overlooked.

Trish Nolan, Irish vocalist and multi-instrumental artist, has spoken publicly about being taken into institutional care with some of her siblings in the 1980s when she was eight years old. Trish and her siblings were taken away without explanation and placed in care, where they remained for the rest of their childhoods. It was only later in life when Trish researched her case that she discovered that the authorities of the time considered her and her siblings 'neglected' because of their parents' low income and nomadic lifestyle. Being placed in care caused emotional scarring and deep-rooted unhappiness for Trish who, up until that point, had remembered life at home as humble but happy. She recalled growing up with no television or electricity but sitting around a campfire at night listening to stories and singing songs. Trish wrote a song about her life called 'Broken Lines' capturing her feelings about her experience of being taken into care.

Broken Homes, broken Hearts, broken Truths
They make for bad starts
Shattered dreams in broken minds
You can't bridge the distance
Between those broken lines.

Trish's songwriting provides a taste of the hurt she felt and the detrimental effect it has had on Travellers who have shared her experiences:

The Irish state was taking many Traveller children into care at that time under an assimilation ideology which sought to deny Travellers their ethnicity with some politicians wanting to eradicate us altogether. They thought they had the moral right to do so, being part of the dominant culture. This stemmed directly from the 1963 report on itinerancy, whose central aim was to get rid of the 'itinerant problem'. The first words on everyone's lips as a result were 'if only we could find a way to civilise them' and one of the ways they sought to do this was taking as many Traveller children into care as possible in the belief that this would reduce the numbers of further generations growing up as Travellers – that those placed in care would forget about their Traveller roots and genes.

Trish Nolan

It is often said that Irish Travelling communities are both secretive and closed. But it is also rigid from within with certain subjects considered taboo. During childbirth, fathers do not usually attend hospital. Usually, mothers or older daughters are present. Women don't tend to talk about female issues in front of men like periods and childbirth and may be careful of what they tell professionals in case they get their husbands into trouble: *'Please don't tell anyone that I told you.'* Some Travellers are not averse to doing fly-tipping close to where they live. Children tend to be better at going to school than in other GRT communities, but they finish school early – often without qualifications.

Every Traveller seems to represent their whole community. Travellers are a minority people with low expectations. Generation after generation have been told 'You are dirt at the bottom of my shoe'. We are talking about massive cruelty and bullying. Here are people who have been swallowed up into settled existence and have been forced to either dispense with or hide their identity. Time and time again, I have met lovely people who switch personalities by the mere mention of Travellers such is their ingrained racism. You must question why this should happen against a branch of our own people. Ireland is a country that survived a famine and survived civil war in Northern Ireland and its atrocities so we should have developed compassion somewhere along the line, but it hasn't happened. For change to occur there needs to be a mass enlightenment of the world. Travellers are not a homogeneous group. They contain every type of personality – some are very traditional and others more liberal and progressive. Some are religious – others are not. You have single parents, couples with large families. What really needs emphasising more is the levels of poverty and disadvantage they face. It's mere words just to say that they should assimilate more with us. Of course, mixing more would be great. It would break down barriers of mistrust on both sides but now and for the foreseeable future until there is a massive shift that balance simply isn't there.

Flynn

John was only 14 and lived in a house a few doors up from me. His dad was in prison in England. He lived with his mother who was a heavy drinker and his two older brothers. I used to say hello to them when passing the house. John often sat on the front wall with one of his brothers smoking weed. They kept to themselves but there was always one of them outside the house watching everyone else on the street to see what they were doing. I had to tell them off once after they played a silly prank on my niece. They must have seen her visiting me. There was a tree beside my house and that night it was dusk when she was leaving to go home when they jumped down from the tree in front of her and scared her to death. The older brother begged me not to call the Gardai when I threatened them with this. He mentioned that John was having a hard time at school and was taking medication for ADHD. John wasn't the only one having a hard time. Neighbours often complained about the noise coming from the house – constant shouting and fighting. Then small offences occurred within a short period of time. The local shop was broken into. Someone on the next street had their front window smashed. The local school reported an attempted break-in. When the Gardai went to the house, they found stolen goods in the house and arrested one of the older brothers. But greater tragedy was to befall the family. One day John hanged himself in the house. Shock, horror and bewilderment followed and questions of what drove him to his death was partially answered through rumour and whispers. Apparently, John had been sexually abused by an older cousin although this was never proven because the accused also took his own life a short time afterwards.

Bernadette

Irish Travellers in Britain

One example of an Irish Traveller family (consisting of about 30 members) migratory pattern in the early 1950s was to cross from Ireland to north Wales for Spring lambing, then travel and work through the English Midlands to eventually reap the harvest in rural Lancashire. They would then return to the north of Ireland to spend some time with relatives and family and finally winter in Wicklow in the southeast before the cycle began again.

(Power, 2004, p 5)

Irish Travellers have lived in the UK for about 150 years. As of 2022 there are over 20,000 Irish Travellers living in Britain (Anonymous, 2019). They, along with Scottish Travellers, are the descendants of a nomadic people who have traditionally inhabited Ireland and mainland Britain. Times were hard and work was limited in Ireland in the 1950s when Irish Travellers routinely emigrated to Britain. They often worked in factories polishing brasses, or found work as tinsmiths, chimney sweeps and farm labourers. Other young Travellers learned to look after horses and harness them before later moving on to buying and selling horses. In the 1960s, others did door-to-door 'hawking' selling items like lino floor covering or asking for scrap metal but made little money. Up until the 1970s, jobs on building sites used the sign, 'Blacks and Irish need not apply'. This was followed by 'No Traveller' signs, which remained in frequent use until the 1990s. Some found steady self-employment as scrap, antique and carpet dealers. Later, many found an opening in tarmacking and block paving. However, many Travellers live on low incomes and are dependent on state benefits.

The British press vilified Irish Travellers in the 1990s and labelled them as unskilled and ignorant – stating that they left their shanty towns around Dublin and came to Britain because the benefits system meant handouts were bigger, better and more easily come by than in Ireland. Mac Gabhann (2011, p 84) states that Irish Travellers in Britain are more interested in their own survival and prosperity than carving out a new and different life than the one they had back in Ireland:

Irish Travellers have not always adapted to the dynamics of contemporary life in Britain. Committed to retaining their strong family bonds and nomadic way of life, many Travellers have refused to assimilate into British society. On occasion, maintaining the Travellers way of life, has, for some Travellers, meant living apart from mainstream society.

Historically, many Travellers emigrated from Ireland to Britain because they were less discriminated against as they were seen as 'Irish' as opposed to Travellers; although those who returned on visits discovered the discrimination they endured before they left still existed. Derek realised this during a visit:

I notice it and see it when I go back to Ireland to visit family graves. People who know you might speak to you and say 'Hello, how are you?' but there will be others who stand back and say nothing. You can see that they are looking at one differently. It does not matter if you are dressed as a lord; they will still treat you like they have always treated us. To them, they have always had a low opinion of us; leopards do not change their spots.

Derek

Some Travellers expect discrimination against them – and accept that people have no respect for them. It is disempowering. It has taken hundreds of years for Travellers to be recognised as an ethnic group of people – before laws were on their side, although many laws are still overlooked with bias and discrimination against Travellers by the police and the courts. Irish Travellers in Britain faced discrimination as both Travellers and Irish people – excluded from official council sites for a long time. They also faced hostility from English Romany Gypsies too in the past by being called 'Chikli', meaning dirty. Many Romanys felt Irish Travellers brought a bad reputation to them. But over the course of the past 20 years, they have called a truce on this and now mix freely with each other, especially at horse fairs, and overall there is less of a divide. It is not uncommon to see Irish Travellers and Romany Gypsies marrying.

Irish Travellers in Britain will travel back to Ireland for weddings, funerals, christenings and First Holy Communions and confirmations. Anywhere there is a large gathering of a family or closely connected clan, it is deemed offensive not to attend. These occasions are an ideal time to catch up with friends and family who have travelled long distances. Here they show off new outfits and perhaps meet potential partners for the first time. However, there is a high proportion of debt in Travelling communities – incurred by purchasing goods from catalogues and loans raised to pay for travel costs, especially those who travel home to Ireland from Britain to attend weddings and funerals. Horse fairs are also a big annual outing: friends and families gather in their finery. Men sell handmade horseboxes, trailers and horse accessories. Women have stalls of Crown Derby China, Waterford Crystal, baby clothes, costume jewellery and shoes. Weddings are often planned over the course of the event, capitalising on the fact that many hundreds of extended family members and friends will be present anyway. It is also not unusual for marriage proposals to take place. There is a lot of entertainment at horse fairs during the evening time, including music and dancing, and even bare-knuckle fights still take place.

Young Irish Travellers and young Romany Gypsies tend to mix quite a lot with each other. They are known to 'link' with each other, which involves playful matchmaking among themselves. An example of this could involve, for example, congregating at some large shopping centre on a Sunday morning at a fixed time. Extra attention is paid to how they dress and how their hair looks (boys included) to make themselves look as attractive as possible. They 'eye' each other up before mustering courage to 'link' up with someone, which entails making a promise that they will remain loyal to each other by not becoming attached to anybody else. A little chivalry is sometimes thrown into the equation when a boy asks a girl's older brother if it is okay to link with his sister. This type of innocent courtship can take place from the age of 12 upwards and rarely involves underage sex. It is mainly about friendship, loyalty and commitment to one person, although some of these associations have survived the test of time and resulted later in marriage, as Irish Travellers and Romany Gypsies still tend to marry young.

Martin's story

I spoke to Martin, who emigrated to Britain with his parents when he was a child. He recalled what life has been like for him and other Irish Travellers who grew up in Ireland before deciding on a new life away from their homeland. Martin said Irish Travellers have crossed over to England since the 1940s and 1950s to work and better themselves. They worked on railway lines, in hospital jobs, potato picking and doing groundwork. His father was one of these men who travelled each autumn to work before returning the following spring or early summer before the cycle was repeated in the autumn time. According to Martin, female Travellers were resilient in those days. When their husbands were away, they would go out selling baskets and clothes pegs and either getting money or asking for 'spuds and eggs' in return so that they could go home and feed their children. Martin added that the thought of any female Traveller these days being able to do the sort of thing that their mothers and grandmothers had to do was unthinkable.

Martin was born in Ballyfermot in Labre Park in the 1970s in a serviced caravan site consisting of a chalet-type building where his parents paid rent to Dublin Corporation. This was at a time when an estimated 1100 Traveller families lived throughout the Republic of Ireland (Watson et al, 2017). Martin's parents emigrated to Birmingham when he was six. This was the first time he had lived in any type of accommodation other than a chalet, but he didn't really notice that much of a difference, which he attributed to his age in the sense that he didn't care where he lived.

The family flat was in a large block of flats where at least 12 other Irish Traveller families resided. They all knew each other and were friends. They constantly went around to each other's places. He made friends with other Irish Traveller boys, and they went to school together. He felt protected and happy. Although Martin has since moved away from Birmingham, he said he has always retained affection for the people of Birmingham whom he described as being welcoming and friendly. He couldn't ever recall anybody being nasty to him through his childhood or early adulthood in Birmingham other than the occasional person calling him a 'paddy', referring to him being Irish which he viewed as humour rather than discrimination.

Martin's father lost his job, resulting in the family moving to Glasgow. Here they lived in a trailer on a council site. By the time he was 13, he went working with his older brothers 'hawking', doing odd labouring jobs and tarmacking. Martin remembers great camaraderie among his community back then when people helped each other out and shared information about where to find work. But things are different now. *'People haven't got time for a fella these days'*, Martin said with sadness, when recalling how things have changed in the past 30 to 40 years.

Although Martin mainly settled in Glasgow for several years, he and his family often travelled about the country for short periods visiting friends and relatives who lived in Sheffield, Leeds, Kent, Norwich and Derbyshire. He said it is in the blood of a Traveller to travel. There is something about its freedom that a non-Traveller can never feel or understand. Travellers, he said, love open spaces, countryside and nature. They love being their own boss. They like to be left alone and to be alone with members of their own community where they are understood. *'We used to go away and then come back'*, but finding work was always the factor for Martin and his family that determined how long they settled in one place before moving on to somewhere else.

Martin got married when he was 24 and started a family with his wife soon afterwards. For many years, he and his wife and their children lived in a mobile home, often travelling to different locations for five days to seven days – seldom any longer than this before the authorities moved them on. It was a way of life that he enjoyed and which provided him with contentment as he travelled up and down the country pulling into new places, seeking out work before upping roots and moving on to the next place.

Although he was contented at the time, Martin could see in hindsight that there were tough times, especially when he would sometimes go to work in the morning and then come home after a hard day's work only to discover that they had to move on immediately with police presence putting pressure on the situation. That meant everybody rushing around the place dismantling the generator and gas cylinders. The children would often be hungry but there was no time to eat before moving on and finding another patch of land to park the mobile home. It would often be late and dark before all the equipment, including the generators, was working and he could eat and go to bed in the hope he could find some work the next day that would help him feed his wife and three children.

Life on the road in those days meant no running water in the mobile home, which meant Martin and his family having to go to a local leisure centre or service station where they would pay between £2 and £5 for a shower. Life on the move got to the stage that getting random jobs in new areas started to prove more difficult and by 2013 Martin decided to move to Kent and buy some land to park his trailer. But life on the road or in authorised sites has waned in the past 25 years resulting, according to Martin, in there being only around 30 per cent of Irish Travellers in the UK currently living in camp sites. He said many people no longer feel safe moving into a site where they do not know anybody because, by doing this, they risk getting placed alongside some 'lunatic' (as Martin referred to younger Travellers who misuse drugs and are involved in criminal activities). He wondered out loud, *'How would a man keep safe? Who would look out for your family?'*

Martin has now put his days on the road behind him, although he still sometimes goes away for short breaks in his mobile home – like to the annual Appleby Horse Fair to meet up with friends and family. He now owns his own plot of land that is home to trailers where he and his wife and each of his children and their families now live. Martin feels blessed being surrounded by his family. He and his sons have carved out regular tarmacking work in their local neighbourhood. *'A settled life means regular work'*, he said, before jokingly adding, *'the gallivanting is over'*. He also said that he is proud to be a Roman Catholic and a believer. *'I try my best; I go to Mass but I am not perfect in any sense'*, he concluded with a wry smile on his face.

Conclusion

When I asked Travellers what they considered were the greatest challenges they face in society, they pinpointed racism and discrimination. These were the key areas of concern which they felt both affected them emotionally and prevented them from reaching their full potential in life. Some of the professionals I spoke to felt that the state and state institutions were to blame for having taken power and rights away from Travellers through various policies and legislation. They felt that the chance to shift this imbalance needs to come from the state and society in general. But they also questioned how this could occur if members of the government deem it acceptable to be openly discriminatory about Travellers.

The voices of Travellers must be heard before viable solutions are found that bring change in key areas of housing, health, education, hate crime and prejudice and discrimination. Many NGOs continue to do sterling work in lobbying government and pressing for key changes in legislation to bring about better outcomes for Travellers. However, while many hold the view that change must be delivered from the state down through public bodies, there are those who believe Travellers must take on board and address the negative public perceptions held about them and accept responsibility. To do so they will need to seek ways within their community to restore their reputation by addressing anti-social behaviour, fly-tipping and acts of extreme violence at funerals of rival Traveller families.

Chapter 5 | Health

Introduction

This chapter looks at the range of health issues affecting GRT communities. Many of the causes of health issues and high mortality rates among the main three communities are the same. These include unemployment, poor accommodation and overcrowding, low income, smoking, poor diet and obesity. Depression, stress and anxiety are very high in GRT communities, but suicide appears to be highest in Travellers and Romany Gypsies. The reasons suggested for the high suicide rate, particularly in Irish Travellers, is both poignant and sobering. Racism and discrimination also play a big part in health inequalities. More healthcare workers are urgently needed who are GRT themselves or trained specifically in working with GRT people and have in-depth knowledge and/ or experience of working closely with these communities to help with targeted intervention programmes. Although some young GRT people are paying far more attention to diet and exercise and healthy lifestyles in comparison to the generations of their parents and grandparents, a major problem running through all the communities is drug misuse, particularly among those aged 20–30 upwards, which has escalated at alarming speed over the past ten years.

Healthcare issues across all GRT communities

GRT communities tend to have younger populations in comparison to other groups and mainstream society. It is estimated that over 60 per cent of Gypsies and Travellers are under the age of 25, compared with 35 per cent nationally, while 42 per cent are under the age of 15, compared with 21 per cent nationally (Sweeney and Matthews, 2017). Statistics from the Northern Ireland Human Rights Commission (2018) have shown that those from GRT communities aged between 14 and 25 represent the third highest group of young people (after Polish and UK young people).

Gypsy and Traveller females live 12 years less than females in the general population, while life expectancy for males in the same groups is 15 years lower than for non-Travellers. Roma across Europe also have the lowest life expectancy (up to 25 years less) and higher infant mortality than any other group of people. Here in the UK, infant mortality rates are 14 per 1000 in comparison to 4 per 1000 in non-Travellers (Equality and Human Rights Commission, 2016).

Health problems among Gypsies and Travellers are between two and five times more common than in the general population owing to high levels of poverty. Forty-two per cent of GRT people are affected by a long-term condition as opposed to 18 per cent of the general population (Bowers, 2016). A strong link is considered to exist between poor health and poor living conditions. Many Gypsies and Travellers live in substandard housing both in local authority accommodation and in that of other social housing providers – particularly in large urban areas in accommodation without central heating, running water and proper sewerage. Inadequate and inappropriate accommodation is often a major contributing factor that leads to poor health in both adults and children. This, along with overcrowding, family conflict and lack of access to basic facilities, impacts greatly on people's overall quality of life.

In the UK, some Gypsies and Travellers live on sites – whether on council land or privately rented land (a small number own their own land). Some of the living conditions are poor, including poor sanitation as well as other amenities that have fallen into disrepair. Some families will live without running water, electricity and proper heating. A lot of older Gypsies and Travellers have developed lung conditions, including cancer, due to not taking sufficient care around dangerous materials like asbestos or burning mattresses.

Common ailments

Common health difficulties and concerns in the Romany and Roma communities include:

- » respiratory problems, including asthma and bronchitis;
- » arthritis;
- » heart conditions;
- » cancer;
- » poor dental care (not everyone is registered);
- » drug and alcohol misuse;
- » lack of knowledge and understanding around sexual health;
- » diabetes;
- » cardiovascular and circulatory conditions;
- » high cholesterol owing to over consumption of sugar, salt and fatty and fried food.

There are problems accessing healthcare services, for example, registering with a GP without being able to provide proof of address, along with language and literacy barriers. There are high levels of digital exclusion in older GRT people. This is coupled with many finding that they are unable to communicate effectively about their physical and mental health problems when seeing a doctor. It is important that doctors and nurses are aware of communication difficulties and social awkwardness, particularly in older GRT patients.

GRT people tend not to seek medical attention until their condition has become very serious and are more likely to turn up at accident and emergency departments in hospitals because of previous poor experiences at their GP surgeries. An overall lack of trust among GRT people has led to a lack of engagement with public health campaigns, resulting in them often having a lack of knowledge about health services and their entitlements.

Young GRT children have higher reported prevalence of hearing, eyesight and speech problems than the general population. Poverty impacts greatly on children with an estimated one in ten children 'going to bed hungry' at least once a month. Children with bad asthma often get lost in the system with no follow-up from their teens. Leaving school early and unemployment has seen high numbers of young people resort to binge-drinking and anti-social behaviour, including dangerous driving. Road fatalities among the Gypsy and Traveller communities are very high. Drug misuse is recognised as being a big problem in younger generations of GRT people and will be discussed later in this chapter.

There appears to be a mentality within GRT communities of 'getting on with life', resulting in high levels of stress, anxiety and depression going unnoticed or living with it without seeking support. GRT people are nearly three times more likely to be anxious and twice as likely to be depressed. Many people hide their true feelings because they fear they will get judged by others in their community. Over 70 per cent of GRT people will have suffered prolonged discrimination, stigma and prejudice in their lifetime (Thompson and Woodger, 2018). Some grow accustomed to this, while others are less resilient. Another major cause is poverty and unemployment, which can sometimes lead to alcohol and substance misuse.

Sex is still considered a taboo subject to talk about although sexual health knowledge has improved, along with an increased use of contraceptives by Gypsies and Travellers.

Mothers tend to be younger in comparison to the general population. Breastfeeding is low in Romany Gypsy and Irish Traveller women but is high in Roma mothers. At least two-thirds of Irish Travellers are married to a cousin, resulting in metabolic and congenital disorders being higher than in the general population (UCD Dublin, 2010). Overall, there is little or no information on the number of Travellers who have an intellectual, physical or sensory disability.

There appears to be low awareness around national screening programmes for cervical, bowel and breast cancer. There is also less contact with health visitors and maternity services. This, however, is two-sided because some health visitors are reluctant to visit Traveller sites and GRT women tend to rely on older women in their communities to talk to about sensitive matters relating to childbirth. The need for professional help is evident though because one in five GRT mothers experience the loss of a child compared to one in a hundred in the non-Travelling community. There is a low uptake in child health services and community support services – low immunisation rates, poor utilisation of maternity services and women's health services, lack of value and poor understanding of ante-natal and post-natal check-ups. The levels of post-natal depression among GRT women are unknown because few seek professional help. There is also a low uptake of developmental paediatric services and specialist child health services, as well as family planning services, and a low rate of breastfeeding. In terms of preventative health and screening, women are getting better at having smear tests or a mammogram.

Irish Travellers

Irish Travellers have a distinctive population profile (particularly in the Irish Republic), which resembles some developing countries. It is noted that there is a higher birth rate and higher mortality rate at a young age than in the general population. Life expectancy as of 2022 is the same as the 1980s for men at 61.7, which is 15.1 years less than men in the general population. The figure for women is 70.1, which is 11.5 years less than for non-Traveller women. Traveller mortality is 3.5 times higher than the general population. The greatest causes of mortality in older Travellers tend to be heart disease and respiratory conditions in both males and females. Traveller infant mortality is estimated at 14.1 per 1000 live births compared to the general population, which is estimated to be 3.9 per 1,000 live births. As Watson et al (2017, p 66) state: *'When we compare Travellers and non-Travellers in the 35–54 age group, we see that Travellers are about three times as likely to have poor health or some type of difficulty or disability'*.

There is excessive cigarette smoking in both males and females, which often leads to high blood pressure. In terms of alcohol, far more men drink alcohol than women – approximately two-thirds of men; however, Travellers drink less alcohol than the general population but those who do drink do so more frequently and in large amounts.

Common health difficulties and concerns in Irish Travellers include:

- » high rates of haemophilia – an inherited bleeding disorder in which the blood does not clot properly;
- » osteogenesis imperfecta – a group of genetic disorders that mainly affect the bones;
- » muscular dystrophy – a group of inherited genetic conditions that cause the muscles to weaken;
- » asthma and chronic bronchitis;
- » rheumatoid arthritis;
- » angina, heart attacks and strokes;
- » diabetes;
- » low take-up of Covid-19 vaccinations;
- » poor diet;
- » excessive use of sun beds (females).

Some NGOs I spoke to claimed the causes of poor health and health inequalities in Travellers is because of racism and discrimination, which has permeated every aspect of their lives. They stated that discriminatory views are getting worse, whereby people casually and regularly express racist views towards Travellers on social media platforms. Many Travellers distrust the system – fearful that their children will be taken off them if they are ill or their kids are sick. Racism and discrimination are multi-faceted and feature in every main organisation. The Travelling community are becoming pro-active in challenging racism and discrimination by having community health workers (many of whom are Travellers) go out to communities and individuals to promote better mental health (anxiety, stress, depression and anti-suicide strategies) and physical health (cardiovascular diseases and diabetes). This also includes culturally appropriate smoking cessation programmes and advice and support on drug misuse, which has become a major problem in the Travelling community in the past ten years and which accounts for many sudden deaths because of overdoses. Travellers who are trained community health workers are listened to and trusted by fellow Travellers. This fresh approach is slowly bringing about the required changes but needs to be further supported to address health inequalities and to lower mortality rates

Those aged over 55 are considered old, particularly men who may suffer from heart problems, strokes, diabetes, cancer and alcohol misuse. It is not unusual to see a Travelling man at 50 whose health resembles the health of an 80 year-old man. This is partly because of a denial of access to healthcare because of racism and poor health education. Another big factor is because Travellers do not feel they are part of society, which is hardly surprising to those who get housed beside a sewage or waste ground or near a river, giving automatic chances of developing asthma, or beside a busy road, causing issues with noise pollution.

Some Travellers move around, preventing them from using their medical card which is means tested and assigned to one address/area. Some GP medical practices are reluctant to take on new patients and are often accused of not making Travellers feel welcome. This in turn results in Traveller patients not getting treatment or being referred to consultants. There is also a failure in medical services not realising that many Travellers are illiterate and/or suffer digital poverty. Eighty per cent of adult Travellers have literacy problems, which seriously impacts on health promotion, including filling out medical card applications and understanding instructions on prescription medicines (Watson et al, 2017).

Some Travellers favour folk medicine and go to see faith healers, seeking out, if possible, a healer who is the seventh son of a seventh son. Cures are often offered through means of prayers and remedies like herbs, oils and flowers. Using a faith healer is often based on strong religious beliefs and a family custom handed down the generation chain.

A barrier for some Travellers is that they don't like going to see a doctor. They are afraid of big words that they won't understand. They feel ashamed and have no self-confidence. Usually a family member goes with them but this means having no privacy. Heart conditions are a big problem that are often inherited. Other conditions are diabetes, cancer, asthma and COPD. Things are getting better. Many community health workers are Travellers. They go out to the halting sites. Travellers are more comfortable around them than they are with settled people. I am a Traveller myself, which means it is easier for them to talk to me and for me to explain things to them in a way they'll understand. The organisation I work for got leaflets printed that are Traveller friendly. They have pictures on them and simple words to read as many Travellers are illiterate. The leaflets have useful telephone numbers on them to where they can contact for help and that includes advocacy services, which I explain to them. I work mainly with families with young children. I give parents advice on dental care, child safety around the home and child development – vaccines and check-ups. I have noticed ongoing difficulties in Travellers being able to find Traveller-specific accommodation. There are so few halting sites for the number of people wanting to live on a site. Trespassing laws have made this intolerable for many people and the knock-on effect of this is their mental health, which it badly affects.

Geraldine – Community outreach worker

Mental health

Key factors in having a mental health problem are as follows.

» It is difficult for someone to admit they are depressed (shame and guilt prevent this).

» Services, including culturally appropriate services, are difficult to access.

» An entrenched inability in mainstream services to understand GRT people and the problems affecting their emotional well-being.

These factors mean that some do not seek out the support they need. There is a lack of research in this area but anecdotal evidence suggests some degree of undiagnosed mental health conditions.

A preponderance of mental health issues exists in Gypsies and Travellers. The fly in the ointment though is endogamy. Our community has had this for over 1000 years. People don't want to talk about this but the reality is that it is one of the root causes of our mental health problems.

John – Romany Gypsy

Racism and discrimination and the feeling that one is constantly under attack enters a person's head space and gets them down. Every time I make a new friend, I am wondering if they will be kind to me when they find out my background or if they will judge me for no reason. Then conforming to people within your community is another factor with a 'keeping up with the Joneses' feel to it. This places massive pressures on people to make sure their children are well dressed, that they are seen to be eating steak for dinner or are driving around in a nice car. This becomes a major part in a person being made to feel their self-worth.

Patrick – Irish Traveller

Many GRT people are not confident enough to go to their GP and admit they have a problem. If asked, they will skirt around the problem and say 'I'm fine' and then end up staying sad, miserable and unhappy.

Moses – Romany Gypsy

Professionals have suggested there may be a growing issue with drugs among young GRT people but there is no evidence to support this yet.

The younger generations have an easier, relaxed approach. They openly talk about it among themselves and often supply to each other. The preferred drug appears to be cocaine as it is seen as the expensive drug that won't do lasting damage compared to other drugs, for example heroin. They see pictures of the harrowing gaunt features of somebody hooked on heroin, which is considered a cheap drug, and this makes them feel they are able to dissociate themselves from somebody like this. It helps them think, 'I will never be like that person. I will never become that damaged'. But with cocaine it is considered a prestigious drug. That's their rationale for taking it because they believe it puts them in a different category. But it too leads to high dependency and is also linked to young people who took their own lives

Shane – Romany Gypsy

There is no proper recognition given to the problem either inside or outside the respective communities. Outreach support is limited and the resources of NGOs are tight. State bodies are not invested in tackling the problem with funding not being made available to set up targeted culturally trained services where GRT people can turn to for help, including phone and online counselling services.

Depression and anxiety rates and mental health problems in general are three times higher in Gypsies and Travellers than in the general population (Travellers' Times, 2020). Anxiety is often linked to them being fearful around their identity and linked to xenophobia, racism and discrimination. This affects young people more than older people. There are also high levels of mental health issues in Roma, including depression, personality disorders, learning disabilities, self-harm and suicidal tendencies, and dependency or misuse of drugs.

The Covid-19 pandemic brought its own share of problems – where Gypsies and Travellers were unable to travel long distances owing to restrictions which curtailed the work of those employed doing tree surgery jobs and paving work, as well as those selling and buying. This added stress had to be endured along with everyday anxiety and depression, resulting in an increase in anti-depressants being prescribed.

I look after my mental health. I go to the gym as well as doing a bit of boxing. I like working out and then going for a swim and to the sauna and steam room. This helps me to level my thinking. Travellers don't speak about how they feel to others unless you are a close friend. We tend to bottle things up. Terrible pressures on young people to have money and many have turned to drugs.

Lee – Irish Traveller

There is great stigma within GRT communities about members who have mental health problems, which means that diagnoses are often kept quiet. There is a lack of understanding about autism and mental health diagnoses for children and young people. One community outreach worker told me a poignant story about a mother whose young son had autism and how she kept this hidden from neighbours and friends. She continuously covered it up. The little boy had speech difficulties and could hardly talk. He attended a special school, but nobody knew about this. She referred to him as a 'poorly boy'. She turned to her religion and prayed and hoped that a 'miracle' would happen to heal her child. She remained very secretive about his condition and was so scared when professionals visited the site in case conversations were overheard and someone would discover the truth.

Travellers are reluctant to engage in mental health services because they don't like talking about their problems to people they don't know. Depression is still a taboo subject among Travellers. The strange thing is that more young people are getting diagnosed with autism and ADHD, but parents are aware that there is money to be claimed if their child gets diagnosed with ADHD, so they pursue this route. But at the mere mention of depression to anyone, it's given a wide berth. Suicide is high, especially in those who feel they have failed. We are high achievers in our own right and for some this unfortunately places undue pressure on people who compare their successes to others. Another taboo among Travellers is sex. This has led to Facebook groups being set up where disgruntled lovers post what they consider 'shameful' pictures to hurt and humiliate and applies equally to men and women. Unfortunately, this spitefulness has led to some people taking their own lives because of the embarrassment it has caused after family members and friends viewed the postings because some traditional families still expect virginity to be the norm before marriage.

Vicky – Romany Gypsy

Suicide

A very high percentage of Gypsies and Travellers experience suicide in their families and this is an issue that affects everybody. There are no statistics for Roma suicides, but it is thought these are significantly lower than in Romany and Traveller populations where it is estimated that 20 per cent of families are bereaved by suicides – most of which are young men.

Among Irish Travellers suicide is six to seven times higher than in the general population and accounts for 11 per cent of deaths. Sixty-five per cent of suicides are males under the age of 30 years old (The Traveller Movement, 2019). The prevailing issues causing Travellers to take their own lives include family problems, psychiatric illnesses, alcohol or drug misuse, violence and sexual orientation.

Other key markers are as follows.

- » Dereliction of Traveller culture since the 1960s, which began the quest to absorb Travellers into mainstream society and make them settled as a form of false 'rehabilitation' because the Travelling community were seen as a culture of poverty.
- » Loss of sense of identity: many feel ashamed of their identity, which has caused them enormous damage to their culture and well-being in general.

- » Travellers feel displaced in their own country: young people feel they don't belong in their country. In fact, some don't feel they belong anywhere, especially when they are denied access to services and refused entry to places.
- » Educational disadvantages: many young men feel they have no purpose – they are poorly educated and feel they lack a role in their community. Those who haven't succeeded in education and are unemployed can't provide for their families, rendering them feeling worthless.
- » High rates of unemployment: there are few opportunities for young Gypsies and Travellers and few initiatives for progressing in life, interspersed with racism and discrimination affecting their self-worth and self-confidence. Some hide their identity to get interviews. The anxiety is overwhelming, coupled with rejection if they are found out and not given the job.
- » Legislation: the criminalisation of the nomadic lifestyle and anti-trespassing laws have had a huge negative impact on Travellers, coupled with a lack of sites and lack of transient sites.

There are many facets to suicide, which includes a cumulative response whereby for example an additional family member dies by suicide after an older sibling takes their life. It is often seen as the only way out for them and is linked to the challenges of their lifestyle. Life becomes so overwhelming for those who find it difficult to juggle cultural expectations, including being expected to present with a macho, stoic and fighter image when their inward emotional well-being is frail and in need of support. Mental health issues can start at a young age given that nine out of ten children and young people from Romany and Traveller backgrounds have suffered racial abuse and nearly two-thirds have been bullied and physically attacked – often for prolonged periods of time, which erodes self-esteem and self-confidence (Greenfields and Rogers, 2020).

Ireland has no appreciation of Traveller culture and fails to see it as an important part of Irish culture. Look at kids who bully Traveller children in the playground. It is obvious they get a negative view of Travellers from their parents. Racism and discrimination impact on the lives of every Traveller. Anxiety is ever present in their lives. It impacts on both physical and mental well-being. One in ten Travellers die by suicide. These premature deaths are closely followed by the high number of deaths related to cardiovascular disease, diabetes and cancer. A lot of Travellers in Ireland live in horrific accommodation – overcrowded and often lacking in basic facilities. It is not uncommon to find two families living in a two-bedroomed house with up to 12 children. Local councils simply don't care and won't listen to their complaints. Travellers to them are an easy group to ignore. You also must look at halting sites where it's not unusual to find them situated next to a dump. This clearly shows the lack of empathy that the council has towards Travellers,

which is overall lacking in compassion and isn't trauma informed. When you see examples like this, it is easy to understand how a person's sense of purpose can become completely deflated.
Thomas – Irish Traveller

One positive thing that is occurring is that more Travellers are having counselling. The Travelling Counselling Service in Ireland, which was set up over a decade ago, offers culturally appropriate interventions by counsellors who are Travellers themselves. Over 70 per cent of referrals to the service are self-referred with the remainder coming from social workers and public health nurses. Based in Dublin, this is a Traveller-specific service, but they have also set up steering groups who are rolling out the service to other parts of the country. The service is available in person to those who can get to a centre but is otherwise available via telephone or by online sessions. Another service that is offering support and a voice to people is the National Traveller Mental Health Network, which attracts a large social media following among Travellers. Its Facebook page is helping lessen stigma around mental illness with people being given the opportunity to talk about their problems. It has been noted that more men are saying things and praising and respecting people who speak out, which is a very encouraging sign that attitudes are changing.

Conclusion

It is said that Travellers have a propensity to live life in the present moment and prefer to live as intensely as possible, irrespective of this bringing immense joy or great suffering. When it comes to caring for their health though, there is a 'stuckness' whereby change is either slow or not forthcoming. There are some hopeful signs in the younger generation who do not tolerate injustices like their forebears and are more vocal and questioning of their rights. A lot of young people register more easily with a GP and address health concerns as they arise. Young people are better aware of issues around their life expectancy and more of them are living healthy lifestyles, including diet and exercise. Suicide remains a phenomenally big problem, particularly in Irish Traveller males. Investment in tackling the causes of this needs urgent action to reduce these staggeringly high statistics.

As mentioned in this chapter, women are better at attending preventative scans but despite this improvement more public health nurses need to be employed to work across the GRT communities. These should either be from a GRT background or be specifically trained in working with GRT people and possess both community development skills and anti-racist skills. They should also be highly knowledgeable in health issues pertaining specifically to GRT communities and be able to plan and implement targeted strategies to improve access to healthcare provision. There are pockets of improvement though in some areas, with health visitors providing outreach to local GRT communities by offering help and advice on immunisations, family health concerns, teeth, healthy eating, blood pressure and weighing babies. Finally, there is a need for more investment in research into the health of GRT people, including research into intervention to address the significant health inequalities that have prevailed for far too long.

Chapter 6 | Education

Introduction

The educational landscape of GRT children and young people is dominated by a lack of qualifications, underachievement and literacy difficulties. Historically, GRT people have had a reputation of being poorly educated. Little value or emphasis was placed on attending school, which was seen as something that wouldn't benefit the financial future of young people from the respective communities. This still exists but it is not recognised as being the sole cause of why so few GRT children complete secondary education and nor is it accurate to say that GRT parents perceive a lack of value in education and don't encourage their children to attend. Sometimes the opposite is true. Bullying, racism and discrimination are commonplace for GRT children and young people in schools and other educational establishments. It is often ingrained, institutional and acceptable. The educational system is flawed and unyielding to the ethnic needs of GRT pupils, resulting in intergenerational apathy and indifference towards education. This is a system that has badly let them down so the obvious question that needs to be asked is when this cycle will break. This chapter explores both the historical and current issues behind educational experiences of GRT children and focuses upon some of the key changes necessary to bring about the required improvements for young people to thrive in education as opposed to the current levels of exclusion and disenfranchisement that prevent successful outcomes.

Key factors

Feedback from professionals and the GRT community has highlighted the following main reasons for the poor educational outcomes of GRT children.

» Problems with attendance, behaviour and adjustment to a school environment.

» GRT children often leave school early (some before they complete primary school) because of pressure from their community to start work, particularly boys.

» Some GRT children are not even registered at school and stay at home without any formal education.

- » Many GRT young people leave secondary school early with no formal qualifications; this rate is three times higher than the national average.
- » GRT children are more frequently identified as having special or additional learning needs than other student groups.
- » Up to 25 per cent of GRT children are not in education or employment after the age of 16.
- » Irish Travellers have the lowest retention rate of GRT people in UK schools and in Ireland they tend to leave school before the age of 15, resulting in serious issues in terms of literacy and other skills.
- » Continuing education and progression to college and university for GRT young people is an exception (less than 1 per cent go on to further education after secondary school).
- » Low expectations from teachers and poor understanding by schools about Gypsy, Roma and Traveller culture and heritage.

There are no inherent reasons why GRT children should not achieve as well as any other child at school. They have inherently the same potential to get GCSEs and other qualifications. Despite the many changes in Gypsy and Traveller lifestyles life over the past 30 years, school attendance is still a major problem.

With regard to primary education, it is commonly expected within many GRT families that when sufficient literacy and numeracy skills have been developed, other aspects of the curriculum may not be regarded as necessary. GRT young people withdraw from school because they feel old enough to be out working, coupled with the idea that they do not need formal qualifications because the family business in which they plan to work has no requirement for formal qualifications. Stories abound about boys being taken out of education to go and work with their fathers – and girls taken out to become homemakers. Many feel that as long as they can read and write so that they can do the driving theory test, it is sufficient of an education. Others simply leave because they do not see the value of education. Mobility is a feature of some Traveller communities like fairground and circus families because the high level of seasonal movement may mean that children remain in one area for only a few days while maintaining a fixed winter base and school. Others easily get excluded for challenging behaviour. This is coupled with some children not completing secondary school because of older siblings also leaving early, resulting in there being little incentive to be different.

GRT parents may have had little experience of formal schooling themselves or have had negative experiences. They may have little communication with parents outside their communities or may have experienced hostility or racism from other parents within their areas. A lot of GRT parents are afraid that their children will lose their cultural identity at school. Some distrust schools and view them as places where cultural pollution among gorgers contaminates their children's mindsets. Other parents dislike their children receiving sex education in school which they do not consider 'moral' – or are worried about drug culture in older teenagers and sexual behaviour among teens – and therefore will not allow their children to stay for long in secondary school.

However, many parents do want their children to receive a proper education but may need extra help, support ánd encouragement in helping ensure their children regularly attend school. More parents are accepting the downside of their children not completing secondary education – coupled with an over-reliance on manual self-employed work. They realise their children will not get any decent job without qualifications and know that a lack of education/qualifications means low-paid unskilled jobs – often for life.

Some Gypsies agree that change is needed – especially for boys who mainly quit after primary school. They are eager to go and work with their fathers, although they must comply with the legality of home tutoring. Many parents feel their sons are impressionable and that by going to secondary school they will be exposed to drugs. They like to 'shield' them from the world and also shield their daughters because they want to teach them the value of things that need to be done at home. However, more girls than boys go to secondary school with many having ambitions of going to college and getting a decent job.

I was in my early thirties before I learned how to read and write. This is not uncommon, and neither is for Gypsies to play ignorant. It is part of a lazy streak in Gypsies [laughs], *particularly in males who are used to asking others to read and explain things to them. I was rebellious at school. Well, more mischievous than anything else. I was good at sport and not so bad at maths. I knew it was important to add up. When it comes to money, none of us wants to be short-changed* [laughs again]. *School is different now than in my day. There are far more drugs knocking about the place. These days the teachers ask the kids if they want to be a boy or a girl* [reference to transgender people]. *Gypsies place a lot of value on a person having common sense and far less value on somebody that is educated. They laugh when they hear of people going to university, getting a degree and then being unable to get a job, which means they end up working in the Co-op. To them, this is a waste of time. They look at those years at university as lost ones and think that person does not have much sense when they could have used that time to work and earn money. They also look at themselves and see how they worked themselves from an early age despite not having much of an education and yet they come up smelling of roses, like their fathers and grandfathers. Many young men follow in the footsteps of their fathers because they want to learn a trade and join in the family business. They do not want to feel trapped in a regular 9–5 job. They want to work whereby they can please themselves. They are 'Free Spirits' by nature.*

Bartley – Romany Gypsy

Education at home

I spoke to several education engagement officers working with GRT children who painted a bleak picture of GRT children and young people in education. Old-fashioned views are still sometimes expressed by fathers: '*I can't read or write and did alright for myself.*' Attendance at primary school is good with most children attending at least 75 per cent of the time but struggling academically. GRT parents rarely buy toys for their children and visits to homes reveal that there are often no books, newspapers or magazines to encourage mental stimulation. The cost of this is that GRT pupils are always 'behind' other non-GRT pupils in terms of restricted vocabulary and ability to develop good literacy skills.

One officer who worked with GRT pupils for over 25 years said that the situation has got worse in the last quarter century with fewer young people going beyond the first year at secondary school. Some mothers might show enthusiasm for their child to attend secondary school, but this is not matched with their child attending. Among young people, there is complete disinterest around the need to study for qualifications which they view as 'worthless' for a Gypsy or Traveller. Boys still tend to think of themselves (or are made to think of themselves) as adults at the age of 11 and girls around the same time start preparing for 'married life'. Those who do start secondary school are teased and bullied from others in their community when seen in a school uniform. Parents sometimes ask if their child can go to school 'part time' so that on the other days, the older boys can go and work with their fathers and the girls can stay at home and help with chores.

GRT culture also interrupts school attendance. Parents sometimes don't hesitate to take their children out of school when attending a horse fair, whether this is in the UK or Ireland, without explanation, and have a cavalier attitude when a 'Child missing education' investigation takes place. In addition to horse fairs, some children also take time off during school terms to go to religious events or to attend funerals and weddings.

Although schools are not supposed to encourage home education, they sometimes do, or they may informally advise parents what happens if they decide to take the child off-roll at the school. The fact is hardly anything happens under education at home. The parents have no obligation to teach any subject linked to the national curriculum, including maths and English, and nor do they have to adhere to any set timetable.

Provided they can provide evidence to the education at home officers (who carry out random visits) that the child is receiving some form of education then no further action is taken. GRT parents get around this by stating that their children are receiving a 'cultural education', which is deemed acceptable within the guidelines. The parents might be telling the truth about educating their children in Gypsy and Traveller culture, but the result is poor literacy and numeracy with no academic qualifications; this is rarely acknowledged. When a parent is asked if they ever take their child to a library, the response may cite discrimination along the lines of the library not allowing them to enter because of their ethnicity. Many professionals agree that these guidelines around education at home are weak and flimsy and often result in the GRT child and young person not receiving any acceptable form of education that will help them flourish and thrive in life. Finding a solution to this imbedded disaffection will not be easy and there are few, if any, solutions on the horizon. One possible answer is middle schools but there are few of these in the country and these only take children from the ages of 11–13. This age criteria would need to be revised to cater for the needs of GRT children.

Some schools offer a foundation course to students who are struggling academically and are likely to not sit their GCSEs. I have seen successful courses like this where some GRT students did well and gained functional skills. The course I am thinking about accepted those aged 14–16 and consisted of about 25 students. Subjects included maths, English and IT designed to increase levels of literacy and numeracy. Some of the GRT students who successfully completed the course went on to college and others found jobs in retail and social care, so the course was well worth doing. It is unfortunate that there aren't more courses like this because I honestly think this could offer real chances to many young Gypsies and Travellers who struggle or dislike attending school.

Janice – Education officer

I would estimate that at least 50 per cent of GRT young people are educated at home after Year 7 – and of those who do persevere at school, only around 5 per cent end up getting some GCSEs. Those who continue after Year 7 tend to be English Romany Gypsies. In my opinion, parents who receive penalty notices for their child's non-attendance are not the least bit perturbed and usually don't pay the fine by stating they haven't got the means to do so. Occasionally young people themselves reach the age of 16 and 17 and display aspirations about going to college to be mechanics, hairdressers, plumbers or to do bricklaying. However, without basic educational qualifications like functional skills in maths and English they simply haven't got a chance. There were colleges in the past that would sign up GRT young people without qualifications but did not have very positive experiences. I'm not saying it would be impossible to get somebody a place without qualifications, but they would have to demonstrate at least they had a good school attendance record and were able to demonstrate strong aspirations of learning in their chosen subject. Unfortunately, this is not something that many GRT young people are able to provide.

Emily – Education officer

Many GRT children and their parents choose to hide their identity and will identify themselves as White British when applying for entry into a school. They do this to protect their children from negative experiences they have encountered. Schools need to address this with GRT parents to ensure they can convince them that their schools will be a safe place for GRT children to learn and thrive and not to have to deal with unpleasant experiences. Priority needs to be given to the following factors to become embedded in school teaching and its overall ethics.

» There is nothing to be ashamed of in being a Gypsy, Roma or Traveller.

» You should be proud of your heritage and culture.

» You should be proud of your family and where you live and not have to hide it.

» You have a right to a good education just like everybody else and it does not depend on you having to hide who you are to receive it.

» No child should be expected to hold a closely guarded secret of who they are – and live with the fear of exposure.

» Teachers should precisely know the culture and background of their pupils, which will enable them to understand problems and dilemmas and to help them best, eg assign a teaching assistant if deemed necessary.

Despite the challenges and institutionalised racism often faced by Gypsies and Travellers in educational settings, some small changes are occurring. GRT History Month is celebrated in June each year with schools beginning to encourage debate among students about the history and culture of GRT people because most young people know little about Gypsies or Travellers. There are no mentions of Gypsies, Roma or Travellers in the curriculum in secondary schools and in primary schools this tends to be pictures for younger children, eg trailers, horses and dogs and caravan painting. What needs close consideration is that teachers know little about GRT culture. How many teachers know a Gypsy or Traveller in their private life or have ever visited a GRT family home or caravan site?

Some GRT people are aware that education is a powerful tool. Young people themselves are more clued up than ever before through social media about what they need to have for success and advancement in their lives. However, the education system must change its perspectives of GRT people. Stereotyping and racism must be stamped out. Every GRT child needs to be properly educated in mainstream schools which include diversity relating to their needs, including having GRT culture and history taught in lessons. Provisions must be in place for GRT children who still live nomadic lifestyles (25 per cent). But there is a shift/change of attitude whereby within the next decade there will be more GRT people completing secondary education, gaining qualifications, going to college, entering apprenticeships and getting into employment than ever before.

Travellers are catching up with the times. Many realise that everything is computer-based and that it's essential to be able to read and write and to be good at maths and English, especially when running your own business and doing invoices etc. More are entering apprenticeships than ever before, and some are even going to college. It's still not high numbers but it's a start. We know the world is changing but the education system needs to realise that we have distinct cultural differences. Take for example when someone dies, we mourn for longer periods than everyone else so there needs to be a curriculum that can adapt for things like this. Schools need to be more creative with GRT children. Why not ask them to do more school projects that address our culture? Young people could be asked to make videos of animals and horses – to take photos and write journals about various aspects of our culture. I know some young use their cultural background as an excuse for leaving school early, but the mentality is slowly changing because there is a shift occurring in their parents and grandparents who see that things are no longer the same as when they were young. For others, their mentality is stuck because for them money equals wealth and they believe that the sooner they start earning money, the quicker that they will get rich.

Kavan – Romany Gypsy

Roma

Roma children do marginally better in British schools with a reported improvement from what they experienced in their countries of origin where they were segregated from other pupils (notably in Slovakia, Hungary and Bulgaria). Most Roma children have been denied access to education in Eastern European countries. Assessment is done in state languages like in Slovakia – if they fail to understand the questions, they are placed in special schools coupled with an institutional belief that Roma are inferior. Many come to the UK with little prior experience of formal education – and together with issues of language and unfamiliarity, many families often find it difficult to adhere to school routines and abide by the formal rules of a school setting. A lot of Roma parents are unable to read and write, which impacts on the way schools communicate with them despite interpreters sometimes being used. However, Roma parents generally think it good for their children to get an education and admire the British educational system.

Roma young people are a little better than Romany or Travellers at completing secondary school in the UK. Unfortunately, education is sometimes disrupted by them moving around from one area to another. It is not uncommon to see a child settled and doing well, only to be suddenly uprooted and moved to another part of the country and have to start all over again. With regard to older Roma children who are 16/17 and do not speak English, it is hard trying to get them on an ESOL (English for Speakers of Other Languages) course given the scarcity of this provision in the country.

Irish Travellers in Ireland

Only 13 per cent of Irish Travellers complete secondary education. Bullying is tolerated, including comments from teachers that imply they have low expectations of young Travellers. The slightest difficulty at school results in many being put on reduced timetables (European Union Agency for Fundamental Rights, 2020).

Young people complain of being misunderstood and that nobody values them, resulting in school being seen as a hostile environment from which parents remove their children consequently. There is also peer pressure to leave school because many look at it as a 'baby' thing and consider staying there until they are 17 or 18 as non-sensical. Some do not see any incentive because they might know of someone who had completed their education and gained qualifications but remain unemployed. Overall, there is no ambition in the Travelling community because there is no encouragement or validation of what strengths and benefits they could bring to the workplace. Travellers make up 1 per cent of the population, and their 1 per cent is not represented in civil service or public sector jobs. Those who attend job interviews tend to hide their identity and often dress differently in fear of being detected as Travellers, such is their internalised oppression and shame that society has made them feel from a young age.

The past in Ireland saw a segregated model of provision. This meant there was a special class in primary school for all ages of Travellers with a designated teacher. This approach placed little emphasis on an age-appropriate and integrated educational model. Thankfully, this discriminatory approach stopped in the 1980s, although, historically and currently, Irish Travellers have never had time for school once they have finished national (primary) school. In the Traveller community there is a saying '*The time has come to run after the pound*', meaning somebody is old enough to work and follow in their parents' footsteps in scrap metal dealing, market trading and horse dealing. The focus is on going to work as soon as possible and earning money.

One young woman told me about the segregation that took place between Travellers and non-Travellers when she was in primary school. The teacher made her sit with non-Travellers in the class because she was considered brighter than her Traveller peers. She still feels resentment towards this because it set her apart from the others and resulted in her not being accepted in the class with non-Travellers and being rejected also by her friends in the Traveller class because they felt she thought she was better than them and that was why she sat away from them. Others reported bias and racism towards Travellers. Some schools use every bureaucratic rule in the rulebook to avoid accepting Travellers into the school, often claiming they are not in the right catchment area or will have to seek references/school records from previous schools etc. Anything to avoid or delay entry.

Gus – an older Traveller (aged 70) – believes that children in his community are better placed at going to school nowadays because they are now more settled than at any other point in history. He said:

In the past, schooling and moving around from place to place were not very compatible for receiving a consistently good education. It was hard to keep approaching schools and then move on to a new place and restart the process. It was very tough on the children, and many ended up hardly ever going to school.

Youthreach

Fifty per cent of Traveller young people aged over 15 do not attend school. They do not see the positive side of doing so and display the attitude of, *What's the point?* Many parents view home tutoring with disdain and place little value on this, coupled with a high percentage of them escaping any legal punishment. However, Irish Travellers face high rates of unemployment – over 75 per cent in the Irish Republic compared with 8.5 per cent of the general population and, in Northern Ireland, 89 per cent are registered unemployed in comparison to 4 per cent of the general population (European Union Agency for Fundamental Rights, 2020). Youthreach provides opportunities for people who leave mainstream school early without formal qualifications to build on their basic education and improve work skills. Up to 10 per cent of young Travellers avail of this learner-centred programme, receiving one-to-one support with a bespoke individual plan for each. Youthreach is a two-year programme where young people can obtain a level 3 qualification (equivalent to the Junior Certificate – GCSEs) or level 4 (equivalent to the Leaving Certificate – A levels). Each student is paid a weekly allowance of up to €50 based on age and attendance. The curriculum is both academic and vocational based and consists of English, maths, SPHE (social, physical and health education), cooking, computer courses, personal effectiveness, career planning, crafts, woodwork, hairdressing, sports and childcare. Students also carry out work experience leading to offers of employment. Feedback from tutors states that young GRT people on the programme don't stand out any differently from other young people and are generally well behaved. Their literacy skills are no weaker than other students. Most of the young people complete level 3 and a few complete level 4 before their 18th birthday with some leaving to get married.

Other key educational difficulties include the following (Anonymous, 2019).

- » Only 75 per cent of Traveller children attend primary school. Furthermore, nearly six in ten Traveller men are educated to, at most, primary level in sharp contrast to the general population, for which the comparable rate is just over one in ten.
- » 92 per cent leave secondary school without having completed secondary level – marginally more females remain and complete their Leaving Certificate. Most Travellers leave before completing the Junior Certificate.
- » 9 per cent of Travellers aged 25–64 years stay in school beyond the age of 16 (compared to 75 per cent of non-Travellers).
- » Only 1 per cent of Travellers enter third-level education and have a college degree compared to 30 per cent of non-Travellers.
- » Traveller children are more likely than non-Traveller children to attend a designated disadvantaged school and have a greater likelihood of being assessed as having a special educational need.
- » Traveller children have a tendency of starting school a year later than non-Traveller children.

There is a ravaging unemployment level of 84 per cent in Travellers, which is often a direct penalty for having a lower level of education (European Union Agency for Fundamental Rights, 2020). Prejudice and discrimination play their part, but the greatest factor is lacking education and qualifications. The chances of unemployment are eight times higher because of a lack of education and qualifications. This is coupled with employers lacking awareness in Traveller culture and therefore there is poor tailoring around recruitment to meet the needs of Travellers. Travellers themselves are fearful of loss of welfare and secondary benefits when seeking employment.

With regards to education, it has been a long-protracted process. Many schools never have had Traveller pupils because they are not allowed entry, which has never been challenged by the state, by society or teachers themselves. Therefore, many Travellers have developed the attitude 'Why should I burst my guts at school because I will never be treated properly with respect?' We non-Travellers have taken everything away from them to live their authentic nomadic lifestyles that they crave. Instead, we have put them in substandard housing, made them dependent on the state and criminalise them at every opportunity. The truth is educational authorities often couldn't care less about the education of Traveller children.

Cathy – Community outreach worker

Conclusion

As mentioned in this chapter, small changes are appearing on the horizon. The Irish government supports legislation to ensure Traveller history and culture become an obligatory part of the primary and secondary school curriculum. The education system must ensure that Traveller children and young people feel their experiences and perspective are valued and be provided with opportunities to reach their full potential. Maybe the British government should consider similar proposals for the UK, including Northern Ireland, particularly if pressure is placed on them to take the GRT children's ethnic and educational needs more seriously. The message should also convey that GRT history must be taught and not just promoted. Putting up posters each June to mark GRT History Month is of little use if schools offer no direct education about GRT traditions, language, skills, culture, arts and music. Sadly, there never has been any inclination to put this on school curriculums. Many Gypsies and Travellers would like to learn more about their languages, but sadly, there has been no investment by the state. Some question whether the narrow-minded views of some educational authorities who believe in capping the promoting and teaching of other cultures are the cause. GRT History Month is often little more than rhetoric and needs addressing if it is to have more substance and worth. Although curriculum changes are a good idea, a concerted effort should also be made to stamp out the bullying and racist behaviour directed at GRT children and young people throughout their school years. These injustices must stop because if no improvements are made, the conversations about this issue will be the same ten years from now, coupled with the same appalling statistics. Furthermore, another generation of GRT children and their families will have been failed by an unjust system.

Chapter 7 | Religion

Introduction

Religion is one of the key values among GRT people. Baptisms, weddings and funerals are usually marked by extended family. This involves large community gatherings with strong religious ceremonial content. Romany Gypsies have traditionally belonged to either the Church of England or the Catholic Church. Roma are mainly Orthodox Christians with a small Muslim population in certain Eastern Bloc countries. Irish Travellers are Roman Catholic and many practise devoutly. Based on that landscape alone, it would be safe to surmise that the GRT communities hold inherently strong religious beliefs.

However, fulfilment is not always found in traditional religious denominations because over the past decade or so a growing Christian evangelical movement has been gathering momentum in Britain called Light and Life, which this chapter will explore in close detail. There is a quest to require a greater meaning of life, which is often found in marginalised groups. Many GRT people simply have a quest for a greater presence of God in their lives and find this in the Bible. This has its advantages and undoubtedly impacts positively in many lives, but the downside is the garnering of judgemental values.

Light and Life Church

This new Pentecostal/evangelical movement has resulted in a radical transformation in British Romany Gypsies in the last 30 years with a growing membership. There are 35–40 established churches in Britain and Wales. Every Romany Gypsy will have heard of the mission. It is estimated that this 'Gypsy' awakening has over 30,000 followers – around a tenth of the estimated Gypsy population – and it is steadily growing each year. Its membership also includes some Roma and Irish Travellers who have become attracted to this type of more radical Christianity which places great emphasis on how God showed us his word which is found in John's Gospel (3:1–21) where Jesus told Nicodemus the Pharisee that unless a person is born again, he cannot see the kingdom of God.

An annual convention takes place each year, usually in Manchester or the Midlands, where up to 10,000 GRT people attend over a six-day period. A big 5000-people capacity tent is erected where three services a day are held during the convention.

The Light and Life Church has grown rapidly in the past 30 years – it claims up to 40 per cent of British Gypsies belong to it. There is no concrete evidence for this claim, but most Gypsies and Travellers will agree that there is a surge in people joining. Twice weekly services are held at a growing number of churches across the UK.

The Light and Life movement in Britain consists of born-again Christians which has come about because more and more people are searching for greater meaning in their lives, resulting in them discovering that the only way this is possible is by living life as outlined in the Bible. Although I was born into the Catholic faith, I no longer consider I have a religion. Instead, I have a relationship with God, and I express this with my brothers and sisters in the Light and Life mission because they share my views in living life through the Bible.

Avalon – Roma

The origins of the Light and Life movement

The words 'Jesus can heal' on the leaflet caught the attention of the Gypsy women in a French market town in Brittany, France, when someone handed them one that advertised services at a local church. These women were worried and troubled. Their friend's 17-year-old son was seriously ill in hospital, and they feared he would die. One of them suggested going to the church and asking the pastor if he could come to the hospital and heal the young man. The pastor explained to the women that it wasn't him or the church that healed people and that it was only Jesus who could do so. After some persuasion, the pastor agreed to go to the hospital and pray for the young man's recovery. A little while later, the young man began to get better and eventually made a full recovery.

The boy's recovery led to Gypsies going to services at the church. Here they were told that their lives would be filled with the Holy Spirit when they were baptised. Sadly, it was here that they ran into a big hurdle. None of them were baptised and it was an adult requirement to be baptised to be a proper member of the congregation. Many left the church crestfallen at this piece of news. However, a little while later a new pastor took over and heard about the plight of the Gypsies. His name was Clément Le Cossec, and he was young, enthusiastic and eager to spread the word of God. He was a little more radical than the previous incumbent and told the Gypsies that they would all baptise each other. And this is what they did. Apparently before the pastor arrived in the village to take charge of the church, he had a dream telling him that he would work with foreign people, but he interpreted this as maybe going off to do some missionary work in India.

Clément grew fond of the Gypsies and noted their religious convictions. He began to teach them to read and write and to read the Bible before deciding to leave his church and set up a new 'church', which he named Vie et Lumière. This new church gathered momentum across Europe in Gypsy communities and by the 1960s had made its way to Britain. Across Europe, at least one in ten and perhaps as many as one-third of the entire Gypsy, Roma and Traveller population are now devout and active followers or have been in a Light and Life church at some time. It is noticed that the movement is also making inroads among the traditionally Roman Catholic Traveller communities.

Sunday service

I attended one of these services and made this observation. Everybody was well dressed. Some arrived with Bibles. Women had their heads covered while praying (as dictated in the Bible). There were hymns accompanied by music – mainly guitar and drums. People clapped and held out their right hand as a gesture of desiring the Lord to come closer to them. Men and women tended to be separate in the church. Only men participate in the running of services. This is seen as a man's job, although women are free to speak at designated times.

The preacher told the congregation *'God rejoices over us and loves us so much'*, before adding, *'You need to thank God that he has saved you. You have been given salvation'*, before rhetorically asking the congregation, *'What does salvation mean to you?'* Then the preacher told a story about a tiny lily flower that was once found in the Egyptian desert and of the many people amazed when it imparted a most beautiful and unimaginable fragrance they had never smelt before in their lives. He told the congregation, *'When you have salvation in your life, you too will be able to smell this beautiful fragrance and not the stagnant, bitter, rotten, putrefied scent the world presents from the shadows of life to those without salvation.'* He then went on to say, *'Don't take from this world because it will pollute and destroy you'*, before citing examples of gay people, and those who engage in extra-marital affairs, drug taking and crime. The preacher then held up two small bottles to illustrate the difference between heaven and hell. One of the bottles contained clean drinking water and the other contained a brown liquid substance. He joked about not knowing what its contents were and said he had hurriedly collected it from his horse stables just before the service. He then told the congregation, *'If you drink from the bottle of clean water, it will refresh and renew you but if you drink from the other bottle, it will poison and make you very sick.'*

After the sermon was complete, the preacher invited people to share out loud their petitions to God. This consisted of people requesting prayers for deceased loved ones or for sick relatives as they cried out loud, *'Please Lord, please save them and grant them salvation.'* It was said in an imploring tone of voice as if they were pleading with God to hear their petitions.

The ideology behind the need for salvation seems to come from the perspective that human beings are wounded, damaged people and sinners, and will remain so until they seek salvation by turning to the Bible and God and by becoming 'born-again Christians'. Parishioners feel the best elements of Gypsy culture are at the heart of the church's energetic services and state that they are encouraged to display joyfulness, loudness, happiness, and sometimes dancing, to celebrate the goodness of God.

Old school GRT don't want anything to do with the born-again Christian movement. My father used to say, 'I don't need to be born again. I was born once, isn't that enough?' He also thought those who joined such a church were looking for forgiveness. That's what he said about my nephew Steve when he joined. Steve cheated on his wife so many times. He also used to collect and sold goldfinches, which are nicknamed 'goldies'. Goldfinches are a popular steal amongst Gypsies who like to have one in their home because it is a bird song and therefore worth money.

Roxy – Romany Gypsy

GRT and marriage

Older generations of GRT people believe that a man and woman should 'marry' for life. However, one man told me that he was one of 12 children and his parents have never married, which led me to discovering some fascinating insights into marriage in general. At least 70 per cent of Romany Gypsies are not 'legally' married but in the eyes of their community (and God) they are in a lifelong union. But for some young couples they adopt the custom of eloping. After a period of dating, they elope and go to a hotel for the night to consummate their union before returning home and telling their parents and family that they have got 'married'. Young people are often chaperoned to ensure that they do not develop relationships because their parents could have somebody in mind for them to marry. Despite this watchful eye and laying down the law by the parents, some young people prefer to find their own partners and hence elope and have sex before returning and declaring their love. This leads to a quick marriage to prevent single motherhood in the event of an unexpected pregnancy. This applies equally to males and females. Some might have a small party afterwards, but 30 per cent do get legally married, and these usually have a lavishly expensive party.

Gypsies believe that if you are married in the eyes of God then that is all that matters. They believe that although there is the Biblical story of Jesus attending the wedding feast at Cana, there is nothing that implies that the couple had an official wedding service beforehand. Older Gypsies believe that materialism has taken over the world and frown upon spending too much on big weddings, which they feel is unnecessary.

As in Romany Gypsy and Traveller families, Roma often marry cousins. They also tend to marry young, usually around the age of 16, to prevent them having sex before marriage. Even in the UK, most get married around the age of 18. Virginity is expected in both boys and girls before marriage. Take Bulgaria for example – as mentioned in Chapter 3 young people aged around 12 or 13 are matched by their parents. This results in the girl moving in to live with the boy's family. They basically grow up together and get to know each other this way before consummating their 'marriage' around the age of 15 or 16. Roma are adamant that these are arranged marriages as opposed to forced marriages and state that love blossoms in this way and that the divorce rate among Roma is low, although it is less frowned upon now than it was in previous decades.

Jump the broomstick

'Jump the broomstick' is a term often used within Gypsy circles. People of all ages still use it when describing people getting married, cohabiting or entering into an agreement to date or marry at some later stage. It was also used when referring to an elopement or a sham marriage that was legally binding. References to 'broomstick marriages' were first mentioned in England in the mid-to-late eighteenth century and were often used to describe a marriage ceremony of doubtful validity. It was even mentioned in Charles Dickens' novel *Great Expectations* when he referred to a couple being married 'over the broomstick'. The term 'jumping over the broom' was also used in other circles when referring to an irregular or non-church union, particularly clandestine marriages outside church circles before the introduction of civil marriages in 1836. Others interpreted the term 'stepping over the broom' as a test for chastity, while putting out a broom signalled that a man in the house was looking for a wife.

Younger Romany

Years ago, marrying outside the community was frowned upon but not so much anymore. Young people socialise better with non-GRT people and live completely different lifestyles to their parents and grandparents. Their culture and values are changing. That is not to say some of them don't face prejudice and discrimination from outsiders with some who are in relationships being rejected after their boyfriend/girlfriend discovered their GRT background, leaving many people feeling broken-hearted in the process.

Attitudes towards sex before marriage have lessened over the past few decades. Before this, sex was widely regarded as something that should only occur within marriage. It was looked down upon if a woman had sex before marriage but was generally more acceptable if men had sex before marriage. There has been a bigger shift in women having sex before marriage in the past 20 years and much the same for men. These days, women tend to have sex outside marriage both within their community and outside of it, given the greater interaction and integration with the wider non-GRT community. It is estimated that 70 per cent of women and 40 per cent of men are virgins on their 'wedding' night.

When I asked representatives of the Light and Life Church what type of morals they thought young people should uphold, they outlined the following:

Boys should live clean lives with no drugs or criminal activities. They should earn an honest living and not sleep around but find a decent girl to marry and have kids.

Silas – Romany Gypsy

Girls should not sleep around. They should not have boyfriends before marriage. They should be taught how to maintain a good home, bring up their children and be a good wife who lives a clean life.

Ramon – Roma

Irish Travellers

Marriage

Although Travellers are historically very religious in nature, some churches have refused to baptise babies after using the excuse that the parents and family do not live in the parish. Churches have been criticised for denying Travellers this fundamental

Catholic sacrament. Marriages too have seen a decline in the past decade or so with some Travellers opting instead for civil ceremonies as well as cohabiting without getting married.

Marriage is often viewed as just a bit of paper. Travellers tend to meet people and stay with them for life and not bother getting married. That goes as much for the older generation as it does nowadays for younger people. You could say we are split into three groups – those who stay together for life, whether they are married or not – those who divorce – and those who marry outside the community, ie marry a gorger. Even with those sorts of couples, many stay together for life. But I know things are changing. I only must look at my own life to know that. My parents are no longer together although I was brought up to believe that marriage was for life and that women should never look at another man once she got married – not even on social media.

Joseph – Irish Traveller

Coming of age for boys is at around 12 years when it is expected in a patriarchal way that they start transitioning from being a boy to becoming a man. Like Romany Gypsies, the family tradition entails boys spending a lot of time with their fathers and going out on jobs with them. Here they are 'educated' to be men. Over time, the boy will now see himself in many ways as an equal to the adults around him and will expect a degree of respect from his mother and sisters. Power, authority, community and familial roles are often very specific and assumed within GRT communities. Men hold power and authority in their families and are expected to be strong and macho.

Up until the 1970s, arranged marriages were commonplace and still are for some traditional Traveller families. However, in the main, most Travellers these days choose their own partners. Marriages still take place at a young age and usually before the age of 18. Marriages between first and second cousins are still quite common as Travellers try to marry within their own community as much as possible. Marriages between first cousins require specific permission from the Catholic Church. In the past, up to 40 per cent of Travellers were married to first cousins but this statistic is believed to be lower these days because Travellers are more aware of the risk factors involved in marrying close relatives, including disabilities and deaths (UCD Dublin, 2010). Fewer Travellers remain single than in the general population. Married couples tend to have more children than non-Travellers and although the numbers are lower than previous generations, most Traveller couples tend to have an average of five children compared to three in the rest of the population.

Young girls aged 12 tend to look after younger siblings and get them ready for school. They become a 'mother' figure to younger children. Girls are expected to jetwash trailers and do household chores, including making beds, washing and cleaning.

A transitional process also takes place around the age of 10 when they start growing their hair long. Once it reaches their waistline or beyond, this will signify that the girl is both fertile and has reached the point of marriage, usually between the ages of 16 and 17. The wedding day is the biggest event in a young woman's life, some dreaming of it since the age of 12 or earlier. Traveller weddings tend not be as ostentatious as depicted in the television show *Big Fat Gypsy Wedding,* which gave a distorted view of the Travelling community around extravagance. However, young brides will have dreamt of marrying their Traveller prince and will put great effort into choosing their wedding dress. Some put a Cinderella touch to the occasion by requesting a coach and horses to take them to the church.

Funerals

Older Irish Travellers are often devout Catholics who attend Mass and say the rosary every night, carrying on the same traditions as their parents and grandparents. Many will have travelled to visit Catholic holy places overseas, including Lourdes, Medjugorje and Fatima. But the biggest religious event is usually funerals. Horse-drawn carriages and expensive caskets are the norm. These days they have their own undertakers who oversee all the arrangements.

The deceased is placed on display for two or three days before the funeral takes place. During this time family members take it in turn to sit by the open coffin. Women and men tend to remain separated during the pre-funeral gathering. The women offer tea and refreshments to all the mourners. The men will light a fire, which will keep burning until the funeral, and other male mourners will sit around the fire, tell stories and drink beer.

Everybody tries to help during this time of sorrow. Some people will bring wreaths, while others will offer a contribution towards funeral costs. Some older Travellers are superstitious so before the coffin is closed, certain items will be placed in it, including money, photos and jewellery to be taken to the afterlife. Certain items are also burnt, including clothing and furniture, with the belief that possessions can go from one life to the next. Years ago, some Travellers took it a step further and burnt the caravan that the deceased once lived in. A similar tradition takes place among Romany Gypsies, who sometimes burn the trailer after the person has died to get rid of bad karma, vibes or omens.

When the body is leaving the site and getting taken to the church, flowers are placed on the back of some lorries, which are formed into a procession. Men and boys carry the coffin. Women openly pray and cry. Hundreds of mourners turn up for the Mass to show their respects. Attending funerals among Travelling communities is expected and reciprocated. While at the church, the congregation might mix (gender-wise) at the service but once they leave the church they go into male and female groups. Older women still might wear black for six months afterwards if a close family member dies. The burial plot in the cemetery is in a particular section bought by Travellers, where they are buried with their parents and grandparents. After the burial, a wake takes place where alcohol is consumed and sometimes among the grief emotions run high, which can result in grievances and fights. It is not uncommon for Travellers to erect expensive large marble tombstones to symbolise the love and respect they have for their loved ones. They are often specially designed with symbols of things that were associated with the deceased (including vehicles and animals), which allows the living to keep that connection with the dead person. Regular visits to the cemetery also take place to show how the deceased are missed and will never be forgotten.

Romany funerals

Attending funerals for Romany Gypsies is still a deeply held tradition in their culture. Some even consider it an honour to be able to be present at the funeral of a loved one or a family friend – or a friend of a friend. Romany people feel an allegiance towards their own people, and this is a way of publicly showing it.

The body is taken home to the family residence. Once upon a time, the body used to be kept for a week but these days it is kept for just two days before the funeral. People stay up all night with the corpse to help it journey over to the spirit world. The taking of the dead person home goes back to the last century when you had body snatchers who stole bodies for organs etc.

Jack – Romany Gypsy

Romany Gypsies dislike having alcohol around the dead with some families requesting that visitors do not bring it along. One woman told me the story of her father's funeral when she found men drinking beer outside around an open fire. She got angry at the men for not showing respect to her father and confiscated the beer. Mourners who come to view the corpse are always offered refreshments, which are often sandwiches and tea and coffee.

I have four sons, so it worries me that the issue of suicide is not more widely discussed or if nothing is done to prevent this fate falling on one of my children. But nobody seems to care because they see it as a Traveller issue. People who attend funerals of young men don't say anything. What can you say? But people go over the top sometimes and take big wreaths along with them or big framed pictures of the deceased. But they don't discuss how or why the person died, especially men who tend not to talk.

Florence – Romany Gypsy

Victoria's story

Victoria worked in the bar of her local village hall where wakes were often held. She said that sometimes just ten people would turn up and have tea and talk for an hour. But there would be no personal touches – no pictures of the deceased. She said she found this strange with it being so calm and impersonal and most unlike what wakes are like in her own community. She said that Travellers take much more effort at celebrating at the end of a life. Firstly, there are always lots of people present: aunts, uncles, cousins, distant cousins, and friends of all ages. Everyone dresses respectfully and never turn up dressed casually in jeans. Men always wear dark suits. Women never dress in bright colours at funerals. Everybody brings something to eat and drink and a wake can go on for several hours. Some laugh, cry or both and tell stories about the person they mourn.

Victoria heard stories from her grandfather about how 100 years ago Romany people would burn all the belongings of the deceased person, including their wagon, to make sure the person had a good afterlife. She didn't know whether he was joking or not, but he said he once heard of how the family of a dead man burned him as well when they set light to the wagon! He also told her another story of a man who died and how his dog was heartbroken without him, so the dog was put to sleep and placed in the coffin along with his master. Part of this tradition of burning items still exists and depends on the traditional nature of the individual or family. Others place jewellery and other personal objects in the coffin. Victoria's mother has asked her to take any photographs or personal possessions she wants before she dies and has given instructions for her clothes and shoes to be burnt after her death because she cannot bear the thought of someone else wearing them. Setting fire to things is always regarded as setting the spirit free. Victoria joked that her mother's furniture won't get burned because her brother still lives in the house and that he will need that! Victoria expanded on the meaning of death in Romany culture and the respect it is given, even when somebody dies in hospital. Extended family members will often sit in the hospital corridors, while others may wait in the carpark. It's a custom called 'sitting in', which starts at the point of death until the person's funeral to ensure that they are never alone before the body is taken home and the 'sitting in' continues.

With regard to periods of mourning, Romany women are expected to mourn for at least a year afterwards. Men tend to mourn for a lesser period, especially if they have young children. People tend to drop hints, 'Those kids need a mother', which often prompts the man to remarry. Romany people visit the graves of their loved ones on birthdays, anniversaries and at Christmas. If a young person or child has died, it is not uncommon for family members to bring a cake, gather around the grave and eat the cake to commemorate the deceased's birthday. Many take great comfort in this.

Roma

Weddings

Things are slowly changing in Roma communities. Previously, in Roma families a boy was considered to grow up, get married and bring his wife into his parents' family – so she can help cook and clean. Forced marriages occurred sometimes and if the girl resisted or rejected her husband, rape was used as a means of control.

Maria – Roma

Arranged marriages (as opposed to forced marriages) are still commonplace in Roma communities, although younger generations have more choice in who they marry. If they strongly object to marrying someone, they are more likely to be listened to than in previous generations. Marriage is often seen as two large families coming together and establishing a new family within this so it's considered important to get it correct. These days, most Roma are marrying a little older than previously and are usually aged between 18 and 20. Any older than this, the person is considered 'old', particularly for women.

It is very important for the bride to be a virgin, otherwise this brings big shame on the family. In more traditional Romanian families, for example those who are Pentecostal, evidence that the bride was a virgin on her wedding night entails her bringing the bed sheet from the marital bed and showing it to the bride's and groom's parents and members of the wider community the following morning to prove her virginity with a bloodied sheet. When Romanian Pentecostal weddings take place in the UK, the practice of showing the bed sheet is done more privately and consists of just the couple and their respective parents. In some very traditional families, some parents request that their son sleeps with his bride the night before the wedding to ensure she is a virgin. Dowries are sometimes given to the bride but this is not seen as if she has been bought. It is seen as providing financial security for the couple and can include giving items of gold jewellery to the bride on her wedding day to ensure this stays in the family.

Music at Roma weddings is very important. There is a wealth of creativity found in Roma communities, including singers, instrumentalists and dancers. Jazz, flamenco and dancing are common features in gatherings. There is a wide variety of musical influences spread across Eastern Europe but mainly two types are used at weddings. One is traditional music entailing musicians playing violins, cimbalom and fiddles, as well as Turkish pop music which has a Romanian origin to it. Everybody – young and old – joins in the celebrations and shares in the happiness of the new couple, so great is the joy expressed at weddings.

We believe in God because nobody else accepts us. Nobody helps us but God. That's why we believe in Him because He loves us and supports us. He accepts and believes in us as we are.

Aluna – Roma

Funerals

Family is everything in Roma communities. When someone dies, people come from far and wide to the funeral. Roma people have huge extended families with family members including cousins who are often regarded as brothers and sisters. The grieving process takes a long time in Roma circles and can last up to two years or longer. The death of an elder or grandfather figure is often viewed as a tragedy because they are seen as advisers of the community whereby no important decision is ever made without their approval. When that figurehead dies, the family and community feel an enormous loss, which sometimes deeply affects more than 100 people. This is a common occurrence in Roma communities throughout Eastern Europe, which is beyond the comprehension of most people who are not Roma. People's mental health is often affected because the grief is so profound.

Traditional Roma customs when someone dies include the following.

» Men don't shave for 40 days.
» Close family members do not shower for nine days after the death of a loved one because they don't want to wash away the touch of the deceased person's spirit.
» Mirrors are covered in the home where the person died while the body is still present in the house – to prevent the spirit getting trapped.
» The home is cleaned to ensure the spirit starts new and fresh in the afterlife.

- » The dead person is dressed in new clothes to appear 'refreshed' before God and to be cleansed of their sins.
- » Roma who die overseas are usually repatriated back to their home countries for burial.

Roma death and funeral traditions are in line with Orthodox Christianity.

Day 3: The funeral service is held. The significance of it occurring on the third day is because Jesus was dead for three days before rising from the grave.

Day 9: The dead person ends their earthly existence, and it is on day 9 that the soul meets God for the first time.

Day 40: This concludes the period that the soul has spent wandering the earth visiting their family home and places they have lived, as well as paying a visit to their grave.

Roma do not agree with post-mortems because they believe that cutting out organs upsets the spirit. They prefer burial to cremation. Burial is very different to Western customs in the sense that the 'grave' is more akin to a burial chamber. Some of the burial traditions were picked up while Roma travelled through Egypt during their exodus from India to Europe in the fifteenth century and resemble aspects of customs belonging to the pharaohs. Roma dislike coffins being placed in the earth where it touches the soil. The size of the grave is also important and mainly consists of a burial area like the size of a room. The 'room' has concrete walls and floor and is tiled. The coffin is placed in the chamber along with furniture, television, telephone, family pictures and sometimes even a bar with alcoholic drinks to ensure the deceased person has a wonderful afterlife. It is usual for there to be couples only per grave although sometimes young children are buried in their parents' plot. The chamber is sealed but allows ventilation to ensure the body does not decompose too quickly.

Roma, if they can afford to, like to place an expensive tombstone on the grave as a sign of deep respect for their loved ones, which often contains religious figurines. After the funeral, the family give away clothing belonging to the deceased to extended family members and friends in the belief that by doing this it will ensure that the dead person continues to 'live' in them and will help ensure a happy afterlife. Word of mouth substitutes funeral invitations. When a person dies, the family plays loud, sad music signalling that a death has occurred in the house. Dancing and crying are not uncommon to show how heartbroken family members are but also to show that they are happy that the dead person will now be able to reap the fruits of the afterlife. Traditional Roma food is cooked for funerals in the belief that the deceased can smell their favourite food and that this helps their spirit elevate towards heaven.

Jewish and Muslim Roma

There are small pockets of Jewish Roma in countries like Ukraine, Russia and Serbia. These communities converted to Judaism during the Second World War when Roma were trying to mix with other nations in order to keep their families safe – or during communism when all the nations were considered equal. Jewish Roma communities in Romania, Bulgaria and Moldova are now quite small in number because many of them proved their Jewish ethnicity and relocated to Germany, Austria and other countries as reparation for anti-Semitism and to live better lives. Roma and Jewish people have a special connection through their shared suffering in the Holocaust and many come together each year to commemorate the International Holocaust Remembrance Day, which is held on 27 January.

There are also small communities of Roma who are Muslim. Ruska Roma, also known as Russian Gypsies, are the largest subgroup of Roma people in Russia and Belarus and in Eastern and Central Ukraine. They have their own special kind of dialect of the Romani language, which contains Russian, German and Polish words as well as a small amount of Russian and Ukrainian grammar. Other Roma groups criticise Muslim Ruska women, stating that they do not fit in because their clothes don't resemble those of either a Roma or a Muslim. Their outfit is usually one bright colour from tip to toe and they always have a scarf covering half of their head. They do not show off any areas of skin, such as legs and arms, so they are usually covered. They marry very young between the ages of 14 and 16.

There are other Muslims as well within Roma communities who are termed Muslimansko Roma (or Muslimanenge Roma), and which date back to the Ottoman Empire. Muslim Roma were preferred in the Ottoman Empire and many converted to Islam. Today they are found in many countries, including Turkey, Bosnia and Herzegovina, Montenegro, Kosovo, Bulgaria and Romania. The largest number though is in Croatia where it is estimated that half of the Roma population are Muslimansko Roma (Sunni Muslims). Male Roma Muslims get circumcised at the age of five because the number 5 is a sacred symbol among the Romani people. The majority of Muslimansko Roma speak Balkan Romani or Kurbetcha, a creole language which entails the mixing of different languages. Some others only speak the language from the host country and deny their Roma background.

Superstitions

Many GRT people are naturally superstitious and believe in stories or customs handed down from their forbears. Superstitions are fear based and rooted in religion. Many

GRT people say they don't really believe in superstition but still do certain rituals out of habit or as one woman told me, '*So nothing bad happens*'. Some Roma people wear red rubber wrist bands to ward off curses. Others believe in the 'evil eye', which is a look or a stare from somebody who is jealous of a person or who dislikes them but is done with a conscious or unconscious intention of harming the person. In order to ward off such attacks, Roma often place a talisman, which is designed in the shape of a blue eye, in their homes or they use a key ring with this symbol in the belief that this brings them spiritual protection from such harm.

I'm not religious but I am a bit superstitious. When I see magpies, I always count them... one for sorrow... two for joy... three for a wedding. When I see two or three of them, I take a picture and post it on my Facebook page. I never walk under ladders and hate being around a cracked mirror in case it brings bad luck. 'If a black cat crosses your path, you will have bad luck, unless you turn around three times and spit on your little finger.' Don't meet someone on the stairs. No shoes on a table. If you drop a knife – let someone else pick it up.

Pamela – Romany Gypsy

The Light and Life movement frowns upon superstitious practices and has warned their practitioners from believing in what they consider to be lies of the devil. However, others see superstitions as harmless fun. One man told me that when he was young, his mother was very superstitious and would never hand wash any clothes over Easter weekend because throwing out the water would mean throwing dirty water in the Lord's face. He also mentioned that some Gypsies still practise psychic services and palm readings, and that 'lucky heather' is still sometimes sold for a donation on high streets. The man laughed about these practices and said he finds it incredibly silly that people still believe in them. He added that anybody who truly believes in the Lord has no reason to fear anything.

Conclusion

Everything in GRT culture and customs surrounds family structure rather than individuals. Second to this is valuing life in the present moment and having gratitude for what they have in life as opposed to what they are lacking. Everything inside and outside of their communities is contextualised in accordance with family life and its values. Marriage for GRT people is the Holy Grail – a rite of passage whereby getting married or forming a lifelong commitment to someone is seen as central to life itself. From a young age, males and females think about the day they get married. This surpasses everything else, including school, what type of job/career they would like and where they would like to live. Alongside this strong belief in marriage and families is the strong belief in God because He is the one who made them into the most resilient group of people alive on the planet today. Their survival skills and ability to shake off adversity and setbacks constantly surpass the abilities of non-GRT people. In Ireland, some Travellers attend Mass but others, like mainstream society, stopped attending following the clerical sex abuse scandals of the 1990s. Despite this, they keep lots of religious memorabilia in their homes, including pictures of the Sacred Heart of Jesus and the Virgin Mary. Visits to Knock in County Mayo where the Virgin Mary appeared in 1879 are an annual event. Travellers remain spiritual people who have a strong connection to nature, land, forests and the countryside, which they view as being part of their connection with their higher being. Many pay visits to holy wells to drink spring water to feel cleansed. Others refer to visiting 'healing priests' – a term used for priests who are open and willing to engage with Travellers, hear their confessions, listen to their woes about life and give advice. Overall, it can be realistically said that religion still plays a big part in the fabric of GRT lives throughout the world despite the changes that have occurred both within and outside their communities in the past 50 years.

Chapter 8 | Crime

Introduction

There are no crime figures or statistical evidence to accurately pinpoint that GRT people are more criminally prone than other groups in the general population. GRT people acknowledge there are some in their respective communities who commit crimes, sometimes serious offences, and in doing so, tarnish the reputation of the majority. Domestic violence is considered high in GRT communities, but that doesn't mean every Gypsy or Traveller beats their spouses. It is not uncommon for GRT males to outright condemn violence and the abuse of women. Travellers are twice as likely to be victims of crime as non-Travellers, but this seldom, if ever, gets reported in the media (The Traveller Movement, 2018).

Research carried out by the Traveller Movement (2018) mentioned social media postings by serving police officers who called GRT people 'pikeys' and stated they knew GRT people were lying *'every time their lips moved'*. Would those officers feel so free to write a derogatory comment about a black person or Muslim? It is also valid to ask why the courts tend to imprison more GRT people than other groups in society. Prison officers and probation officers receive little or no training in GRT culture and history and are sometimes completely ignorant of their lifestyles, customs and traditions. Much more emphasis needs to be placed on GRT training in equality and diversity within the criminal justice system.

Police feedback

There is terrible mistrust between the police and GRT communities and vice versa. Police have been accused of using discriminatory methods by informing local residents and business owners to be vigilant if they live close to a Traveller site, especially if new Travellers arrive in the area. GRT people have complained of police harassment when officers call to sites, often at unsociable times, and randomly ask questions when there is no apparent explanation other than them finding some stolen goods on the off chance. Police in return complain of being met with aggression during these visits. Police also state that more 'mini-Travelling sites' are on the increase. The reason behind this is an increase in GRT buying land and placing motor homes on it, which can increase rapidly from two motor homes upwards to 10 or 15. Denials to council officials that the homes are not static results in lengthy legal processes which can take several years before a resolution is found, by which time some of the Travellers will have left the area.

Having spoken to several police officers, I was informed that there are certain types of crime they associate with GRT communities, such as burglary artifice. An example of this is a bogus water board official who gains entry to a property, usually that of an elderly person, and steals items of value once inside. Other fraudulent crimes involve cold calling. Two or more fake builders will stop at a house and tell the resident that they are working in the local area and have noticed that some tiles on the roof are broken and need replacing, which they can do at a reduced cost, maybe as little as £20–£50. Once they have gained access to the roof, they pretend to find a problem requiring urgent attention that involves extra cost but unknown to the owner they will have broken a tile, bored a hole in the roof and poured water in the hole to make it look like a leak. Once these 'repairs' are carried out, they demand payment of up to a couple of thousand pounds.

Police also associate the 'ringing' of motor vehicles to be a popular crime among GRT criminals. Transit vans are stolen, the number plates are changed and the engine number is ground off and replaced with a new number, or in some cases a new engine is inserted or the engine is taken out and the rest of the van is scrapped. Thefts of motor homes and caravans also occur, including those of European tourists who travelled over by ferry to holiday in the UK.

Drug supply has become a big business in some GRT circles. Cannabis cultivation occurs frequently in those who have access to land in remote locations. Those who evade capture are known to make upwards of £300,000 per assignment. Police have also noticed an increase in drug using and drug supply in some Traveller sites, which has become more prevalent in the past five years. The financial incentive of this outweighs the risks of getting caught. An increase in the use and supply of cocaine, amphetamines, ketamine and MDMA has been noted in younger Travellers.

Other offences include the operation of 'puppy farms', which involves dog smuggling and the sale of dogs which often cost £3000 upwards. Suspicion exists that some dogs are made to have two litters a year as opposed to the recommended one litter. Accusations of tax evasion are plentiful surrounding cash-in-hand jobs, even by self-employed GRT builders who are skilled and capable of carrying out block paving and tarmacking to a good standard. Police have arrested some of these builders for fly-tipping afterwards when they discovered the work was carried out at a reduced cost because they did not have a waste disposal licence.

Feuds among GRT members often result in threats of extreme violence.

My research discovered that the police have made some attempts to better improve their relationship with the GRT community. They are aware of their fractured relationship and believe that a better understanding needs to be reached. One police force I spoke to told me that to commemorate GRT History Month, they flew the GRT flag over their headquarters as a gesture of goodwill. However, this decision received massive criticism from serving police officers who questioned why this was done, especially as the court case of three teenage Travellers convicted of the manslaughter of PC Andrew Harper in Berkshire in 2019 was still fresh in people's minds. PC Harper was dragged to his death behind a speeding car being driven by one of the teenagers after becoming entangled in a tow rope attached to the car they were driving when he attempted to arrest them on suspicion of stealing a quad bike.

Crime in the GRT communities

The causes of crime in GRT communities include four pivotal areas: poverty, health, employment and discrimination. Drug misuse is also a key factor, particularly among the younger generation with some involved in large-scale supply of Class A drugs. This tends to be more drug dealing as opposed to regular personal drug misuse. Some GRT males tend to travel around for work purposes, including going to Europe to countries like Germany doing tarmacking jobs and this leads to them bringing drugs back to the UK and Ireland in the attempt to sell them for huge profit. Gypsy and Travelling communities were once regarded as anti-drug communities but a shift has occurred in the past decade. Those aged 30 and above are still relatively ignorant about drugs and have never taken them.

Some Travellers will break the law more easily than others. Some may get done for tax evasion because they don't understand the system. Others don't realise that you need a licence to deal in scrap metal – or they choose to ignore this. Among young people, there is a fair bit of anti-social behaviour, but this is often no more than being loud. Young people in groups who are out late at night leads to some people feeling intimidated. Travellers are fast talkers. We are naturally defensive people but to others this can come across as being aggressive when it is not meant to be aggressive. I'm always telling people to slow down when talking to outsiders. Fighting is at the core of our culture. We are born to defend our honour. Bare-knuckle fights are one thing but in recent years, knives are appearing more and more. That's not good and neither are drugs, which have also been on the increase including dealing the stuff. I agree there is a mentality among our communities that doesn't respect the rightful ownership of others. If they see something they want, their impulse is to steal it – anything to get their hands on a quick pound.

Felix – Romany Gypsy

Reports of crime and anti-social behaviour from Traveller sites across the UK are sadly a common feature that causes much anguish to residents living in these areas. In some cases, after years of putting up with intolerable anti-social behaviour, neighbours living close to these sites have been known to sell their homes and move away for their safety and peace of mind. Those who remain live in fear and are afraid to talk openly of their anguish in case there are reprisals, which often have meant physical threats or assaults or damage to property.

The arrival of Travellers to an area has often resulted in lives being changed for people living in surrounding areas with some afraid to go out on their own at night-time. Reports of people having bricks or other objects thrown at their cars by youths as they passed sites are not uncommon in trouble spots. Prosecutions rarely take place owing to insufficient evidence.

Some people feel Traveller sites have been made into lawless compounds. Some sites are known to have access to guns, particularly in sites containing feuding families. People are afraid to make reports to the police in case it worsens matters or fear reprisals, while others have lost trust in the police who they feel won't do anything and conclude that some GRT people generally get away with crime, irrespective of whether this is true or not.

Some people question if Gypsies are criminally minded. Some would say that they are more victims than perpetrators and that many GRT people fall victim to 'top dogs' in their communities who keep them in line. It is not uncommon for a person to get badly beaten or murdered if they speak out. Many remain silent of crimes committed against them by their own people.

Society is often afraid of being considered racist and discriminatory towards the GRT communities if they speak openly to the press or media. There is also awkwardness with political correctness where some people – and police – are reluctant to highlight the problems associated with Traveller sites and crime. Police officers are often hesitant to go to sites because of the level of violence they face. This is particularly relevant in rural areas where police numbers and resources are stretched. There is a high concentration of crime in some areas linked to Traveller sites in rural areas. Farmers have had trouble with trespassers on their land causing damage to crops during illegal hare coursing. This too is part of organised crime with thousands of pounds generated in betting activities. When challenged, those responsible have responded with threatening and aggressive behaviour to farmers and landowners.

There is so much violence around. This is not just in the Gypsy community. I still think there are still more good Gypsies than bad ones. But it takes only one bad apple to spoil a bunch. It's hard for kids growing up. Have you seen cartoons on telly? These days it's nothing but characters beating each other. It's ugly and horrible to watch and isn't good for young kids to see.

Nicolas – Romany Gypsy

Crime is a problem in our community. There is a lack of self-respect and self-value in some of our people. Remember, we have often been made to feel ashamed of who we are and have had to cover up by lying about our identity. That still happens to this day. Unfortunately, this means that some people turn to crime because they have no hope in their lives by the devalued way they feel about themselves and the world. We need to break the cycle but how?

Sabina – Roma

GRT trust in the police

Trust in the police is limited in GRT communities, where it is claimed that almost every GRT person will at some point or other in their lives have had a bad experience or will know somebody closely connected to them who experienced racism, prejudice and bigotry at the hands of the law. The 2018 Traveller Movement qualitative crime survey entitled *Policing by Consent: Understanding and Improving Relations between Gypsies, Roma, Irish Travellers and the Police* looked at relationships, policing issues and how better to build trust between the police and GRT communities. The survey consisted of contributions from 17 serving police officers and 14 members of the GRT communities. It found that some officers were willing to treat Gypsies and Travellers better and as individuals. Other officers, however, were ingrained with hearsay and institutionalised prejudice. GRT participants highlighted a generational cycle of mistrust and lack of confidence between GRT communities and the police with a long history of police harassment. It was also found that the police prioritised enforcement over engagement with GRT participants encountering prejudice and harassment at the hands of the police, where sometimes it was deemed acceptable to be openly racist towards GRT people.

Other key findings from the survey included the following.

- » GRT communities are always viewed as a 'risk factor' by police who inextricably link them to criminality with widespread stereotyping of the communities as being engaged in criminal activity.
- » Limited police awareness of GRT communities whereby they are not seen or treated as individuals – rather, they are treated as a community.

- » GRT people rarely report crime to the police – although they are a vulnerable group, they are rarely seen as victims.
- » Roadside Travellers without access to an authorised stopping place reported police officers in various forces being hostile, heavy-handed and carrying out evictions late at night, while others took a more respectful, non-enforcement approach.
- » There is a need for GRT police officers as well as better GRT training in police training – and a greater crackdown on racism and prejudice in police forces towards GRT communities.
- » There appear to be more lenient police disciplinary procedures taken against officers in cases of racism and discrimination involving those from GRT communities, yet again signalling that it's okay to be racist towards members of the GRT communities.

Generally, GRT people often complain that they have a terrible relationship with the police. One of the biggest complaints GRT activists have about the police is that they feel they have become the bogeyman of the crime world. It has become a fallacy whereby GRT people become guilty by association. If a crime takes place in an area where GRT people live, the finger of blame is automatically pointed at them along the lines of '*Oh, he's a Traveller; he'll know something about the crime*' (Mattey – Romany Gypsy). It is felt that police need to do more basic research by looking at crime figures prior to some Gypsies or Travellers moving into an area and compare them every six months. Often, there will not be any difference.

GRT people have therefore become 'guilty' simply because of their ethnicity. It is noted, for example, that GRT people are targeted within the remit of police ethnic profiling for 'stop and search', which is disproportionally higher than for other ethnic groups in mainstream society with the exception of black people. GRT people feel that if things are to change, attitudes must change. Hate crimes towards GRT people are often ignored, which will be addressed later in this chapter. However, GRT people acknowledge that not all police officers are harsh or racist towards them and that some good officers exist among them, who include GRT police officers who have a member organisation called the 'GRT Police Association'. Unfortunately, many of these officers hide their identity and are not open to colleagues about their ethnicity due to fear of reprisals, bullying and racism. Often in reply to accusations of racism and heavy-handedness towards members of the GRT communities, the police have responded by saying that they constantly face opposition from the GRT communities when doing their job, including threats of violence. They state that GRT people don't like to be told what to do and believe this is a male macho power dynamic. Police feel

GRT people set out to intimidate officers during their line of duty. It is not uncommon for officers to be told, *'You are only doing this because I am a Gypsy or a Traveller because if I wasn't, you wouldn't be doing such and such'* (*Kent Police*).

Domestic abuse, coercive control and gender-based violence

Gender-based violence takes many forms and while it can affect some men, it mainly affects women and girls and is usually in the following forms:

- » physical;
- » sexual;
- » psychological;
- » domestic violence;
- » sex-based harassment;
- » forced marriage;
- » online abuse.

GRT communities are often male dominated. GRT men are often regarded as the person in overall control as part of their gender role in relationships. Reporting of domestic abuse is significantly lower than in other communities. Abuse is seen as something that is confidential and to expose this is viewed by many GRT women as something that is shameful, embarrassing and stigmatic and a sign of weakness if they were to report it or even tell someone outside their community.

Some women do find support in their community by turning to an elder for support but while a listening ear is extended in such cases, it comes with the advising message of needing to remain in the relationship. To do otherwise, they are told, would be detrimental to the couple's reputation and that of their families were the abuse to be reported. If the wife leaves her husband, this will almost always lead to being ostracised by their community. Instead, they are expected to deal with their issues and carry on in the relationship, often accompanied by the attitude that domestic abuse is a normal part of life.

There are no statistics which give an accurate figure of the number of GRT women who endure domestic abuse and likewise the number of men. In mainstream society, it is estimated that one in four women and one in six men are subjected to domestic abuse at one point or other in their lives. However, statistics recorded by organisations and charities who help victims of abuse have noted that hardly any of these are from GRT communities. One counsellor from a domestic abuse charity I spoke to told me that out of 250 referrals she dealt with over a three-year period, none were from the GRT communities. Furthermore, it is noted that it is rare that any women's refuge centre receives anybody from the GRT communities. Some local authorities have funded victim outreach workers to tackle the issue, but these are often time limited owing to funding coupled with confidentiality issues, which has prevented reporting on the number of cases and scale of the abuse. Proper time and investment must be given if respect and trust is to be gained from people who already feel the heavy weight of levels of discrimination against them and who do not want to become more 'labelled' than they are already.

It is estimated that abuse is experienced by three out of four GRT women at some point in their lives. When I spoke to community outreach workers about domestic violence, I was told this is due mainly to pressures because of poverty, mental illness and exclusion from society, as well as alcohol and drug abuse. The workers also told me that patterns of abuse tended to follow family lines, meaning that, in some families, abuse is the accepted norm whereas in some it is non-existent.

As a Traveller woman, you do not have the support of family. If you leave, you lose your community and you lose who you are because you are leaving everything you have ever known and everyone behind.

Elaine – Irish Traveller

Domestic abuse tends to remain undetected because very few women feel able to report it. Some women feel or are made to feel that marriage is for life, and if marriage breaks down, women can be ostracised not just from their family but also their wider community. They feel they bring shame on their family and believe their children will be punished for their actions. A lot of these women are brought up to believe that they are their husband's property.

The feeling among GRT communities – even with young men – who have witnessed this from a young age is that women are subservient to men and that this concept is so strong it can entail young boys abusing their mothers. When is this outdated attitude towards women going to be challenged – and changed? There are small traces of younger women who are careful about getting into abusive relationships by getting to know their partner better before they enter into commitment, but family and community pressures do not make having a choice easy. Parents can be reluctant to let their daughters mix with non-Traveller young men – or young men from different cultures.

Even when girls and boys are young, the girl is always at home. The girls have strict upbringings and are not allowed to go off anywhere. Their father is the boss. They are raised to babysit, clean and cook, and know they will get married young. Boys are expected to protect their sisters and have power over them; even from a young age this is instilled into them. If a father leaves or dies, the eldest son (irrespective of age) will become the 'head' of the family and asks everyone to do what he says. This can lead to child–parent abuse. For many GRT people, marriage is for life and if a marriage does break down this can lead to women being ostracised from the community, which could explain why reporting of abuse is low.

I knew a girl who was 21 when her marriage broke down. She had a young baby at the time. The fact that she was no longer living with her husband was kept secret from extended family members and friends. She and her immediate family always made the excuse that he was working away from home. Her father and brother forbade her from leaving the site. She wasn't even allowed out to go the supermarket or shops. They were worried that if she went out by herself, that she would tell people that her husband left her, bringing shame to the family, or worst still that she would start dating somebody new. The likelihood was that she would probably never be allowed to divorce or remarry.

Charity – Romany Gypsy, NGO employee

Domestic statistics are not collated anywhere so it's impossible and unjust to say that this type of violence or broader gender-based violence is higher in GRT people than in other communities or to say that this is part of any community when there isn't the evidence to back this up. Women are not always the victims – men can be too.

Noah– Romany Gypsy, NGO employee

The Equality and Human Rights Commission (2016) suggests that woman who do report domestic violence and coercive control will often have suffered it more severely and over a considerably longer period than other women. Cultural barriers mean that GRT women stay in violent relationships far longer than other women. Women are taught to stand up for themselves as strong Travelling women. It is seen as weak if a story is leaked out that domestic violence is occurring between couples. Only a tiny minority consider an injunction, which might have been advised by probation services if a husband is in prison specifically for attacking his wife and where future violence is likely to occur upon release from prison.

Changes will not occur quickly. I have spoken to domestic abuse experts who state that the key to bringing about change is education and raising awareness. This is about engaging GRT women to learn the difference between what is normal and what is not. However, when someone has lived all their life within a closed community and does not have any non-GRT friends and is poorly educated, they assume it is a normal part of life. Often GRT women see it as something that goes on in families – if it isn't happening to them it's happening to their mother, sister, aunt, friend or neighbour. It simply does not create any level of shock or surprise in them.

Some feel that there is a growing number of Gypsy and Traveller women who want better equality in their relationships – it is okay for a man to remarry but not for a woman. Solas Anois (Gaelic for Comfort Now) is the UK's only refuge for Gypsy and Traveller women. More mothers are willing to assist their daughters in leaving violent relationships. There are those who are sick and tired of violence – who know that it is wrong – and are willing to stand up because they know that getting a beating from a man has nothing to do with GRT heritage. However, the concept of GRT women going into a refuge is still limited. Greater consideration needs to be given to women who may not have lived in a house before. Campaigners believe that it needs to be more culturally sensitive, for example, having perhaps a refuge centre based in a private caravan site.

For change to occur, this needs to be an inward community approach. It is considered very shameful to ring the police. The current approach is to deal with things 'in house'. This needs to stop. We need to teach young girls more about healthy relationships and what is and isn't acceptable. We need more domestic abuse advisers. There are a lot of violent homes out there where couples openly batter each other. There are also homes where couples have toxic and negative relationships where they shout at each other but don't resort to physical violence although if you don't know the couple and overhear them rowing, you might automatically think violence is involved. People are talking about it more and more within the communities, which is a good thing, and what is more encouraging is that young men are open to talking about it. So, there is hope for change.

Duke – Romany Gypsy

It is a myth that it is accepted as part of Traveller culture. It is never right to hit a partner. It's a myth that men beat their wives. Often, they worship their wives. I strongly condemn people who commit domestic violence. It should be reported to the police. Women should become more aware of their rights. I know that a lot of education is being given by outreach workers on the subject as well as signposting victims to counselling services.

Eugene – Irish Traveller

Culturally, women like to keep to themselves and don't want to voice themselves over men. Bear in mind that up until 50 years ago, it was the norm for wives, daughters and mothers to be homemakers where their main role was to look after the children and look after the house. Gypsies still hold on to these old-fashioned traditional values. Many Gypsies view leadership as something that comes from a man. Religious people in GRT communities consider this as something that was outlined in the Bible, where men led and women followed.

Women are not overlooked or neglected in Travelling communities. There is protection of them that goes back to the 'tribal' gene. We originated in India. Our instincts are not that dissimilar to that of Turks, Arabs and Jews in the way women are viewed and treated and for me that is basically protection.

Buddy – Romany Gypsy

We know our place – when men are talking to other men, we would never interrupt them because they might be talking business. The man is seen as head of the home. Women stick together. We like it that way. Our women dress respectfully. Gypsy women are wise women who live on their wits. Historically, they dressed very conservatively with long dresses and skirts down to their ankles, like how Roma Gypsy women still dress. A woman is never allowed to disrespect a man.

Georgina – Romany Gypsy

Women often face discrimination in family court and in the main judiciary system. This occurs even with legal advisers who often are redundant in providing a full and equitable service to Roma women based solely on their ethnicity.

Henri – Roma

Greater numbers of women work than men but the number is still small given that the unemployment rate for Travellers is 87 per cent.

Martina – Irish Traveller

Irish Travellers in the criminal justice system

The landscape of Irish Traveller prisoners in Ireland is similar to the UK in being disproportionate. It is estimated that almost 10 per cent of the Irish prison population comprises Irish Travellers with these mainly being nine-tenth males – very high considering that Travellers represent less than 1 per cent of the total population. The risk of imprisonment for Travellers is 11 times higher than that of the general male population and Traveller women are 22 times more likely than non-Traveller women to be imprisoned (The Traveller Movement, 2021).

Irish Travellers in the British prison system are massively overrepresented. Four to five per cent of the prison population identify as Traveller or Gypsy (The Traveller Movement, 2021). The system is seen as being very discriminatory – starting in the courts with pre-sentence reports. Once the court picks up on the convicted as being from a GRT background, it sees them as being of higher risk than non-GRT people.

With regard to applying for and getting bail, in addition to Irish Travellers being seen as a flight risk, several problems arise in relation to their living arrangements which are taken into consideration. It is very difficult for a prisoner to get bail if they live on a communal site – or if they travel around the country to various sites as this is considered 'no fixed abode'. Many Travellers are forced into permanent accommodation against their will or risk getting remanded into custody. Likewise with getting early release as they won't be considered for an electronically monitored curfew tag (EMC) if the person lives on a site. Even with 70 per cent of Travellers now living in houses, they might have a large family or have extended family members living with them. This can result in them not having free access to their own bedroom, which is not deemed a suitable location for an EMC to be fitted.

Many Irish Travellers have no proper means of identification before they are released from prison. If somebody can potentially be released to a Nacro hostel, they will need to apply for housing benefit and Universal Credit but to do so they will need identification, including their National Insurance number. This is a condition of the person's release. The London Irish Centre based in London works with Irish Travellers to ensure they get these essential requirements, along with help obtaining birth certificates. However, Traveller culture is based around family, and many do not want to go and stay in probation hostels; they want to live with family. Being close to family plus other Travellers is a safeguarding measure. There is a trust and loyalty towards each other, and they understand problems around their lifestyle. Therefore, many first-generation Irish Travellers serving custodial sentences in British prisons request that their supervision on licence upon release from prison is carried out back in Ireland, especially if the man's family including his wife and children live there.

Take for example somebody who is given a three-year prison sentence and is released after 18 months with a further 18 months on licence. They may get returned and supervised by probation in Ireland provided they have no outstanding matters and are not a risk threat. Otherwise, it means staying in Britain where the person has no family in the country and few networks, making it more likely for them to reoffend. Returning to Ireland means they can do their period on licence under the Irish Probation Service and rebuild their lives at the same time. However, repatriation to Ireland to an Irish prison during a custodial sentence is far more difficult. This is trickier and carries legal challenges. Few achieve this because of legislation in Ireland that is not favourable, owing to a difference in remission rates. Prisoners serve half of a fixed-term sentence in prisons in Britain, whereas prisoners in the Republic of Ireland serve two-thirds of their sentence in prison before they become eligible for early release. Irish Travellers have in the past taken the Irish prison service to court over this difference. They had to serve longer in the Irish prison that they would have served in England or Wales where they were originally sentenced.

Clan fights

Clan fights go back to the point of Travellers being 'fighters', intermixed with struggles relating to defending family honour. This is seen as a pride thing with the motto '*My people are the best*' coupled with '*We are not going to let them get away with that*' and '*We have a family name to uphold*'. Two men can have a fight and shake hands afterwards, but the winner knows that he has earned himself a better reputation for winning the fight. For others, getting into fights or being violent is seen as a normal part of their upbringing. This normalisation of violence in Traveller life has led to it becoming an exciting spectator sport, bringing large numbers to watch when two men fight to settle a disagreement or perceived injustice. If two Traveller boys have a fight that results in neither of them winning, then it resorts to their fathers to have a fist fight to determine which family is the better fighter. Sometimes this can be between two families, or it might be just two individuals who have expressed a grievance towards each other.

Acts of extreme violence occur between rival Traveller families, including weapons like pickaxes and machetes resulting in catastrophic injuries and death. Some Irish Travellers have even carried out acts of extreme violence against rivals at funerals, such are their levels of unrest and grievances. The root of the anger may lie in somebody having disrespected the other, which they feel they must not let go without a fight. It is very egotistical, but some parents organise a wedding to end longstanding intergenerational feuding by agreeing to the marriage of two of their offspring in order to break the cycle and make peace.

Mediation

Feuds in the Travelling community can go on for two to three generations. Travellers have pride in their family name but unfortunately there are some families who have never got along with each other. This might be for something simple that is multiplied and magnified over time regarding an act of theft or someone leaving rubbish behind on a halting site. There is often a hierarchy among Travellers with some families not wanting to live beside other Travellers. Some feuds have resulted in extreme violence with some victim either being stabbed or dying in horrific circumstances. Some experts claim the main reason for this brutality is because of internalised oppression felt by Travellers at being ostracised from the 'settled' world around them. These vicious attacks and murders do not occur as regularly as reported in the tabloid media.

The Traveller Mediation Service in Ireland was formed in 2009 and helps sort out disputes before they escalate to violence. The mediators, both male and female, are trusted because many are Travellers themselves or have been trained by Traveller mediators – so they are equipped with knowledge about Traveller culture and heritage, making it easier for them to gain acceptance in Traveller communities.

The Traveller Mediation Service covers the entire 32 counties of Ireland. Mediation takes place wherever the Travelling families feel most comfortable – in their homes, on halting sites or at other arranged locations. When the service started, 90 per cent of referrals came from the police and the courts but these days 90 per cent are self-referrals, so good is the trust that the service has established in families and communities. Trust and confidentially are key to this success. The Mediation Service has good working relationships with the police, who often discuss cases with them that might otherwise have led to prosecutions. Violent crime rates have come down – fewer stabbings, fewer shootings, fewer petrol bombs. The main aim of the service is to sort out the feud/problem to the extent that it no longer impinges on daily life or impacts on outer circle family members who get drawn into taking sides.

Some Traveller men only feel comfortable being around other male Travellers and often get accused of having a 'bantam cock syndrome', implying some like to stick their chest out and fight because they desire to be regarded as being brave, strong and fearless. Bare-knuckle fights still take place between Irish Travellers (and between Romani Gypsies in the UK). Say for example two men have a feud they wish to sort out; they decide to arrange a fight. Both men will have their respective supporters, sometimes as many as a hundred each;

irrespective of whether these 'followers' agree or disagree with the men, they are expected to turn up at the fights through a sense of obligation. They may get told *'If you don't stick up for me, then I won't stick up for you if you get into a fight'*. The fights take place in the back of a yard. No weapons are allowed – only bare-knuckle boxing. An independent referee is selected, and the fight is videoed to ensure foul play or cheating does not take place. Referees are often thought to steer the fight to conclude with a draw, which means that both men can walk away afterwards with their heads held high.

The two feuding families each choose the best fighter in their family – usually a man in their 20s to early 30s. Many are experienced boxers. After the fight is over, the men usually shake hands and a line is drawn under the matter. This prevents a festering of bad blood between the families, but it does not mean that they become the best of friends afterwards. They make peace and can be civil to one another, which is important. However, not every man or family likes or wants to fight. There are opportunities for men to say no to a fight if challenged. The Traveller Mediation Service has helped with this. A man can say, *'I'm not a fighter... let's work this out another way'*.

However, after the fight is over and forgotten about, a video clip may surface on social media or on YouTube that stirs up trouble again. Bullying takes place with one party posting menacing messages like *'My uncle beat your uncle – ha ha ha – my uncle was the best fighter'*. New bad blood gets generated because of these messages and results in second-generation family members challenging each other to fight, resulting in the feuding cycle to start all over again.

Other services provided by the Traveller Mediation Service include prison work. Fifty per cent of prisoners in Castlerea Prison are Travellers, although only 0.7 per cent of the Irish population are Travellers. The Traveller Mediation Service runs conflict resolution courses in six prisons in Ireland in total and has seen a high level of reduction in the levels of conflict since starting the courses. Mediation inside prison impacts on what is going on outside – sometimes something is occurring and leading up to a feud taking place outside – and vice versa if something is brewing inside and word gets out inside the prison about this. The conflict resolution courses have often helped de-escalate feuds before they lead to violence. There are also specially designed conflict resolution courses which take place in the community for women (women-only groups) as well as for young men aged 18–24. These are designed to help individuals teach others how to mediate after being equipped with the necessary skills.

Prison life

Traveller prisoners are of all ages – although over the past five years there has been an increase in older people imprisoned for historical sexual abuse offences. Crimes for men include non-fatal violence, burglary and drugs, especially those found in possession of Class A drugs with intent to supply. Crimes for women include burglary, robbery and violence. Fifty per cent of offences from both genders are in relation to unlawfully obtaining property.

Key issues that affect GRT prisoners include:

- » mental health problems;
- » learning difficulties and low levels of literacy;
- » discrimination and racism;
- » addiction;
- » family breakdown.

Statistics

The Traveller Movement (2021) state that prison statistics are disproportionately high for GRT prisoners with many campaigners calling for an inquiry into injustice in the criminal justice system. Questions are constantly being raised as to why the most vulnerable have become targets with lengthy sentences in comparison to others in the general population, and whether GRT people are being made an example of in what is largely considered an unfair and discriminatory system.

- » 5 per cent of the prison population is from the GRT community, showing an overrepresentation.
- » 10 per cent of the male prison population consists of GRT prisoners.
- » 6 per cent of the female prison population is from a Traveller community.
- » 13 per cent of GRT young people (under 18) are in either a secure training centre (STC) or a young offender institution (YOI).
- » Over 50 per cent of GRT prisoners have only had a basic education or are illiterate.

In addition to the research carried out by the Traveller Movement, HM Inspectorate of Prisons carried out a prisoner survey in 2019/2000 among ethnic minority prisoners and found some notable data in relation to GRT prisoners (HM Inspectorate of Prisons, 2020).

- » 64 per cent of Travellers are recorded as having mental health problems, compared to 46 per cent of non-Travellers.
- » 53 per cent are recorded having a disability, compared to 35 per cent of non-Travellers.
- » 66 per cent have children under the age of 18, compared to 47 per cent of non-Travellers.
- » 37 per cent said they had been prevented from making a complaint when they wanted to, compared to 28 per cent of non-Travellers.
- » 29 per cent of Travellers recorded drug and alcohol problems compared to 17 per cent of non-Travellers.
- » 24 per cent had spent one or more nights in the segregation unit in the last six months, compared to 9 per cent of non-Travellers.

Hate crime

The Equality and Human Rights Commission publishes a research paper every five years entitled *Is Britain Fairer?* which examines human rights for GRT communities. The last publication in 2019 remarked that the treatment of GRT people in the UK is getting worse and not better. Anecdotal evidence is rich indicating that there is endemic racism, discrimination and hate crime in GRT communities, which is not found in any other ethnic group. It is intergenerational, involving or affecting several generations. Examples include the education system, which is not supportive for GRT pupils. It is an embedded structure that gives up too quickly, too often and is often shrouded in embedded racism towards GRT pupils and families. In policing, it was found that out of 44 police forces in the UK, only nine of them record GRT communities as ethnic groups, meaning that they cannot be ethnically recorded as victims of crime, which is basically institutionally racist. Voyeuristic and sensationalist broadcast programmes have been proven to increase negative and stereotypical attitudes and opinions, and society's role in normalising intolerance, stigma and discrimination, including persistent stereotyping on social media. The *Is Britain Fairer?* report pointed out that people really need to become more vigilant to dehumanising behaviour and comments or else society is fast-tracking itself into turning its back on becoming committed to being a society that is grounded in equality and solidarity.

National Hate Crime Awareness Week takes place in October every year. In recent years, it has highlighted how hate crime towards GRT communities can be experienced in a variety of ways and outlets, including but not exclusive to:

- » social media abuse;
- » media incitement;
- » reinforcing negative stereotypes;
- » intimidation, harassment and violence;
- » exclusion and discrimination from and within services;
- » bullying at school and work.

Hate crime and speech alienates and isolates GRT people, which makes them incredibly vulnerable. Refusal at being served in shops, public houses and restaurants adds to existing exclusion. So does workplace bullying or being turned away from work when ethnicity has been discovered. Everyday hurtful name calling and racial slurs are commonplace with examples including '*Go and commit suicide*', '*You need to wash*', '*Learn to read*', '*Pikey retards*', '*Hitler had the right idea*'. This is coupled with ongoing racism within their neighbourhoods with graffiti containing racist words daubed on walls. GRT people are also tired of reading comments on social media including accusations that they don't pay tax or their TV licence, or comments implying that they make a mess wherever they go, questioning how they tax their cars if they have no fixed address, or remarking that it costs the council money to put up portable toilets for them, to clean up their mess and give them skips. Then there are physical threats against GRT people as well as criminal damage done against their vehicles and property. Crimes against GRT people are often met with indifference from the police with perpetrators rarely convicted.

Anti-Gypsy hate crime research in Europe

Roma and Travellers have a long history of experiencing discrimination, persecution and exclusion in Europe. Roma are still being deprived of their basic human rights in Europe. The European Union Agency for Fundamental Rights carried out research in 2020 in six countries, Belgium, France, Ireland, the Netherlands, Sweden and the United Kingdom, to look closer at the extent of anti-Gypsyism given that Roma and Travellers are the largest minority ethnic group in the EU, with an estimated 6 million to 8 million people. The survey collected information from 4659 respondents aged 16 and over who self-identified as Roma or Travellers.

It found that hate-motivated harassment because of someone's Roma or Traveller background included:

- » offensive or threatening comments in person;
- » threats of violence in person;
- » offensive gestures or inappropriate staring;
- » offensive or threatening emails or text messages;
- » offensive comments online.

Almost every second respondent in the survey had experienced at least one form of hate-motivated harassment because of being Roma or Travellers in the 12 months before the survey. On average, the proportion of Roma and Travellers who felt discriminated against was higher among younger respondents.

Not reporting hate-motivated incidents was common: 93% of hate-motivated harassment and 88% of physical attacks that happened in the past five years were not reported anywhere. More than half (53%) of respondents who did not report the most recent hate-motivated physical attack believed that nothing would happen or change if they reported it. Meantime, 16% did not know where to go or whom to contact about it.

(European Union Agency for Fundamental Rights, 2020, p 33)

Key recommendations of the survey included the following.

- » The fight against anti-Gypsyism and discrimination should be a distinct priority in the EU's equality and inclusion policy.
- » EU member states should ensure that the authorities record hate crime incidents to facilitate investigation and prosecution.
- » Member states could consider employing Roma and Travellers in law enforcement to improve relations and raise awareness among law enforcement officers.

Conclusion

Perhaps the most significant point readers should take from this chapter is that GRT people are more likely to be victims of crime than perpetrators. The NGOs I spoke to in the UK and Ireland strongly explained this point by emphasising that hate crime is increasing, particularly on social media platforms, without fear of prosecution. The research mentioned in this chapter by the Traveller Movement highlighted the need for improved cooperation between the police and GRT people. Trust is clearly needed from both sides to dispel the stereotypical views of GRT people held by the police and for GRT victims to freely report a crime to the police without fearing they won't be taken seriously or treated with respect.

Although I have included examples of crimes that police currently associate with GRT people, these are only examples. These types of crime are also indicative of people from other communities and non-GRT groups. Ultimately, readers need to know that no research is available that categorically states GRT people are more criminally inclined than any other group in mainstream society. In fact, there might be reasons to suggest otherwise given that a large percentage of Romany Gypsies (as well as small numbers of Roma and Irish Travellers) have become born-again Christians in the past 30 years, which in itself would indicate they are law-abiding citizens. Young people in the GRT communities (as in other communities) carry responsibility for their future. Greater awareness of domestic abuse and a strong ability to refrain from keeping it quiet will bring about change. Substance misuse among the young is still a big hurdle to overcome. It is hoped, though, that new research, education and initiatives will target this malaise before it takes a firmer grip and destroys thousands more lives and futures.

Chapter 9 | Discrimination

Introduction

We live in a world where nearly every GRT person whose identity is revealed is either ignored, dismissed or treated with contempt. It is estimated that more than 70 per cent of GRT individuals try to hide their ethnicity, suggesting that stigma and fear of discrimination is very real for them (Thompson and Woodger, 2018). That impacts on whether they can get a job, rent a house, have a taxi come and pick them up from their site or have an ambulance come to the site, among other examples. Most of the information and knowledge people in general hold about GRT communities has come from TV programmes and media outlets – and is a one-sided perspective. Therefore, society forms an understanding of Gypsies and Travellers from media sensationalism, tabloid press releases and entrenched stereotypes and prejudices. When somebody thinks and speaks about the GRT community, they do so from a prejudicial and uninformed position. Many are seen as vagrants, beggars and thieves. Racism towards most ethnic groups is now hidden, less frequently expressed in public and widely seen as unacceptable. However, towards GRT people it is still common, frequently overt and seen as justified. A prime example of this is when seeking accommodation. GRT people feel they are not offered sufficient opportunities to raise concerns about their accommodation, particularly in social housing as well as when accessing private rented accommodation, because of the racism shown by some landlords towards their ethnicity.

Everyday discrimination

Many GRT people face discrimination daily consisting of verbal and physical abuse purely because of being a Gypsy or Traveller. This leads to them feeling socially unacceptable and inferior to other people, as well as experiencing a lack of pride in their culture as a result, which can also lead to high levels of anxiety and low self-esteem. Richardson and Ryder (2012, p 46) succinctly quote this by referring to Macionis and Plummer (2002): *'It is the racialisation of Gypsies and Travellers, based on their supposed "undesirable characteristics", that had led to their exclusion, and in reinforcing it, has such a profound impact on many levels'*. 'Racialisation' is a preferred term for the process of ranking people on the basis of their presumed 'races' and is described as being at the heart of a system of inequality and social exclusion.

Different types of discrimination

1. Interpersonal discrimination: This is at an individual level and is the most common when a GRT person seeks access to any of a range of goods, services and facilities to which access is denied purely because of their identity as a Gypsy or Traveller. Many GRT endure being followed around shops and being refused entry to sports halls, cinemas and nightclubs.

2. Institutional/structural discrimination: This consists of national policies that have failed to recognise the deep levels of racism and discrimination experienced by GRT people by not advocating for a more comprehensive policy and legal framework that protects them as distinct ethnic communities.

Trust is low in GRT communities towards public services due to historical and ongoing discrimination. They feel they are at best ignored and at worst actively discriminated against and singled out in public services and policy making. Some people take the course of having as little to do with the society that rejects them as possible. Others react by rejecting their traditions and culture to fit in.

Although GRT people are not often seen in public spaces, including pubs, clubs and other social settings because they are often refused entry, many don't feel comfortable in such places because they fear being judged by their ethnicity. No other ethnic culture is judged like this by their community issues rather than individual personal qualities. Many Gypsies and Travellers make spelling changes to their surnames to avoid detection of being a Gypsy or Traveller. Many GRT people do not feel the law protects them and none more so than those who have lost tribunal cases for discrimination after being told they did not look 'Gypsy' or 'Traveller' enough. Some GRT parents are reluctant to claim certain social welfare payments because of fears that they would be considered 'sick' and have social services come and take their children away. Other GRT people I spoke to felt that discrimination against them is still commonplace and said the UK government is not interested in preserving Gypsy culture because it had made it very difficult for them to buy land. The legislation resulted in much of the travelling coming to an end because of the lack of sites. The men were also painfully aware of the general reputation levied against members of their community because of the actions of a minority among them – mainly around theft and dishonest behaviour. One referred to their community as 'condemned' because they are often used as scapegoats when any crime where they live takes place, even though nine out of ten times they are not responsible.

Gypsies are fearful of revealing their identity in case it results in discrimination, stereotyping or prejudice towards them, especially in areas of employment. Younger ones are instructed by their parents to be quiet and neither boast or declare anything about their identity or culture. In my experience, even the nicest person can change and turn against someone after they discover a person is a Gypsy – or there are people who may otherwise appear nice and decent who have a deep-rooted dislike towards Gypsies and will openly use words like 'pikey' and 'gypos'.

Connor – Romany Gypsy

Some GRT people are reasonably confident at hiding their identity because they feel they 'blend in' with few guessing their background, and that they escape the more direct racism experienced by black and Asian communities because they conceal who they are. Many knew of restaurants that have turned away people after becoming aware of their background. When I asked one man what the worst piece of discrimination he'd experienced was, he told me about being at a football match some years ago between Tottenham Hotspur and West Ham. There were hundreds of men in the Tottenham stand shouting and yelling at the West Ham players, saying things like, '*Gypos, go back to your caravans*' and nobody batted an eyelid. The Romany Gypsy, who is a Tottenham Hotspur fan, said he stood there and had to absorb the racist chants, making him realise that society accepts that it is okay to be racist towards Gypsies because people know they will get away with it.

Others feel a lot of prejudice towards their communities comes from programmes like *Big Fat Gypsy Wedding*, which they think gives a negative, unrealistic and distorted portrayal of how the majority of Romany Gypsies and Travellers live their lives. One person I spoke to said that this was the equivalent of thinking that every black person listens to rap music all the time, while others consider it as a form of 'poverty porn' that is attractive viewing to those who like sensationalist television.

One man mentioned Tyson Fury, who he feels is a good role model for the community. He admitted that a percentage of his community are involved in crime and that some Gypsies have gone 'hawking' around to houses with some preying on the elderly and vulnerable. He also felt there are others who are unruly and have no manners, but he added that every community has this type of people, which is not an indication that everyone in the community is dishonest. He believes that changes are occurring and that more Gypsies are trying harder to lead law-abiding lifestyles, especially those who run legitimate businesses and those who have become born-again Christians.

Dale Farm

Television scenes covering the 2011 mass eviction of Travellers and Romany Gypsies from Dale Farm in Essex showed violent clashes between its residents, the police and members of Basildon County Council. Dale Farm in Essex was Europe's largest Traveller site and the eviction affected 80 families (400 people in total), who were asked to leave their illegally built homes. Dale Farm was a six-acre plot of land on Oak Lane near Basildon. During the 1970s, 40 English Romany Gypsy families were allowed to live beside the next-door scrap yard but over the years this grew after Irish Travellers bought some of the land in 1996. The council started clamping down on new applications in the late 1990s, but the site continued to expand. Many blamed this on an influx of Irish Travellers from Ireland, which caused a rift because Romany Gypsies lived on the site resulting in the two groups not getting on well together because of cultural and heritage barriers. Despite an apparent 'overcrowding' on the site, the council asked why many unoccupied sites on the farm were there, leading to them discovering that many families spent much of the year travelling, between April and October, only using it as a home over the winter months. But a few were staying longer because they knew the threat of eviction was looming.

The site had a long and contentious court history with various court eviction hearings which resulted in appeals. The arrival of the bailiffs in October 2011 was the climax of one of the most contested and ugly evictions the UK has ever seen. Hundreds of riot police and 200 bailiffs in large numbers cleared the site. The cost to Basildon Council for the eviction was estimated to be around £4.8 million. Essex Police put their bill at an estimate of £2.4 million. Many commentators noted that had this happened to any other ethnic group in the UK, there would have been a huge national media outcry depicting the public's anger at this violation of human rights right before the eyes of the British public. Instead, there was no empathy or compassion at the plight of the families being evicted, which was met with indifference, silence or blame towards those who were made homeless.

Equality Act

GRT people face some of the starkest inequalities of any ethnic group in the UK. NGOs state there has been a persistent failure by both national and local policy makers to tackle these in any meaningful way. The Equality Act (2010) says that public bodies must comply with public sector equality duty and ensure public authorities carry out their functions, as well as making concerted efforts at eliminating unlawful discrimination. An example is turning GRT people away from health services despite patients not needing proof of identification, address or immigration status to register at GPs and dentists. Many GRT people consider the Equality Act to not always be effective enough while acknowledging that it plays a part in combating racism and discrimination against them.

There is still widespread ignorance in society regarding not knowing that GRT communities are distinct ethnic groups as opposed to a lifestyle choice. This lack of awareness also extends to public service bodies, who often do not understand GRT people and sometimes consider them as ill-defined communities. It is crucial that the Equality Act has a more public mandate and to examine how it should be implemented more widely to ensure it is embedded in the practices of all public bodies. An equality assessment should form part of every state body as opposed to it sometimes being tagged at the end as a tick-box exercise. This is the only way that GRT people will get a fair deal and will begin the process of them being freed from policies and institutions that have discriminated against them – both overtly and covertly – for centuries.

NGOs continue to be a driving force for change for GRT people. Most of these organisations are made up of 50 per cent plus of GRT staff and board members as well as peer researchers, which provides extra gravitas to campaigning as the message comes from lived experiences. These authentic voices speak for their communities when campaigning to make breakthroughs in breaking the cycles of institutional racism.

GRT communities and the police have had a longstanding negative relationship based on mutual distrust and poor communication, including police harassment and the prioritising of enforcement over engagement. While relations are slowly improving across the various police forces, pockets of unconscious bias, racism and discrimination exist between the police and GRT communities, mainly because there is still an inherent belief that GRT people should be treated as a risk factor because of their ethnicity. The impact of this means higher levels of stop and search, including vehicle stops close to where Travellers live. There is also criticism regarding the large numbers of police officers attending callouts to Traveller sites and homes even when investigating minor offences. The Traveller Movement (2018) carried out research into improving policing and GRT communities and some of the key recommendations to improve police and Traveller relationships included the following.

- » A complete review of each police force to assess the extent of institutional bias towards GRT communities and how policing differs from that in non-GRT communities.
- » Better collaboration between the police and local licensing authorities to ensure GRT people are not refused entry to public houses because of their ethnicity.
- » Police forces across Britain should support the reporting of hate crime aimed at GRT communities and ensure these are investigated and appropriate action is taken.

» All police forces should set out to recruit members of the GRT communities whereby GRT officers have a visible presence as opposed to being officers who have to hide their ethnicity because of being fearful of discrimination.

Victimology

The police should serve and protect the community but instead they pay a scant regard to Gypsies and Travellers and the fact that crime affects their lives like everybody else. They seldom, if ever, reach out to GRT communities and tell them that they are there for them if needed if anybody harasses their children – or refuses to serve them in a shop, which is a crime. When they visit encampments, they don't ask if anything is stolen from its occupants. A prime example of theft from encampments is dogs that are allowed to roam and are often stolen. Does anybody ever realise that the theft of a dog can leave a child heartbroken?

Caroline – Romany Gypsy

Police, Crime, Sentencing and Courts Act 2022

This legislation makes trespass a criminal offence and is aimed explicitly at Gypsies and Travellers. While there are no exact figures for the number of people who travel full time or for part of the year, 3000 people who reside illegally are estimated to get arrested for trespassing. This has stark consequences for individuals and families who live nomadic lifestyles. Facing fines of £2500, six months' imprisonment, and the removal and confiscation of caravans and cars will make many people homeless. This Act is not widely supported by all political parties or some local authorities as it goes far beyond the call to close down unauthorised encampments. If rigorously enforced, it will result in extra pressure being placed on local authorities to accommodate families and children in urgent need of help.

Many GRT people and NGOs have viewed this legislation as inhumane and unjust and see it as another step the state is taking to eradicate the nomadic lifestyle. How this legislation will affect large gatherings at Appleby Horse Fair, and others, remains to be seen. There were far better options that could have been given consideration. Some local authorities have developed initiatives to help Gypsies and Travellers with schemes that assist with negotiated stopping. An example of this is Leeds County Council, which drafted plans to seek encampments where Travellers could reside for 28 days rather than park illegally in places like car parks due to having no alternative.

Instead, they are directed towards a specially convened council encampment where they sign a behavioural contract to keep the area tidy and not to leave mess or rubbish behind. The Leeds initiative has proven very successful and is seen as a means by which local authorities form good alliances with Gypsies and Travellers.

Anti-Gypsy and Roma Travellerism

The world has moved on in every aspect in the past 50 years apart from the attitude society has towards Gypsies and Travellers. Anti-Gypsyism is sometimes not viewed as a form of racism but there are communities who are constantly racialised through negative stereotyping and, like all forms of racist anti-Gypsyism, this is intrinsically harmful. Greenfields and Rogers (2020, p 2) define anti-Gypsyism as follows:

...a specific racism towards Roma, Sinti, Travellers and others who are stigmatised as 'Gypsies' in the public imagination and by the council of Europe as an ideology founded on racial superiority, a form of dehumanisation and institutional racism nurtured by historical discrimination, which is expressed, among others, by violence, hate speech, exploitation, stigmatisation and the most blatant kind of discrimination.

Anti-Gypsyism and hate crime impact greatly on people's mental health and wellbeing and often lead to suicide and para-suicide after persistent feelings of hopelessness and feeling untrusted. Persistent exclusion and racist incidents often lead to depression, low confidence, lack of employment prospects, anger issues, and drug and alcohol dependency.

Society from the state downwards is appallingly ignorant on GRT people with an attitude of 'We don't know, and we don't want to know' but there are a few organisations campaigning for change. One of them is René Cassin, who have extended the hand of friendship to Roma people in recognition of those who were murdered by the Nazis by attending the Roma Genocide Memorial Day held in Hyde Park in London every August. René Cassin take the view that as a Jewish organisation they need to be there for the Roma community to show solidarity and the true meaning of being an ally. In 2018, they launched a campaign entitled *Cut It Out*, which challenged parliamentary debate and its use of derogatory language when discussing GRT issues including the Police, Crime, Sentencing and Courts Act, and the Home Office access to land debate which effectively criminalised GRT people by default. Little or no thought was put into either of these policies – or those that preceded them – considering the needs of GRT people or using any methods of consultation with the respective GRT communities. This campaign evolved to another in 2020 entitled *Reach Out*, where René Cassin asked themselves about what methods they needed to invoke when reaching out to GRT communities – how do we become better allies; how do we lend you the hand of friendship and acceptance from the point of view where we ourselves have experienced discrimination, hate and racism? They knew what it felt like to belong to a marginalised and minority group. They asked what bound them together with GRT people. GRT people need to be consulted about the changes that need to be made. This needs to be led by the GRT communities with emphasis on doing so. Then organisations who want to be allies need to amplify their story, stating how unfair and unjust it is but that it is also their story by default.

Issues affecting young people

Young people may feel guilty about their identity and history, and feel anger and shame about the intergenerational disadvantages that have occurred in their families. Education experiences for young Travellers remain very difficult and although there are now reduced timetables being put into place in both primary and secondary schools to stem early school leaving, bullying is rife, which is a major deterrent preventing Travellers engaging fully in education. This is often coupled with schools and teachers putting minimal investment in Traveller children, resulting in children and young people being at the receiving end of discrimination whether implicitly or explicitly. This is matched with a lack of ambition in government to advance progress and equality for Travellers in the education system by failing to address early school leaving by proposing alternative provisions, including educational outreach programmes. Young Gypsies and Travellers marry young and many have children by their early twenties but have to remain living with their parents and extended families because of the chronic shortage of social housing. They often double up in a mobile home behind their parents' mobile on a halting site. This lack of space often results in having just one toilet for up to 20 people.

Young people are filled with inherited trauma from their family lineage. Racism, prejudice and discrimination have impacted on every aspect of their lives. The current level of equality for GRT people resembles something that is stuck in the 1960s. While the world has moved on for other communities, GRT people have been left behind by the state and society in general. It's still considered okay to call us 'pikey' – it remains socially acceptable whereas nobody would dare use the 'n' word towards black people with such readiness because they know it is not socially acceptable. It's interesting that society recognises the moral implication in one instance but not in the other. The word 'pikey' is freely used in everyday speech, on social media and there are even websites that freely advertise themselves as 'pikey watch' whereby information is swapped about GRT people living in their area and consists of appalling racist slurs, lies and misinformation and invites the public to add comments in likewise fashion. This is both allowed and condoned.

Tim – Romany Gypsy

Article 12

Article 12, which is applied in Scotland, is part of the United Nations Convention on the Rights of the Child (UNCRC) and is a legally binding international agreement setting out the civil, political, economic, social and cultural rights of every child, regardless of their race, religion or abilities. NGOs in Scotland use Article 12 more frequently than in other parts of the UK and it is proving to be very successful. It focuses on young Gypsy Travellers up to the age of 25 (although older young people are often married with children) to have a voice in representing their community. Groups are set up across Scotland with around 50 volunteers at any one time to empower them to learn the skills and knowledge base to be able to assert their voices in fighting inequalities. It addresses violations in state systems and enables and educates other young Gypsy Travellers in knowing their rights. Many see this as a method of ensuring that the voices of today's youth will break down barriers of prejudice that have invaded their communities for centuries.

I have seen so many success stories brought about as a result of promoting Article 12. I knew one young girl who left school at 14 because she endured terrible bullying. The teachers used to make her sit in a room and give her a chessboard to play with by herself. She joined a local group and over time her self-confidence grew and with this her passion for justice and equality increased too. She became a mentor to other young people in the group before becoming a peer educator. She seemed to go from strength to strength and eventually went to college before getting a job in community development. Now she is helping hundreds of others to find their voice and speak out against discrimination and prejudice.

Lynne Tammi – Scottish Traveller, University of Dundee

Roma

During his trip to Romania in 2019, Pope Francis met with Roma and issued a formal apology on behalf of the Catholic Church and Christians on how badly the church had discriminated against and mistreated them. He said his heart was heavy and weighed down by the experiences of discrimination, segregation and mistreatment experienced by Roma before asking for a pardon from the Roma communities for all the times in history when they have been discriminated against or mistreated or when the church looked askance at them – as well as being unable to acknowledge, value or defend them in their uniqueness. Pope Francis spoke about the distinctive gifts that mark Roma culture and their history, before adding that Roma are renowned for the respect they have for the value of life and the extended family, their concern for the vulnerable within their communities and appreciation for the elderly as well as their spontaneity and joie de vivre.

Eighty per cent of Roma in Europe – mainly Eastern Europe – live below the poverty line resulting in many migrating to Western Europe where they are usually employed in low-skilled jobs, but their quality of life slightly improves compared to the levels of oppression and discrimination in their home countries, as already mentioned in Chapter 3. However, Roma remain Europe's most disadvantaged and ostracised minority. A prime example of this is in Romania where despite the fall of communism, the social and economic circumstances of Roma largely remain way under par and mainly unchanged.

Anti-Roma discrimination is widespread across Eastern and Western Europe, where members of the mainstream population feel that only drug addicts, homeless people and those with large criminal records are less desirable than Roma, such is the level of disdain towards them. The greatest risk factors preventing Roma from inclusion and a greater quality of life rest with institutional discrimination from all state bodies, which has continuously placed them at risk of profound poverty, hate-motivated attacks and frequent harassment that ultimately prevents their inclusion in society. Only 10 per cent of crimes committed against Roma people are reported to the authorities and even then crimes are seldom investigated but met instead with indifference, anger and blame from the police (Greenfields and Rogers, 2020). One of the problems is that Roma in Eastern Europe are not considered an official minority group and as such are not covered by legal protections and rights. Many, including those in Western Europe, are at risk of being stateless because of a lack of official data confirming their existence.

It is difficult to imagine the government of any country issuing an apology over its treatment of GRT people over the course of history. But even if such an apology was hypothesised in greater detail in terms of what it would look like, it would be meaningless until there were concrete plans to end the injustices still taking place against GRT in almost every country of the world. Such an apology would have to explain the change governments were going to implement, what was going to be different, and what steps were going to bring about change both in the short and in the long term. This would need to take a bird's-eye view of the true extent of discrimination and oppression occurring because of policies – or lack of them – in all major states and public bodies because no change can occur until this is acknowledged and tackled. GRT inclusion in society can never otherwise take place. The task of NGOs to pursue this goal is herculean given the indifference and disinterest towards GRT issues in world governments and state bodies.

Irish Travellers

It is not unusual to read of discrimination in newspapers, for example, in 2021 *The Guardian* reported how certain UK holiday parks and resorts retain lists containing the surnames of well-known Irish Travelling families commonly found in Ireland and within the Irish diaspora in Britain, such as Doherty, Gallagher, Murphy, Nolan, O'Brien and O'Connell. The purpose of such lists is aimed at stopping Gypsies and Irish Travellers from staying at their facilities, which contravenes the Equality Act and Human Rights Act. Banning people from services based on their race is discrimination and is unlawful, and is reminiscent of signs displayed in hotel windows 50 years ago explicitly barring Irish people and black people. But discrimination of this kind is still found in pockets of society with some UK public houses displaying signs on their doors which state 'Travellers by appointment only'.

Back home in Ireland, planning a wedding can prove very stressful for some Traveller couples. There is always a fear the wedding reception will get cancelled if the bride and groom divulge beforehand that they are Travellers because it is not uncommon for reception venues to get cancelled at short notice or on the day of the wedding. This sends a strong message demonstrating blatant discrimination. Often when wedding receptions are allowed to go ahead, guests will be denied access to various parts of the hotel, including its public bars and nightclub.

You learn to live with it. We were raised that way. It was something we grew up with. We passed no heed of it. Is this because of racism against its own people or racism in general? Ireland has never been accepting of others coming to their country and up until the 1970s the only people of colour in Ireland were doctors in hospitals. Ireland is very territorial. Irish Travellers have always been persecuted in Ireland. They have always been viewed as troublemakers and drunks. Some Travellers did behave in a poor way but there were many more that didn't drink and never got into fights or trouble. My father was a very moral man and my mother, unlike a lot of other Traveller women, never drank alcohol. We were very poor, but my mother never failed to make a cup of tea for every person who came to our place to visit. I came from a family of thirteen – nine boys and four girls. None of us were ever in trouble with the law. My father always said that if someone didn't work for what they had, they weren't entitled to it. Once we got to an age of understanding – it wasn't nice to be ignored or singled out. But it wasn't all bad. I remember my brothers and I playing football – soccer – at school. We loved the game and we made friends and were accepted.

Robbie – Irish Traveller

Some Travellers feel discrimination and hate speech on social media is getting worse against them and feel that articles in newspapers too are full of hate towards them. Travellers read all these things and soak up the abuse. Young Travellers are afraid to tell anybody who they are and therefore try to hide it. It puts terrible pressure on them and affects their mental health. There is little trust in the Gardai (police). Some female Travellers I spoke to said that if a woman reports domestic violence to the Gardai, when they come out they are not interested in the woman's story. They just start sniffing around the place asking if the car or van is taxed or insured and don't care about the victim. Others felt that Travellers who were living nomadic lifestyles were forced into houses with no thought put into their culture regarding allowing space for a caravan or a horse. Many were placed in apartments and housing estates. Some were forced to live alongside rival families, or they are placed in sites with no proper sanitation. They felt that officials had no idea or appreciation of Traveller culture and knew nothing about what wagons, trailers, horses, dogs and goats mean to them as a people.

There is a lot of discrimination towards Travellers in Ireland. We are often called knackers and tinkers. People are suspicious of us even when we keep ourselves to ourselves and are minding our own business. Even to this day, they still come up to me in shops and if I am standing in a queue, one of the shop assistants will run out from the back and say, 'Can I get you anything?' I always play it cool and say, 'No thanks but perhaps you could ask the person in front of me if they want any help'. They usually get the message before walking off. I know that some Travellers cause trouble in pubs but when this happens, they bar everyone who knows that person and that is not fair. I love playing bingo... that's all I go for and nothing else. I talk to anybody who talks to me. Some behaviour within the community shames me but I do not behave like that – and neither does any of my family. None of my brothers or sons has ever gotten into trouble.

Geraldine – Irish Traveller

Conclusion

GRT communities have every right to live their lives according to their values and beliefs, which applies to every other UK citizen – but actions that fall outside the law are not as effectively tackled by local authorities, law enforcement agencies and other public bodies than when dealing with similar issues in non-GRT communities. As mentioned earlier in this book, discrimination has a profound effect, which starts from a young age with bullying in the playground and covert discrimination by teachers in the classroom. This starts a lifetime of mistrust in systems, coupled with an unwillingness or inability to access services because of negative experiences – either direct or indirect – of constantly being at risk of exposure to a hostile environment from the state, public bodies, schools, healthcare and youth clubs. As it stands, society has low expectations of GRT people and GRT people have low expectations of society and of themselves. Society expects GRT people to behave badly and to fail without considering the way they are treated by public bodies.

Most GRT people have battled the system all their lives and are so disillusioned that failure often becomes a self-fulfilling prophecy. There are small winds of change on the horizon with NGOs receiving solidarity from other agencies and charities who lend their support. An example of this is those who offered support and stood alongside GRT organisations and challenged legistation that directly affected GRT people's right to travel and live nomadic or partially nomadic lifestyles when they had no personal invested interest themselves in doing so.

Chapter 10 | LGBT issues

Introduction

It seems that the world holds a fascination about gay GRT people, partially because of their lack of visibility. The first public exposure came about in Mikey Walsh's book *Gypsy Boy*, published in 2009, which details the extreme struggles of being gay as a Romany Gypsy. Gay Gypsies and Travellers are often seen as exotic and mysterious, accompanied by the curiosity of seeing what it is like to be gay or lesbian in GRT communities. Life is indeed hard for Gypsies and Travellers who identify as LGBT. Tight communities and strong family values mean there is often disdain for external influences and little room for difference among the status quo. While stigma is seen to be slowly ebbing away among the younger generations, this progress is still reasonably limited. Therefore, being gay, lesbian, bisexual or transgender often remains a contentious subject, especially for those who are particularly religious and fear LGBT people as a threat to family honour and the continuing of traditions in their communities.

It's not what I think that matters. I am going by the word of God. The God of discipline – the God of order. We are all capable of sin, but we need to have the strength to fight our weaknesses. God designed marriage and sexual relations between a man and a woman – not a man and a man or a woman and a woman. That simply is not part of our DNA structure. I don't think for a second that God hates homosexuals, but he hates their practices. I do not believe in cutting and pasting the word of God to suit people and their sexual desires.

Robert (Romany Gypsy) – Light and Life Church

Sexual identity

'Monosexuality' is a term American psychologists use to describe the belief that someone can only consider sexuality from the heterosexual narrative (Nadel, 2013). They refute the idea that anyone could identify with a different sexual orientation. There are, in the main, defined gender roles in GRT communities where men are viewed as the head of the family and like to be seen as strong and macho, powerful and dominant. They are expected to be masculine and fearless in what is predominately an alpha male and patriarchal culture. On the other hand, women are submissive and generally stay in the background looking after the home and children. They are seen but not heard in the sense that their husbands speak on their behalf. There is meekness and a suppressive element to this. It has been learned and passed down from one generation to the next. Monosexuality is also prevalent in GRT communities. Even those in each of the respective communities categorically believe that there is no such thing as a gay Gypsy or Traveller. Ignorance, denial and naivety are more commonplace than often realised. There is currently a trickle of GRT people coming out as LGBT, more than perhaps a decade ago when there were hardly any. It is becoming less of a shock these days, with more families and individuals facing up to the reality that GRT communities are the same as any other community in the sense that they contain a percentage of people who do not identify as heterosexual, as well as those who don't accept the gender assigned to them at birth. But the road ahead is long. Nevertheless, homophobia and transphobia, coupled with violence and emotional abuse, side heavily with the prevailing monosexual, heteronormative narrative. Some commentators will even say that GRT communities are at least 20 years behind in accepting LGBT people than those in mainstream society.

We were brought up in the Anglican faith to believe that it is a sin. It's disgusting – not normal for two men to be together. This is something that is always down to the family. We have old-fashioned traditions. In a religious sense, there are many struggles with it. Others don't want to talk about it because they feel uncomfortable, and some mix up homosexuality and paedophilia. They think they are both the same, and these people are perverts who shouldn't be allowed around children. A few will view someone who is gay as if they are a sex offender, and if a Traveller commits a sexual offence, they are kicked out of the community. Some parents are okay with it provided their son or daughter doesn't rub their face in it or ask to take partners home. When I told my father I was gay, he asked me to keep quiet about it because he was worried that he would have to physically fight other men if they made remarks about me to him. I know of many gay men who got married young and then came out in their twenties after they realised they couldn't live their lives in the closet. They married young after being pressured into doing so but didn't really know themselves at the time.

Llewellyn – Romany Gypsy

Rejection and stigma

GRT people who keep quiet about being LGBT do so for a variety of reasons. Some will have heard negative stories about gay people and are fearful of being 'outed' (a person's sexual or gender identity being revealed). Others will be battling self-hatred and internalised homophobia after listening to family members or others in their communities who say scathing things about gay people – referring to them as unclean, problematic and threatening. This homophobia almost mirrors mainstream society's discriminatory beliefs about GRT people. For GRT people who are gay or lesbian, there comes a point when they realise they must wade through double discrimination. However, the second discrimination is a bitter pill to swallow, especially coming from the community from which they most crave to receive support.

Overall, there are still only a tiny minority of people who are open about their sexuality. Therefore, there isn't a way to fully determine how people in their community will react, but a negative response is highly likely. Families don't welcome conversations about LGBT issues, and often it is in an uncaring and unkind manner when it does get mentioned. There is also the mistaken assumption that if someone becomes close to a gay person, they will influence them into becoming gay. The subject of homosexuality is quashed through ignorance and fear. Culture and religion are not necessarily a barrier to the acceptance of LGBT people. There will be those with open hearts who accept a family member who is gay or lesbian. More often, non-acceptance is because of cultural conservatism and family pressure to get married and have children.

Gypsies and Travellers often feel shunned by mainstream LGBT culture and their own communities, where there is sometimes a high emphasis on 'traditional' gender roles and the 'nuclear family' and procreation as part of conservative religious values. Homosexuality is not tolerated and, therefore, becomes part of a dark and secretive way of life. Some religious Roma families consider homosexuality to come from the devil. They believe that people who experience same-sex attraction are fast-tracking their journey to hell. Many gay people and lesbians feel alienated from the community and develop an ambivalent or conflicted relationship about their own GRT identity. The shame and guilt inflicted upon those who are LGBT is enormous, forcing many to live their lives in denial and in secret, fearing for their health and emotional well-being. By the age of 18 or 19 – and sometimes younger – most are married. Some gay young people even get married to escape suspicion. 'Coming out' in GRT communities verges on the impossible as it's inevitable that these people will face intimidation, bullying, rejection or violence. Older men who are not married and are suspected of being gay get beaten up. Some have been known to become dependent on alcohol or drugs.

LGBT spaces and organisations are not always Traveller friendly and often come with the same prejudices, racism and discrimination that GRT people receive from mainstream society. LGBT support services are also not culturally representative or trained in GRT culture. Furthermore, it is felt by gay and lesbian GRT people that the gay community is very prejudiced and unwelcoming towards them, making it hard for GRT gay people to reveal their ethnicity. The same applies to GRT trans men, who have been on the receiving end of comments by gay men that they are not 'real men' and 'snowflakes' in attempts to discredit them, although this applies to other trans men as well as those from GRT communities. This prejudice is the result of years of being teased or bullied about their own sexuality that has resulted in some gay people becoming protagonists against what they see as 'outsiders' entering their community. Either way, this exclusion has done terrible emotional damage to LGBT people, especially those fighting internalised homophobia and transphobia.

People are born that way but, in our community, it is 1000 times harder to be gay. I believe people are better off keeping this private part of their lives to themselves. Parents don't want to see their sons kissing and cuddling other men or women kissing other women. They don't have to tell anyone their business – they don't have to do it in people's faces. They should keep it hidden because this is something that will never go down well with Gypsy people. I know a man who went off and lived with another man in another part of the country. He used to come home to his parents, and they used to never talk about it – no questions were asked – and they got on fine – no problems. I also know another man who told his parents he was gay, and all hell broke loose. They disapproved and wanted him to change – to get married and have children. He told someone that he regretted telling anyone because of the problems it caused him.

Wayne – Romany Gypsy

Passing

The term 'passing' is used to describe somebody's right to conceal their sexual orientation to fit in. The pressure to 'pass' as heterosexual is like constantly wearing a mask, and the struggle this presents is sometimes unbearable, but many prefer to remain in the 'closet' by not publicly revealing their sexuality.

Historically, both gay people and Gypsies have been well placed to employ strategic 'passing' and determine when and where to pass as straight or non-Gypsy. Here, ethnicity and sexuality mirror each other within cycles of concealment and revelation. GRT people often already live life on the edge and trying to conceal being LGBT means living life on the very edge of that edge. They start early in life by hiding their ethnicity, so when it comes to hiding their sexuality, they have often mastered the skills of managing double invisibility. They do so because they don't want to feel the same inferiority and oppression they experienced when they revealed their GRT identity outside of their communities.

Staying in the 'closet' and passing as heterosexual has its advantages and disadvantages. It can offer safety from attack and homophobia, but it also lures the person away from being themselves and makes it harder for other gay people in their communities to come out. It prevents self-discovery and makes it difficult for GRT gay people to identify themselves to each other, which adds to the collective belief that being a gay Gypsy or Traveller is bad and wrong. This results in individuals and communities being prevented from progressing with LGBT issues. Increased visibility builds better confidence and community cohesion, but the anxiety of being found out is often too overwhelming and is considered a contributing factor to the high suicide rate among young GRT people, particularly young men.

Some queer GRT people may choose to stay in the 'closet' fully or partially to maintain the vital social, community and familial ties, bonds and relationships they depend upon for survival, safety and protection from anti-Gypsyism. Few attain the ability to be hyper-visible as both GRT and gay outside their community while also managing to stay invisible as GRT and gay within their communities. A choice is often made, if possible, but it is not that simplistic in terms of being accepted as GRT within the wider gay and LGBT community. Some manage this better than others, but sometimes certain personal characteristics can inadvertently reveal one of their identities. Some may be willing to reveal they are gay but not GRT and vice versa, depending on the situation and how safe they feel in revealing themselves. Many choose to conceal or reveal their ethnic/racial, sexual or gender identity. Some who do come out often detach from the GRT community if the community is unwilling to fully embrace them. Although some are very proud of their GRT roots and culture, the detachment is only a result of being unable to combine being gay with being GRT.

Lesbians

With the emphasis mainly on young men, there is often little consideration given to young women who are lesbian and married with children. Lesbians are often overlooked, with little or no thought given to young women coming to terms with their sexuality. This often leads to them covering up who they are or fearing they will remain stuck in a marriage or domestic situation where the chances of living an authentic and free life are remote. Women are overlooked because invisibility surrounds LGBT women in GRT communities and this creates mystery around what it means to be a lesbian Gypsy or Traveller in today's world. The expectations of women in GRT culture often mean they get married young and train to be homemakers. Social circles are limited and often difficult to break free from because everybody knows everybody else. If a woman is having an affair with another Romani or Roma woman, everybody will find out. It is very difficult to meet other women outside the community because women, particularly in traditional families, are seldom allowed to go out by themselves. They also have limited privacy when accessing the internet. Only those who work can seize the opportunity to meet other women. Those who do form relationships usually do so with a non-Romani or non-Roma woman to preserve their privacy and feel safe that they won't get 'outed' by somebody from their community. Sometimes women are pushed into child-arranged marriages which become a 'trap' for life, and should it be suspected or confirmed that they are lesbian, the quest for parents to get their daughters married doubles. Although more GRT women are coming out as lesbian than ever before in history, the numbers are still relatively small because LGBT people in GRT communities still face enduring stigma, exclusion and marginalisation from those closest to them.

My grandmother totally loved me although I knew if I was anybody else, she wouldn't have been as accepting. But with me, she accepted me, all my girlfriends and later my wife. She said to my wife, 'I am your granny' and when she'd send her a birthday card, she would sign it off as 'Granny', which was so lovely and sweet. There was silent homophobia with my other family when I came out. Some didn't even come to my wedding. My wife was upset and didn't want anything more to do with them, but I wasn't bothered about it. Many people in my community know I have a wife and are fine with it – or at least to my face anyway. I have straight friends in the community who are allies because they defend LGBT people in their families when the topic comes up. Before I switched to girls and came out, I had a boyfriend. I thought I was bisexual for a time and thought my family would be more accepting of this, but they used to say to me 'why do you want to be with a woman when you can also fancy a man?' When I first came out, I thought that I needed to look like what I considered a stereotypical lesbian so instead of wearing my usual girly dresses and make-up I dressed as androgynously as possible and even sometimes wore men's clothing. But I then realised how stupid this idea was before switching back to female clothes. At that point, I was feeling very proud to be gay. Some Romani Gypsies have never come out because they fear being shunned, although these days there is better support than in previous decades. There are lots of LGBT charities for GRT people, along with Traveller Pride. I know of some gay men who were rejected by their families but returned years later and were accepted. It really depends on the person and their family. There are bigots in every family who will make life difficult for others. It is easier for lesbians to come out than gay men because with men there is a lot of camaraderie about being a man and having sex with women.

Rebecca – Romany Gypsy

Gay and bisexual men

Machismo is defined as a strong sense of masculine pride, whereby you are expected to act a certain way and being gay is not part of this. There is an expectation in

GRT communities that men will procreate and carry on the family name. Therefore, many hide the fact that they are gay, fearful of the hurt, rejection and ostracism they will suffer after perhaps having witnessed others in their community suffering a similar fate. Even when this fails, they stay in the marriage, and some may have gay encounters. Others get divorced and enter gay relationships away from their communities.

I have a live-and-let-live attitude to it provided none of them try it on with me! I don't see it as a problem. Each to their own is my motto.

Daniel – Romany Gypsy

There are signs that some younger GRT men in general are breaking away from confined roles and are developing a growing ability to conform to less structured lifestyle expectations than those that exist in their communities. But nevertheless, the vast majority of GRT men are seen, and like to be seen, as icons of manliness. Physical strength and male camaraderie are commonplace in the Travelling culture. While this can have its advantages, it also leads to toxic masculinity, noxious opinions and a masculine mindset that often becomes a pit of anger and resentment against the world that they perceive as rejecting them. To be gay among this is not easy as there is little room for difference. Being gay is seen as a weakness, an outside malaise that does not fit well in the GRT lifestyle of strength and solidarity. Gay Gypsies and Travellers who are effeminate have a tough time and are forced to pass as 'straight' by their fathers and brothers. Some are pushed into marriage in the belief that this will cure them, toughen them up or straighten them out. This is particularly prevalent in Roma communities where rugged masculinity is generally a preferred way for men to present themselves.

Many people in GRT circles are of the mindset that someone being gay in the family hurts their family honour and their culture is seen as family orientated, while others believe in the expectation that everyone should be heterosexual, especially in traditional families. Although religion impacts massively, there is also a community denial that LGBT issues exist in Roma communities.

Fremlova (2021), who was the first author in the world to write a book about LGBT Roma, referred to roles within male sexual relationships (top and bottom) and the surprise that some men have when they enter sexual relationships with Gypsy men at discovering that some of them are 'passive'; it is expected that all GRT men will penetrate their partner given the perceived stereotypical societal view of their machismo.

There is a shielding in Eastern European countries where Roma people have little opportunity to become exposed to liberal attitudes. The culture of the community often doesn't allow outside exposure. As a result, LGBT issues remain very sensitive and taboo in most of these countries. Large parts have declared intolerance against LGBT ideology or ideologies that undermine the family. Post-communism has seen a regression of LGBT issues and the ability to lead an open gay lifestyle in certain former communist countries – Poland, Czech Republic, Slovakia and Hungary. Communism was never accepting, but in the past ten years, complete regression and rejection of LGBT lifestyle has seen harsher laws, hostility and attacks against LGBT people. However, some countries have started to backtrack after the EU said it would freeze funds if these human rights violations continued. The majority of those who are openly gay or lesbian in Eastern Europe are not from traditional Roma families, where homosexuality is totally rejected. Gay Roma in the UK have expressed the freedom they felt at being allowed to enter relationships and avail of support from LGBT organisations, which is something they would never see happen in their home countries.

My father advised me to go and live in Dublin. It was not that he or my mother had a problem with me being gay, but he pointed out to me that I had younger siblings. He was worried what people might say to them about me and how they would feel, and react, and how it would affect them. My parents wanted to protect me and wanted to do what they felt was safest for me to do. In every community you get people who peddle myths and lies (with or without malice). This was easier to do before the age of the internet because people didn't always have that much access with the outside world or mix with outsiders. So, if someone said wrong things about HIV/AIDS it was easy for them to be believed. But these days, the younger generation is very clued up on everything because they are regular social media users.

Bernard – Irish Traveller

I knew from an early age that I was gay. My mother knows. My father died when I was four. I never married but I have two children, which some people find strange. The reason for this is that I wanted my name to be passed on to future generations. The mother of my children was aware that I was gay but didn't mind because I was well hung! I didn't feel awkward having sex with a woman because it was worth it to have my babies. I have ten brothers and sisters. They all know and although not all of them like the fact, they have learned to accept it. I have always been open about my sexuality. My attitude has been that if people don't want to talk to me, then that's fine. I was sleeping with men for cash from the age of 12 and nobody in my family knew. I never saw it as abuse when I was younger. It just felt normal for me. Sex equalled cash. Gypsies still come to me for paid sex. Some are married – others not. I have regular customers. I charge them for what they want. Some are okay with oral sex. I don't do boyfriends. The nicest part is that I get to meet different guys and have lots of different fun.

Romesh (38)– Roma Gypsy sex worker

Trans people

There is no formal data to indicate how many transgender people there are in GRT communities, but anecdotal evidence suggests low numbers. While attitudes are generally becoming more liberal within GRT circles about LGBT members in their communities, making it easier for gay and lesbian people to come out, it is notable that the same does not apply to trans people. Many GRT people find the concept of transgender difficult to believe.

There will be people in my community who see them on television and say they are freaks, mentally ill or question if they are from a foreign planet. They think it is a choice.

Aleko – Roma

Ruby, an Irish Traveller, spoke to Warde (2021) about her experiences of being a trans woman. Ruby first came out as gay before trans because she thought it would be easier for her parents to process. It took Ruby several years to figure out she was trans and not gay. She even believed she was just a feminine gay boy because she knew so little about transgender issues and could not express exactly how she felt. Coming out as gay went well, but from the moment she told people she was trans, things between her parents and friends began to change as they could not accept or understand it. Ruby thinks that many other GRT people come out as gay even though they are trans because they fear being ostracised if they reveal their true gender identity. This is simply because gay Travellers are a minority within a minority, and therefore the community is ignorant towards it. But being trans results in another level of prejudice completely. Ruby moved from her native County Kerry to London to build a new life, but was assaulted by a group of Travellers. She explained:

I was attacked one time in London, while out with my female cousin. It came from Traveller lads driving around in a van. I even had to call the police. They firstly threw eggs at me as they drove past while also shouting transphobic slurs at me, words like 'tranny' and others. Then when they stopped driving, one of the men got out and came towards me and punched me.

(Warde, 2021, p 27)

The Romani Cultural & Arts Company (2021) conducted research with some LGBT+ people working in the arts across the UK, Ireland and Europe. One of the interviewees was Sandra, an actress from Serbia who was a non-binary (gender fluid) Roma person. Their (*preferred pronoun*) early life experiences comprised their parents expecting them to marry and have children. At 16, it became clear that they couldn't follow these traditions and, at the same time, they realised they were becoming more and more attracted to women, so they left and went to work in a city. After they moved, they avoided contact with the wider Roma community, knowing it would disapprove of their lifestyle. They also avoided Roma LGBT+ people and groups as they felt these were overly dominated by men. They summed this up as follows: *'It doesn't matter if men are gay or not, there is still a kind of machismo or sexism or that men still occupy too much space in our community'* (Romani Cultural & Arts Company, 2021, p 162 – *Gypsy, Roma and Traveller LGBTQ+ Spoken History Archive*).

Fremlova (2021) mentions in her book how trans visibility in Pride marches throughout Western and Eastern Europe is increasing. Although not in large numbers, their presence is there even at Pride events in places like Bucharest, Budapest and Prague. Small numbers of GRT people are also gaining visibility in UK Pride events. Fremlova interviewed some trans people who spoke about their lives and the challenges they face. Here is one such example:

I'm a gay Roma trans guy. But I don't feel part of the Roma community. I'm a bit afraid how the Roma community will react if they know I'm trans because I don't know how transphobic the straight hetero community will react. I identify just as a guy. It's also really hard to see how my sex life is changing because I'm more and more attracted to other guys. I always heard from friends who were transitioning that afterwards they're just into gay guys. It's really hard because I don't have a dick and they expect me to have one. The gay community is really transphobic. They fetishise trans women as objects, and trans men are non-existent because they don't have a dick.

(Fremlova, 2021, pp 158–9)

Conclusion

Hope hinges on the younger generation of gay and lesbian Gypsies, Roma and Travellers to break down barriers by becoming more visible in their respective communities. This will entail bravery because they will face hostility both within their own communities and in the outside world, but the more people who are open about their sexuality, the greater the chance that stigma, rejection and homophobia will eventually weaken or subside. Admittedly, it is still harder for women to reveal their sexuality than men. Men can easily move away from their community, but women find it harder to build a new life alone in a town or city away from family support. This too needs brave souls to break the cycle that prevents such change. There are those who consider GRT communities to be at least 20–25 years behind mainstream society when it comes to LGBT issues, but this could change direction within a decade. Future aspirations lie with those willing to embrace change and challenge backward attitudes and homophobia in their communities. Social media platforms and Pride gatherings are changing perceptions by offering hope to those feeling trapped. However, afterwards they must return home to perhaps a place that is not that safe and once again they have to cover up their sexual identity. If LGBT organisations address their negativity towards LGBT people from GRT communities, this too could prove a catalyst for great change and progress in improving the lives of those often marred by confusion, loneliness and secrecy.

Epilogue

Bob

Since the late 1950s (and from the age of 11), Robert (Bob) Dawson has been collecting Gypsy and Traveller stories. This involved going to camp sites and listening to the elders telling tales that fascinated him – and still do to this very day. Bob has kindly given me permission to write an abbreviated version of one of the stories, 'Four Tasks and Mother Hedgehog', from his book *Gypsy Traveller Folk Tales – England, Wales, Scotland, Ireland*.

Bob told me that in addition to entertaining listeners, a high proportion of stories were about survival and overcoming adversity. The stories were created to answer almost any question. For example, *'what would you do if a gorger asked you that question – or posed a threat – or put you in a difficult situation? How would you get around that problem?'* Therefore, the stories were for specific purposes and to help with learning and explaining how to cope with the world.

Many of the stories held a key to how someone would get out of a difficult situation because Gypsies and Travellers have, in the main, no trust of gorgers and feel that they have been conned and persistently lied to by officialdom. Bob went on to say how Gypsies and Travellers have low self-worth because society has made them feel lousy and to believe that they are 'crap' at things. This only intensifies the need to keep trying and not to give up hope. Most of them have been taught from an early age to watch gorgers and, when they do, they will come out on top in time.

Hedgehogs held a special place in the lives of Gypsies and Travellers and often meant the difference between having something to eat or enduring starvation. They were a particular favourite to catch each autumn time when quite fat. Bob told me that he too has eaten hedgehog, cooked by some Gypsies he knew, and that it tasted like a cross between rich pork and chicken. Parents often gave hedgehog legs to their children to nibble on. A by-product of hedgehog was its grease, which would be poured into a pot to gel. Hedgehog grease was used like a Brylcreem to style both men and women's hair and used to have the most amazing shine.

Another lost art in today's 'settled' society of Gypsies and Travellers is their tenacity in setting up camp near forests and woods. In doing so, they knew that they would be close to where things they needed would be available, including animals and birds but also plants and shrubs. Their resourcefulness meant that through their eyes, everything had a use or purpose. Bob once collated a list containing over 400 different purposes for wood, while acknowledging the different types of wood including blackthorn, hazel and willow and how all of these were used differently. For example, blackthorn was used to make clothes pegs and larger pegs that could hold up a tent – but it was also used to make needles and hat pins which Gypsies would also sell. Wood was also very important in cooking. They used different types of wood to cook meats and stews as they believed certain things tasted better that way. Being superstitious, Gypsies avoided burning elder, believing that if they did, they would end up seeing the devil because certain chemicals in elder are known to induce hallucinations.

Bob feels sad that many of these stories are at risk of getting lost. He laments that younger generations of Gypsies and Travellers are not interested in them. The modern world belongs to them, and this does not consist of sitting around a campfire listening to their father or grandfather tell stories. Bob added that older generations of Gypsies and Travellers have told him of their fears that the younger generation are only interested in earning money – as much as they can – or engaging in shameful behaviour like crime, drug dealing or breaking into people's houses.

***

Folk story

Four Tasks and Mother Hedgehog

This is a story about a king who cared much for all his subjects. Whenever he came upon people who were poor or hungry, he ordered his servants to help them. One day a group of Romany Gypsies called at his castle. The king ordered his servants to let them in before ordering that a great feast be prepared for them. The Romanies entertained the king with music and dancing. The king loved their company and invited the Romanies to stay for as long as they liked. Unfortunately, soon afterwards the Romanies got sick with a terrible illness which killed all of them except a little boy called Raklo and a little girl called Rakli. Sadly, the king's wife, the queen, also caught this terrible illness and died. The king decided to adopt the two children and he had none of his own. He loved Raklo and Rakli and decided that one day they would inherit his kingdom.

One of the late queen's ladies-in-waiting saw a weakness in the king during his time of grief and seized upon the opportunity. She was an evil woman and one day she told him, '*Oh King, I love you more than my own life*'. The king was flattered and soon afterwards they got married. Raklo and Rakli were pageboy and bridesmaid at the grand wedding. After the honeymoon was over, the evil queen announced she was pregnant with a boy and knew of the promise that the king had made to Raklo and Rakli about inheriting his kingdom one day. She began to poison his mind against the two children telling him that they carried disease and would cause great suffering like what had happened in the past. *'Very well, my dear – I don't want you to be worried. They can go and live in my house in the country until our son has grown up but when the time comes, they will of course succeed to the throne.'*

The next day the wicked queen pretended that she was going to take Raklo and Rakli to the country house but instead she dropped them in the middle of the forest and left them with the intention that they would get devoured by wild animals. On the way home, in order to convince the king that something terrible had happened during the journey she tore off a part of her dress and gashed herself with a knife to look like she had received bite marks. She told the king that she was certain that wolves had eaten Raklo and Rakli during the attack. The king wept with great sadness. He erected a special memorial to the two children and said he would always remember them. Later that year when the king's son was born, he made him his heir.

Raklo and Rakli huddled up in the woods for warmth and shelter. Wild beasts roared all around them as they shivered as much with fear and hunger as cold. Then they were found by Mother Hedgehog. She fed them with her own milk and took them back to her home under a hedge. In the years that followed, she suckled them and taught them the ways of the wild. Raklo and Rakli learned the ways of their people so that they became experts in music, metal work and looking after the health of animals and people. Over time they fell madly in love with one another. After all, they were the only remaining people alive in their clan. Mother Hedgehog loved them and treated them the same as her own children. But time was running out for her as she neared the end of her life. She gathered up Raklo and Rakli and her other children and said, *'Listen, you Romanies are the rightful king and queen of this land. Your step-father was a good and wise man, who was misled by his queen'* before then telling them the story of how they had arrived in the forest. Mother Hedgehog then said to them, *'You must try to restore your kingdom'*, before adding *'Go – see your step-father, the old king, to be restored to your rightful place.'*

Raklo and Rakli walked to the castle and were reunited with the king and the evil queen and there they met their step-brother, the future king, for the first time. They told the king their story, but the evil queen instantly rubbished it and called them liars, beggars and imposters in front of the king. She asked for them to be taken to the dungeons for lying and trying to cheat the king. The king was unsure and didn't know who to believe. The evil queen reminded him of her injuries that day when she returned from the woods. The king pondered over it for a while before he said that that there was a way to check if they were telling the truth. He said he would give them three tasks to do and that if they successfully carried these out that they would inherit his kingdom. Before he could say anything else the evil queen interrupted him and asked if she could add another task to the list. '*Very well*', said the king.

For the first task, the king told Raklo and Rakli that in his stable they would find his favourite black stallion. He asked them to use their knowledge to restore the animal's youth. When they found the horse, they saw he was in a terrible condition and was stiff and lame with arthritis. They decided to go and ask Mother Hedgehog what to do. She told them, '*I have only a few days to live. Take off my leg, cook it and rub the horse with it.*' They protested against doing this. Rakli took off her mother's leg with tears in her eyes before cooking it and rubbing the leg over the stallion. Instantly, its grey hair turned black and shone. It was alert and pawed the ground, longing to canter and gallop as it once had before illness and old age had stopped it. When Raklo and Rakli brought the stallion back to the king, he was most impressed with the results and couldn't believe his eyes.

For the second task, the king requested '*With your skills with metal, you must make me a sword which is so strong as to cut down a great tree with one stroke, which will never rust and never be blunted.*' Once again, they turned to Mother Hedgehog for guidance. '*Pull out a handful of my prickles*' she ordered. '*And when you beat the white hot metal into a sword, place my prickles on the metal and beat them into the iron.*' The king liked the new sword and put it to the test. He hewed through a block of stone, but the sword was not even dented. He then dipped it in seawater but still it did not lose its shine. The king was amazed and once again lavished praise on Raklo and Rakli.

For the third task, the king said '*In my grounds, there is a lake. I no longer want it where it is but moved away with the selfsame water and all the fish and creatures that live in it to a new place at the far end of my estate. But the task must be completed by dawn tomorrow.*' Raklo and Rakli went to Mother Hedgehog and told her of the task. She was near death and spoke only in a whisper. She asked them and her children to take her to the shore of the lake. They carried her gently and laid her on a bed of leaves near the lake. She said, '*Play me some music that my passing will be eased.*' As they sang and played the music, Mother Hedgehog died. Raklo and Rakli's sorrow and tears knew no bounds. They tore their clothing and, in their grief, sang the songs of the woods and the heaths. As they sang, their sorrow spread to the lake. The water was turned to thick ice of grief. So, they broke up the ice and for the rest of the night, weeping as they worked, they carried blocks of ice to its new location with fish and other creatures frozen in the ice itself.

EPILOGUE

The king was amazed – and overjoyed when he saw the new lake. He could clearly see they were telling the truth but before he could say anything, the evil queen piped up and said, '*You promised me, oh king, that I could give a fourth task. If they succeed, it is my own beloved son who will lose the crown.*' The evil queen ordered Raklo and Rakli, '*Go, travel to the villages and towns. Ask the people if they want Gypsies to be the king and queen of the land. As soon as you find one of your subjects who agrees with you, bring him or her to me and you will indeed be king and queen.*' Raklo and Rakli visited every town asking people, '*Will you allow us to stay? Will you let us be your king and queen?*' But everywhere they went people laughed at them and said '*We want no Gypsies here! Be our king and queen? Why, you are dirty and scruffy and smell of the woods and the fields. You are thieves and you leave mess. Begone!*' before taking sticks to them and making sure they went far away.

References and suggested reading

Acton, T and Mundy, G (1999) *Romani Culture and Gypsy Identity*. Hatfield: University of Hertfordshire Press.

Advicenow (2018) *A Survival Guide to Child Protection for Roma Parents*. [online] Available at: www.advicenow.org.uk/guides/survival-guide-child-protection-roma-parents-1 (accessed 31 May 2022).

All Ireland Traveller Health Study (2012) *Selected Key Findings and Recommendations for the All Ireland Traveller Health Study – Our Geels 2010*. Dublin: Pavee Point.

Allen, D and Adams, P (2013) *Social Work with Gypsy, Roma and Traveller Children*. London: CoramBAAF.

Allen, D and Hulmes, A (2021) Aversive Racism and Child Protection Practice with Gypsy, Roma and Traveller Children and Families. *Seen and Heard*, 31(2).

Allen, D and Riding, S (2018) *The Fragility of Professional Competence: A Preliminary Account of Child Protection Practice with Romani and Traveller Children*. Budapest: European Roma Rights Centre.

Amnesty International (2010) *Human Rights on the Margins – Roma in Europe*. London: Amnesty International.

Anonymous (2019) *Traveller Culture and the History of Curriculum: A Curriculum Audit*. NCCA: National Council of Curriculum and Assessment.

Banari, R (2020) *Voluntary National Review. Youth Power – on the Implementation of the 2030 Agenda for Sustainable Development*. Chișinău: National Youth Council of Moldova.

Bhopal, K and Myers, M (2008) *Insiders, Outsiders and Others: Gypsies and Identity*. Hatfield: University of Hertfordshire Press.

Bhreatnach, A (2006) *Becoming Conspicuous: Irish Travellers, Society and the State 1922–70*. Dublin: University College Dublin Press.

Bosujak, B and Acton, T (2013) Virginity and Early Marriage in Relation to Children's Rights Among Chergashe Roma from Serbia and Bosnia. *The International Journal of Human Rights*, 17(5–6): 646–67.

Bowers, J (2016) *Gypsies and Travellers: Their Lifestyle, History and Culture*. Travellers' Times.

Buchbinder, D (2013) *Studying Men and Masculinity*. London: Routledge.

Cemlyn, S (2012) *Research in Social Work with Gypsies and Travellers – 1983–2012*. Bristol: University of Bristol for Policy Studies.

Clark, C and Greenfields, M (2006) *Here to Stay: The Gypsies and Travellers of Britain*. Hatfield: University of Hertfordshire Press.

Collins, T and Ward, A (2010) *Irish Traveller Women in London: A Celebration of History and Culture*. London: London Irish Women's Centre.

Cressy, D (2018) *Gypsies: An English History*. Oxford: Oxford University Press.

Dawson, R (2011) *Gypsy Traveller Folk Tales: England, Wales, Scotland, Ireland*. Self-published.

Dawson, R (2000) *Gypsy Codes and Taboos*. Oxford: Blackwell Publishing.

Donegal County Council (2012) *Respecting & Connecting Communities. Building Positive Relations between the Traveller and Settled Communities*. Donegal: Social Inclusion Unit, Donegal Country Council.

Donegal Travellers Group (2021) *Strategic Plan 2021–2026*. Donegal: Donegal Travellers Group.

Equality and Human Rights Commission (2016) *England's Most Disadvantaged Groups: Gypsies, Travellers and Roma*. [online] Available at: www.equalityhumanrights.com/sites/default/files/is-england-fairer-2016-most-disadvantaged-groups-gypsies-travellers-roma.pdf (accessed 31 May 2022).

Equality and Human Rights Commission (2019) *Is Britain Fairer? The State of Equality and Human Rights 2018*. [online] Available at: www.equalityhumanrights.com/sites/default/files/is-britain-fairer-accessible.pdf (accessed 13 June 2022).

European Roma Rights Centre (2015) *Roma Rights: Nothing About Us Without Us? Roma Participation in Policy Making and Knowledge Production.* Journal of the European Roma Rights Centre. [online] Available at: www.errc.org/uploads/upload_en/file/roma-rights-2-2015-nothing-about-us-without-us.pdf (accessed 31 May 2022).

European Union Agency for Fundamental Rights (2020) *Roma and Travellers in Six Countries. Roma and Travellers Survey.* Luxembourg: Publications Office of the European Union.

Foucault, M (1979) *The History of Sexuality: Volume 1: An Introduction.* London: Allen Lane.

Fraser, A (1995) *The Gypsies.* Oxford: Blackwell Publishing.

Fremlova, L (2021) *Queer Roma.* Abingdon: Routledge.

Gallagher, M (2019) *Position Paper – Anti-Gypsyism.* London: The Traveller Movement.

Gast, L and Bailey, M (2014) *Mastering Communication in Social Work: From Understanding to Doing.* London: Jessica Kingsley Publishers.

Goldblum, P (2015) *Youth Suicide and Bullying: Challenges and Strategies for Prevention and Intervention.* New York: Oxford University Press.

Greenfields, M and Rogers, C (2020) *Hate: As Regular as Rain – A Pilot Research Project into the Psychological Effects of Hate Crime on Gypsy, Traveller and Roma Communities.* Buckinghamshire New University for GATE Hertfordshire. [online] Available at: https://gateherts.org.uk/wp-content/uploads/2020/12/Rain-Report-201211.pdf (accessed 31 May 2022).

Haiao-Hung, P (2013) *Invisible: Britain's Migrant Sex Workers.* London: The Westbourne Press.

Hancock, I (2013) *We Are the Romani People.* Hatfield: University of Hertfordshire Press.

Hawdon, J, Ryan, J and Lucht, M (2014) *The Causes and Consequences of Group Violence: From Bullies to Terrorists.* London: Lexington Books.

Her Majesty's Inspectorate of Schools (HMI) (1983) *The Education of Traveller Children.* London: HMSO.

HM Inspectorate of Prisons (2020) *Minority Ethnic Prisoners' Experiences of Rehabilitation and Release Planning: A Thematic Review.* Section 7: Gypsy, Roma and Traveller Prisoners. London: Her Majesty's Inspectorate of Prisons.

Horne, S (2019) *Gypsies and Travellers: A Teacher's Guide.* Amazon UK.

House of Commons – Women and Equalities Committee (2019) *Tackling Inequalities Faced by Gypsy, Roma and Traveller Communities.* London: House of Commons.

Housing Executive Belfast (2020) *Irish Traveller Accommodation Strategy 2020–2025.* London: Housing Executive Belfast.

Hutchinson, P, Chihade, R and Puiu, A A (2018) Predictors of 'the Last Acceptable Racism': Group Threats and Public Attitudes Towards Gypsies and Travellers. *Journal of Applied Social Psychology*, 48(5): 237–47.

Keet-Black, J (2013) *Gypsies of Britain.* Oxford: Shire Publications.

Knott, C and Scragg, T (2013) *Reflective Practice in Social Work.* 3rd ed. London: Sage Publications.

Kovats, M and Guy, W (2006) *EU-funded Roma Programmes: Lessons from Hungary, Slovakia and the Czech Republic.* London: Minority Rights Group International.

Lane, P, Spencer, S and Jones, A (2014) *Gypsy, Traveller and Roma: Experts by Experience: Reviewing UK Progress on the European Union Framework for National Roma Integration Strategies.* Cambridge: Anglia Ruskin University.

Lau, Y H-A and Ridge, M (2011) Addressing the Impact of Social Exclusion on Mental Health in Gypsy, Roma, and Traveller Communities. *Mental Health and Social Inclusion*, 15(3): 129–37.

Le Bas, D (2019) *The Stopping Places: A Journey Through Gypsy Britain.* London: Vintage.

Lemieux, P (2014) *Who Needs Jobs? Spreading Poverty or Increasing Welfare.* New York: Palgrave Macmillan.

Liddle, R (2013) What Do You Call Travellers When They Are No Longer Travelling? *The Spectator*, 26 October 2013, p 7.

Loveland, M T and Popescu, D (2016) The Gypsy Threat Narrative. *Humanity & Society*, 40(3): 329–52.

Mac Gabhann, C (2011) *Voices Unheard: A Study of Irish Travellers in Prison*. London: The Irish Chaplaincy in Britain (ICB).

Mac Laughlin, J (1995) *Travellers and Ireland: Whose Country, Whose History?* Cork: Cork University Press.

Macionis, J J and Plummer, K (2002) Racism, Ethnicities and Migration. In Macionis, J J and Plummer, K (eds) *Sociology: A Global Introduction* (pp 259–64). 2nd ed. New York: Pearson Education Limited.

Mayall, D (1997) Egyptians and Vagabonds: Representations of the Gypsy in Early Modern Official and Rogue Literature. *Immigrants & Minorities*, 16(3): 55–82.

Milner, J, Myers, S and O'Byrne, P (2015) *Assessment in Social Work*. 4th ed. London: Palgrave.

Morgan, J (2016) 'Counterfeit Egyptians': The Construction and Implementation of a Criminal Identity in Early Modern England. *Romani Studies*, 26(2): 105–28.

Nadel, K L (2013) *That's So Gay: Microaggressions and the Lesbian, Gay, Bisexual and Transgender Community*. Washington, DC: American Psychological Association.

National Council of Curriculum and Assessment (2019) *Traveller Culture and the History of Curriculum: A Curriculum Audit*. [online] Available at: https://ncca.ie/media/4324/ncca_draftaudit_travellercultureh istory_0919.pdf (accessed 31 May 2022).

Nelson, A (2012) *Social Work with Substance Users*. London: Sage Publications.

Northern Ireland Human Rights Commission (2018) *Out of Sight, Out of Mind – Travellers' Accommodation in Northern Ireland*. [online] Available at: https://nihrc.org/uploads/publications/Out_of_Sight_Out_of_ Mind_Travellers_Accommodation_in_NI_Full_Report.pdf (accessed 31 May 2022).

Okely, J (1998) *The Traveller-Gypsies*. Cambridge: Cambridge University Press.

Pierce, A J (2014) *Collective Identity, Oppression, and the Right to Self-Ascription*. Lanham, MD: Lexington Books.

Power, C (2004) *Room to Roam: England's Irish Travellers*. Research commissioned by the Community Fund. London: Action Group for Irish Youth.

Quarmby, K (2014) *Romani Pilgrims: Europe's New Moral Force*. London: Newsweek Insights.

Race Disparity Team, Ministry of Justice (2020) *Beyond Acronyms, Gypsies, Roma and Travellers in the Criminal Justice System – Guidance, Information, and Intersectionality*. London: Race Disparity Team, Ministry of Justice.

Rice, C (2021) *A Preliminary Report into the Proposal to Criminalise Trespass*. Cuffley: GATE Hertfordshire.

Richardson J and Ryder, A (2012) *Gypsies and Travellers: Empowerment and Inclusion in British Society*. Bristol: Policy Press.

Romani Cultural & Arts Company (2021) *Gypsy, Roma and Traveller LGBTQ+ Spoken History Archive*. [online] Available at: www.romaniarts.co.uk/voices/grt-lgbtq-spoken-history-archive (accessed 31 May 2022).

Ryder, A, Cemlyn, S and Acton, T (2014) *Hearing the Voices of Gypsy, Roma and Traveller Communities*. Bristol: Policy Press.

Shaw, M (2015) *What is Genocide?* Cambridge: Polity Press.

Stewart, M (1997) *The Time of the Gypsies*. Oxford: Westview Press.

Swann Report (1985) *Education for All: The Swann Report*. London: HMSO.

Sweeney, S and Matthews, Z (2017) *Friends, Families and Travellers: A Guide for Professionals Working with Gypsies, Roma and Travellers in Children's Services*. Brighton: Friends, Families and Travellers.

Taylor, B (2008) *A Minority and the State: Travellers in Britain in the Twentieth Century*. Manchester: Manchester University Press.

Taylor, B J (2011) *Working with Aggression and Resistance in Social Work*. Exeter: Learning Matters.

Taylor, B (2014) *Another Darkness, Another Dawn: A History of Gypsies, Roma and Travellers*. London: Reaktion Books Ltd.

Teater, B (2014) *Contemporary Social Work Practice: A Handbook for Students*. Maidenhead: Open University Press.

The Traveller Movement (2018) *Policing by Consent: Understanding and Improving Relations between Gypsies, Roma, Irish Travellers and the Police*. London: The Traveller Movement.

The Traveller Movement (2019) *Policy Briefing Addressing Mental Health and Suicide among Gypsy, Roma and Traveller Communities in England*. London: The Traveller Movement.

The Traveller Movement (2021) *A Profile of Prisoners in the Adult Prison Estate*. London: The Traveller Movement.

Thompson, N and Woodger, D (2018) *Recognise, Report, Resolve: Everyday Hatred against Gypsy, Roma and Traveller Communities*. London: Goldsmiths' University of London for GATE Hertfordshire.

Travellers' Times (2020) Gypsies & Travellers: Lifestyle, History & Culture. *Travellers' Times*.

Turbett, C (2014) *Doing Radical Social Work*. Basingstoke: Palgrave Macmillan.

UCD Dublin (2010) *Our Geels: All Ireland Traveller Health Study*. Dublin: School of Public Health, Physiotherapy and Population Science, University College Dublin.

Verkuyten, M (2014) *Identity and Cultural Diversity: What Social Psychology Can Teach Us*. Abingdon: Routledge.

Walsh, M (2009) *Gypsy Boy*. London: Hodder & Stoughton.

Warde, M (2021) LGBT+ Travellers: 'A Lot of the Community Are Ignorant Towards the Trans Issue'. *The Irish Times*, 25 April 2021, p 27.

Watson, D, Kenny, O and McGinnity, F (2017) *A Social Portrait of Travellers in Ireland*. Dublin: The Economic and Social Research Institute.

Webber, M (2015) *Applying Research Evidence in Social Work Practice*. London: Palgrave Macmillan.

Weyrauch, W (2001) *Gypsy Law: Romani Legal Traditions and Culture*. Berkeley and Los Angeles, CA: University of California Press.

Wilkin, A, Derrington, C, White, R, Martin, K, Foster, B, Kinder, K and Rutt, S (2010) *Improving the Outcomes for Gypsy, Roma and Traveller Pupils: Final Report*. London: Department for Education.

Useful contacts

Here is a list of some key organisations, mainly in the UK and Ireland, that lend support and guidance to Gypsies, Roma and Travellers. They are mainly the better-known organisations and the list is by no means exhaustive. This should not deter anybody from seeking further information or support from their nearest local organisation – details of which can be found using Google to search the local area or by asking the larger organisations (such as the Traveller Movement or Friends, Families and Travellers) for details of other organisations closer to where you live.

The Traveller Movement helps address Romany Gypsy, Roma and Irish Traveller inequality, exclusion and discrimination while promoting their rights.

> **The Traveller Movement**
> 40 Jeffrey's Road
> Stockwell
> London SW4 6QX
> **Telephone**: 0207 607 2002
> **Email**: info@travellermovement.org.uk
> **Website**: www.travellermovement.org.uk

Friends, Families and Travellers is a leading national charity that seeks to end racism and discrimination against GRT people and to protect the right to pursue a nomadic way of life.

> **Friends, Families and Travellers**
> Community Base
> 113 Queens Road
> Brighton
> East Sussex BN1 3XG
> **Telephone**: 01273 234777
> **Email**: fft@gypsy-traveller.org
> **Website**: www.gypsy-traveller.org

London Gypsies & Travellers supports Gypsies and Travellers to gain greater control over their lives and offers opportunities to end racism and the discrimination they experience.

USEFUL CONTACTS

London Gypsies & Travellers
Mildmay Community Centre
Woodville Road
London N16 8NA
Telephone: 01273 832630
Email: info@londongandt.org.uk
Website: www.londongypsiesandtravellers.org.uk

Roma Support Group offers a variety of services to Roma to improve their quality of life and to overcome prejudice, isolation and vulnerability.

Roma Support Group
P.O. Box 23610
London E7 0XB
Telephone: 07949 089778
Email: info@romasupportgroup.org.uk
Website: www.romasupportgroup.org.uk

Luton Roma Trust helps Roma people in Luton and surrounding areas to access accommodation, education, welfare, healthcare and employment.

Luton Roma Trust
9–10 Crystal House
39–41 New Bedford Road
Luton LU1 1HS
Telephone: 01582 414142
Email: office@lutonromatrust.org.uk
Website: www.lutonromatrust.org.uk

The Romani Slovak Czech Community Organisation offers youth diversion activities and crime prevention as well as general advice and support services at its drop-in centre.

The Romani Slovak Czech Community Organisation
20 The Hive
Northfleet
Kent DA11 9DE
Telephone: 07865 080 161
Email: info@romani.top
Website: www.romani.top

European Roma Rights Centre is a Roma-led organisation working to combat anti-Romani racism and human rights abuse of Roma people in Eastern and Western Europe.

>**European Roma Rights Centre**
>c/o Amnesty International
>Avenue de Cortenbergh 71, 4th floor
>1000 Brussels, Belgium
>**Telephone**: Non-directory
>**Email**: office@errc.org
>**Website**: www.errc.org

Gypsies and Travellers Wales helps find suitable accommodation and improve effectiveness of public services and challenges discriminatory attitudes towards Gypsies and Travellers.

>**Gypsies and Travellers Wales**
>Trowbridge Community Centre
>Caernarvon Way
>Trowbridge
>Cardiff CF3 1RU
>**Telephone**: 029 20 214411
>**Email**: info@gtwales.org.uk
>**Website**: www.gtwales.org.uk

MECOPP Gypsy/Traveller Carers Project uses community development approaches including outreach work, community-led research, film-making, casework and training.

>**MECOPP Gypsy/Traveller Carers Project**
>Norton Park
>Conference Centre and Hub
>57 Albion Road
>Edinburgh EH7 5QY
>**Telephone:** 0131 467 2994
>**Email:** info@mecopp.org.uk
>**Website:** www.mecopp.org.uk/gyspytraveller-carers-project

Bryson Intercultural offers floating support and guidance on homelessness enabling Travellers to find appropriate accommodation, maintain tenancies and gain independence.

Bryson Intercultural
2 Rivers Edge
13–15 Ravenhill Road
Belfast BT6 8DN
Telephone: (028) 90325835
Email: info@brysonintercultural.org
Website: www.brysonintercultural.org

Travellers' Times is a magazine that enables GRT people to challenge negative media and discrimination, and celebrate their history, culture and achievements.

Travellers' Times
c/o Rural Media
Packers House
25 West Street
Hereford HR4 0BX
Telephone: 01432 344039
Email: travellerstimes@ruralmedia.co.uk
Website: www.travellerstimes.org.uk

Republic of Ireland

Pavee Point Traveller & Roma Centre is an NGO working to improve the quality of life, living circumstances, status and participation of Travellers and Roma in Irish society.

Pavee Point Traveller & Roma Centre
46 Charles Street Great
Dublin 1
Telephone: +353 (01) 8780255
Email: info@pavee.ie
Website: www.paveepoint.ie

Irish Traveller Movement is a national network covering over 40 organisations working with Travelling communities across Ireland.

Irish Traveller Movement (ITM)
4–5 Eustace Street
Dublin 2
Telephone: +353 (01) 6796577

Email: info@itmtrav.ie
Website: www.itmtrav.ie

Traveller Counselling & Psychotherapy Service works from a cultural perspective with knowledge and sensitivity towards Traveller culture, identity, values and norms.

Traveller Counselling & Psychotherapy Service
6 Cabra Road
Phibsborough
Dublin 7
Telephone: +353 (01) 868 5761
Email: info@travellercounselling.ie
Website: www.travellercounselling.ie

Traveller Mediation Service works with Travellers to assist and find ways to prevent, manage, transform and overcome conflicts in a peaceful and effective manner.

Traveller Mediation Service
c/o Athlone Community Taskforce
Ball Alley Lane
Parnell Square
Athlone
Co. Westmeath
Telephone: +353 (0) 834322076
Email: tms.chrismc@gmail.com
Website: www.travellermediation.ie

Southside Travellers Action Group provides support and outreach in healthcare and accommodation support for Travellers including programmes for young people.

Southside Travellers Action Group
Unit 5
St. Kieran's Enterprise Park
Furze Road
Sandyford
Dublin 18
Telephone: +353 (01) 295 7372
Email: info@southsidetravellers.ie
Website: www.southsidetravellers.org

Donegal Travellers Project is a community development organisation helping to articulate Traveller identity in Ireland and to work towards the realisation of their rights in society.

> **Donegal Travellers Project**
> Port House, Port Road
> Letterkenny
> Co. Donegal
> **Telephone**: +353 (074) 912 9281
> **Email**: travcomdtp@gmail.com
> **Website**: www.donegaltravellersproject.ie

Offaly Traveller Movement is Traveller-led working to address issues including health, accommodation, youth, education, cultural and ethnic identity and human rights.

> **Offaly Traveller Movement**
> Harbour Street
> Tullamore
> Co. Offaly
> **Telephone**: +353 (0) 57 93 52438
> **Email**: info@otm.ie
> **Website**: www.otm.ie

Galway Traveller Movement advocates for equality and social justice for Travellers and for their meaningful participation in social, economic, political and cultural life.

> **Galway Traveller Movement**
> The Plaza
> 1 Headford Road
> Galway
> **Telephone**: +353 91 765 390
> **Email**: info@gtmtrave.ie
> **Website**: www.gtmtrav.ie

Sligo Traveller Support Group aims to address issues such as accommodation, health, youth, childcare, education, training and employment and to combat discrimination.

> **Sligo Traveller Support Group**
> 1A St Annes
> Cranmore Road
> Sligo
> **Telephone**: +353 (0) 71 914 5780
> **Email**: stsg@eircom.net
> **Website**: www.stsg.ie

Cork Traveller Visibility Group is an independent Traveller-led community development organisation pursuing social justice and equality for Travellers in Cork and the South East.

> **Cork Traveller Visibility Group**
> 25 Lower John Street
> Cork
> **Telephone**: +353 (0) 21 4503693
> **Email**: tvgcork@gmail.com
> **Website**: www.tvgcork.ie

National Traveller Women's Forum challenges racism and sexism experienced by Traveller women and promotes self-determination, human rights and equality.

> **National Traveller Women's Form**
> 4–5 Eustace Street
> Dublin 2
> **Telephone**: +353 (0) 1 7383874
> **Email**: info@ntwf.net
> **Website**: www.ntwf.net

Travellers' Voice Magazine covers a wide range of stories both nationally and internationally about Travellers and the role they play in society.

> **Travellers' Voice Magazine**
> Involve
> Nestors Business Complex
> Monksland
> Athlone
> Co. Roscommon
> **Telephone**: +353 (0) 90 64 98017
> **Email**: info@travellersvoice.ie
> **Website**: www.travellersvoice.ie

Index

abortion, 28
accents, 61
adaptability, 27
ADHD, 99
adoption, 36
advocacy groups, 19, 96
alcohol, 32, 80, 93, 94, 123, 138, 147
Allen, D, 35
Amnesty International, 52
ancestors, 43, 81
annual gatherings, 31
anti-Gypsy laws, 17
anti-Gypsyism, 148, 157, *see also* hate crime, *see also* racism
anti-social behaviour, 48, 58, 90, 93, 133
apologies, 159, 160
Appleby Horse Fair, 17, 31, 89
Article 12, 159
assimilation, 26, 49, 74, 86
asylum seekers, 55
authorised sites, 8, 9, 16, 29, 92, 134
autism, 98
aversive racism, 35

bail, 142
banned surname lists, 161
bare-knuckle fighting, 77, 87, 133, 144
Barge Travellers/Boatpeople/Liveaboard Boaters, 21
Big Fat Gypsy Wedding, 122, 153
Big Issue sellers, 67
birth registrations, 76
blood bond, 8
blood sports, 42
Border Gypsies, 20
Bosses, 60
Bowers, J, 6, 25

breastfeeding, 94
Brehon Law, 81
bride markets, 54
Bulgaria, 13, 48, 52, 53, 54, 62, 119
bullying, 100, 103, 110, 145, 148, 159, 162
burglary artifice, 132
burials, 29, 123, 127

cancer screening, 94
cannabis, 132
Cant, 80
caravans/mobile homes, 8, 13, 16, 33, 74, *see also* nomadic lifestyles
care, children taken into, 36, 64, 82, 83
Cassin, René, 157
caste systems, 65
casual work, 9, 29, 77, 132
Catholicism, 6, 55, 72, 89, 115, 117, 121, 122, 159
census, 4, 17
charity fundraising, 32, 33
child abuse and neglect, 35
Child and Family Assessments, 37
'Child missing education' investigations, 106
child protection, 64
Child Protection Plans, 36
childbirth, 14, 84, 94
children. *see also* younger generation
  coming of age, 121
  communication with adults, 49
  girls' household responsibilities, 121
  health issues, 93
  mental health, 60
  rights, 159
Children's Services, 35, 82
Christianity, 16, 55, 115–18, 127
Church of England, 115, 166

INDEX

Circus People, 19, 22
clan feuds, 20
clan fights, 143
clan groups, 48, 81
classification, 10
cleanliness, 13, 27, 28
close-knit communities, 27, 63
clothing, 27, 54, 63, 69, 72, 141, 171
cocaine, 97
cock fighting, 42
coercive control, 137–41
cold calling, 132
colonialism, 81–2
coming of age, 121
community attributes, 27
community health workers, 95, 96, 101
community outreach, 58, 138, 158
community spirit, 27, 88
concealing of identity
   changing names, 152
   history, 6, 10
   LGBT, 166, 168
   passing, 168
   police, 136
   Roma, 55, 61
   schooling, 108
   self-preservation, 17, 32, 39, 153
   statistics on, 151
   versus pride in identity, 26
contraception, 93
council tax, 12
counselling, 101
courtship, 82–5, 87, 118, 119
Covid-19, 30, 98
crime, 12, 13, 66, 89, 131–50, 152
Criminal Justice and Public Order Act (1994), 21
criminal justice system, 60, 141–7

Dale Farm, 153
Danny Cooper New Forest Drive, 32
Dawson, Bob, 176–7
De Gammon, 80
debt, 86
dialects, 10, 61, 65, 80, 128
digital exclusion, 93, 96
disability, 94, 147
discrimination, 151–63, *see also* racism
   Children's Services, 35
   crime, 133
   criminal justice system, 142
   education, 103, 110, 158, 162
   health inequalities, 91, 95
   Irish Travellers, 71, 73, 74, 80
   LGBT, 63, 167
   police, 131, 136
   Roma, 49, 50
   Roma in Ireland, 68
   suicide, 100
   women, 141
divorce, 13, 39, 119, 139
DNA and identity, 7–8, 26
dogs, 27, 28, 42, 132, 156
domestic violence, 34, 37, 39, 60, 79, 131, 137–41, 162
dowry payments, 54
driving, 104
drug-induced psychosis, 97–9
drugs, 97–9
   criminal justice system, 147
   dealing in, 132, 133
   domestic violence, 138
   Irish Travellers, 80, 89
   overdoses, 95
   poverty, 93
   Roma, 66
   younger generation, 44, 91, 93, 133
dyslexia, 43

economic abuse, 60
education, 103–13, 158
  attendance, 106
  dropping out of school, 53, 61, 104, 158
  further education, 104, 105, 107
  GRT in the curriculum, 108, 113
  incomplete secondary schooling, 26, 75, 103, 104, 106, 109, 111, 158
  Irish Travellers, 75, 82, 84
  lack of necessary skills and qualifications, 53, 103, 104, 105, 107, 111, 112
  legal right to, 12
  nomadic lifestyles, 9
  primary education, 104, 106
  Roma in UK, 62, 65
  segregation, 53
  special education, 53, 109
  special educational needs, 104
Egyptians Act (1530), 6
electricity, 12, 92
electronically monitored curfew tag (EMC), 142
elopement, 118
emotional expression, 49, 63
employment
  casual work, 9, 29, 76, 132
  crime, 133
  economic abuse, 60
  education, 105
  exploitation, 60
  Irish Travellers, 85
  modern era, 5
  Roma in UK, 62
  seasonal, 29
  self-employment, 12, 29, 62, 77, 105
  settlement for, 9
  work ethic, 12, 27, 28, 161
  zero-hour contracts, 62
endangered race, 6
English, 10, 58, 60, 62, 67

Equal Status Act (2000), 73
Equality Act (2010), 6, 14, 16, 17, 154–6, 161
Equality and Human Rights Commission, 139
eradication, attempts at, 6
ethnic group, GRT as, 3, 15, 17, 73, 79, 86, 147
European Union (EU), 51, 56, 148, 172
evangelical Christianity, 115
eviction, 52, 61, 68, 77, 154
evil eye, 129
exploitation, 59
eye contact, 49

Facebook, 40, 44, 78, 99, 101
Fair Grounders, 21
faith healers, 96
falsehoods about GRT, 12–14
family bonds and networks, 16, 36, 83, 85
family events, 17, 27, 28, 86, 106, 115
family-orientated culture, 27, 41, 61, 63, 65, 126, 129, 142, 167
Ferentari, Romania, 50, 69
ferrets, 27
festivals, 21, 80
feuds, 133, 144, 145
fighting, 40
fights, 34, 123, 133, 143
fires, 14, 29, 78, 122, 124
fly-tipping, 84, 90, 132
folk medicine, 96
food, 42, 51, 63, 127
fortune-telling, 5, 6, 13, 129
foster parents, 36, 83
Four Tasks and Mother Hedgehog, 177–80
France, 48, 50, 116
Fraser, A, 25
fraud, 132
freedom, 30, 33, 76, 88
Fremlova, L, 171, 174
fruit-picking, 28, 29, 33

funding, 51, 98, 101
funerals, 90, 109, 122–5, 126–7, 143
further education, 104, 105, 107
Fury, Tyson, 153

Galway Misleór Festival, 80
gambling, 66, 134
gang-masters, 60
gay and bisexual men, 170–2
gender-based violence, 137–41, *see also* domestic violence
genetic disorders, 94, 95
genocide, 56, *see also* Holocaust
goldfinches, 118
GP registration, 9, 93, 96, 154
Greenfields, M, 157
GRT History Month, 108, 113, 133
guns, 134
gym-going, 31, 41, 98
Gypsy (terminology), 10
Gypsy Boy (Walsh, 2009), 165
Gypsy code, 31
Gypsy Diaspora, 5
Gypsy Horse Fair, Stow-on-the-Wold, 32

haemophilia, 95
hair styling, 69, 122
Hancock, I, 7
hand-crafted items, 5
Harper, PC Andrew, 133
hate crime, 14, 136, 147
hawking, 5, 74, 85, 88, 153
health, 34, 51, 91–102, 133
  mental health, 37, 60, 79, 91, 93, 94, 97, 98, 100, 126, 147
health visitors, 94, 102
healthcare
  access to, 9, 93, 94, 96, 101, 154
  GP registration, 9, 93, 96, 154
  language barriers to healthcare access, 93
  returning to home country for, 62
healthcare workers, 91
hedgehogs, 176
high-rise blocks, 51
history, 5–7, 25, 47, 49–50, 71, 72–4, 81, 85, 108, 128
Holocaust, 55, 128, 157
homelessness, 53, 61, 77
honour, 28, 31
horse fairs, 5, 17, 31–2, 74, 86, 89, 106
horse races, 32
horse-drawn vehicles, 5, 28, 29, 30, 122
horses, 17, 27, 28, 30, 74, 179
hospitality, 27, 161
housing
  health inequalities, 92
  housing shortages, 9, 75
  Irish Travellers, 75, 76, 78
  living in, 4, 8, 9, 13, 16
  overcrowding, 36, 51, 52, 60, 76, 92, 100
  poor-quality, 60, 61, 92
  social housing, 8, 52, 59, 67, 75, 151, 158
  typical living arrangements, 8–10
Housing Miscellaneous Provisions Act (Trespass Act) (2002), 73
Hulmes, A, 35
Human Rights Act (1998), 15, 161
human rights violations, 50, 53, 147, 172

ID documentation, 62, 142, 154
identity, 7–8, *see also* concealing of identity
  DNA and identity, 7–8, 26
  loss of, 99, 105
  mixed heritage, 7, 26, 43
  self-identification, 10, 17–18
  sexual identity, 165–6
illiteracy, 11, 62, 67, 93, 96
India, 5, 7, 47, 49, 65
inequalities, 6, 82, 91, *see also* discrimination

infant mortality rates, 91, 94
institutional discrimination, 152, 160
institutional racism, 103, 108, 147, 157
Ireland, Roma in, 67–9
Irish Travellers, 71–90
   criminal justice system, 141–7
   discrimination, 161–2
   education, 104, 110–11
   funerals, 122–3
   health, 94–6
   history, 3
   housing, 13
   identification, 10
   in Britain, 85–7
   legal recognition, 16
   marriage, 8, 120–2
   religion, 115
   suicide, 99
Italy, 53

Jewish communities, 128
Joe Grey (meal), 42
jump the broomstick, 119

Kalderash clans, 54
Kale, 19
Keet-Black, J, 12, 25
Kurbetcha, 128

ladge, 10
land ownership, 30, 77, 92, 131, 152
Lane, P, 59
language
  bans on, 49
  barriers, 58
  education, 109
  history, 10–12
  identity, 43
  Irish Travellers, 80
  language barriers to healthcare access, 93
  loud speech, 49

pride in, 26
Roma, 61
large families, 36, 76, 77, 84, 121, 142
Le Cossec, Clément, 116
legal recognition, 15
legal sites. *see* authorised sites
legislation, 3, 6, 15, 17, 19, 21, 100, *see also* trespassing laws
LGBT, 40, 63, 165–75
Liddle, R, 15
life expectancy, 51, 75, 91, 94, 100
Light and Life Church, 115–18, 129
literacy, 11, 62, 67, 93, 96, 106, 107
Liveaboard Boaters, 21
lobbying, 19
local authority sites, 9, 16, 92, 96, 100, 156
London Irish Centre, 142
long-term health conditions, 92
looked-after children, 36, 82
lotteries, 63
loud speech, 49
loyalty, 27
lucky heather, 129
lung conditions, 92

Mac Gabhann, C, 85
Macionis, J, 151
Mac Laughlin, J, 71
manners, 27
marriage
  arranged marriages, 54, 119, 121, 125
  consanguine marriage, 16, 28, 94, 119, 121
  elopement, 118
  as an end to a feud, 143
  jump the broomstick, 119
  moral codes, 13
  non-legal, 118
  outside community, 7, 26, 28, 43, 79, 120
  religion, 118–22
  young, 28, 37, 53, 54, 79, 87, 119, 166

media, 14, 35, 38, 50, 79, 80, 147, 151, 153, 161, *see also* social media
mediation, 144–5
men
  attitudes to education, 105, 106
  boys transitioning to, 121
  clothing, 55, 124
  crime, 146
  drinking, 94, 123
  health issues, 96
  Irish Travellers, 76
  life expectancy, 91
  mourning rituals, 122
  prone to trafficking, 60
  religion, 117
  roles and expectations of, 57, 61, 100, 121, 137, 139, 165, 170
  toxic masculinity, 79, 171
mental health, 37, 60, 79, 91, 93, 94, 97, 98, 100, 126, 147
metal trades, 20, 28, 41, 62, 73, 77, 110, 133, 179
Methone, Greece, 5
migrants, 16
Mincéir, 72
Misleór Festival, 80
mixed heritage, 7, 26, 43
Moldavia, 13
Moldova, 53
moral codes, 13, 34
mourning rituals, 109, 122, 126
music, 4, 19, 21, 57, 59, 61, 67, 69, 73, 80, 87, 126, 127
Muslim communities, 16, 55, 115, 128

Nadel, K L, 165
National Hate Crime Awareness Week, 148
National Insurance numbers, 62
Nawkens/Nachins, 20
Nazi Germany, 48, 55, 157

negotiated stopping, 156
New Travellers, 21
Nolan, Trish, 83
nomadic lifestyles, 8, 13, 17, 30, 52, 72, 156
non-binary, 173
non-government organisations (NGOs), 1, 14, 19, 51, 76, 90, 95, 149, 154

offensive terms, 10
old ways of life, 29, 40, 44, 54, 78
oral cultures, 49
oral storytelling, 1, 44, 73, 176
organised crime, 134
Orthodox Christianity, 55, 63, 115, 127
outdoor cooking, 14, 17, 78
overcrowding, 36, 51, 52, 60, 76, 92, 100

Pavee, 72
Pavee Point, 19
Paylaree, 22
Pentecostal churches, 63, 115, 125
permanent address, need for, 9
permanent bases, 9
persecution, 17, 49, 55, 59, 69
planning permission, 9, 16
Plummer, K, 151
Poggadi Jib, 10
police
  being stopped by, 4, 136
  concealing of identity, 136
  discrimination, 131, 136
  domestic violence, 162
  evictions, 88
  racism, 147
  Roma, 55, 61
  trust in, 134, 135, 155
Police, Crime, Sentencing and Court Act (2022), 9, 156
politicians, 14, 19, 50, 83
pollution, 96

INDEX

Porrajmos (Holocaust), 55
poverty
    Children's Services, 36
    crime, 133
    health inequalities, 92, 93
    Irish Travellers, 79
    Roma, 48, 50, 52, 57, 60
Power, C, 85
prejudice. *see also* discrimination
    Children's Services, 35
    health inequalities, 93
    Irish Travellers, 71, 80
    Roma, 49, 53
pride, 7, 14, 26, 108, 151
primary education, 104, 106
prisoners, 16, 141, 146-7
probation, 38, 142
promises, 34
prostitution, 66, 172
PTSD, 37
puppy farms, 132
purity, 55

Quarmby, K, 49

Race Relations Act (1976), 14, 15, 16
racialisation, 151, 157
racism
    anti-Gypsyism, 157
    aversive racism, 35
    designation as 'white', 7
    Eastern Europe, 50
    education, 103, 108, 111, 147
    hate crime, 148
    health inequalities, 91, 95
    institutional racism, 50, 103, 108, 147, 157
    media, 14, 15
    police, 136, 147
    Roma in Ireland, 67, 68

Roma in UK, 57
suicide, 100
Rajasthani, 5
rape, 59, 125
refugees, 55
refuges, 140
religion, 16, 55, 63, 78, 96, 98, 115-30, 165, 166, 167
remarriage, 125, 140
resilience, 27, 68, 87, 93, 130
respect, 27, 34, 39, 41
Richardson, J, 151
Riding, S, 35
rights, 79, *see also* human rights violations
ringing (crime), 132
road fatalities, 93
roadside sites, 8, 9, 13, 77, 136
robbery, 6
Rogers, C, 157
Rom Romensa thai Gadjo Gadgensa, 10
Roma, 47-69
    discrimination, 159-60
    education, 109-10
    funerals, 126-7
    hate crime, 148
    history, 3
    life expectancy, 91
    living arrangements, 8
    marriage, 7
    mental health, 98
    religion, 115
    use of term 'Gypsy', 10
    weddings, 125-6
Roma Genocide Memorial Day, 157
Romanes/Rummaness/Romany/Romani (language), 10, 11, 35, 61, 62, 128
Romani Cultural and Arts Company, 173
Romania, 13, 48, 49, 50-2, 62, 160

Romany Gypsies, 25–45
  funerals, 122, 123
  history, 3
  Ireland, 72, 86
  language, 10
  legal recognition, 16
  living arrangements, 8
  marriage outside community, 7, 8
  religion, 115
  suicide, 99
  use of term 'Gypsy', 10
rough sleepers, 61, 77
rubbish/waste, 10, 157
Ruska Roma, 128
Ryder, A, 151

sanitation, 51, 53, 75, 78, 92, 162
Sanskrit, 10, 49
Scottish Gypsy Travellers, 3, 19–21, 85
screening programmes, 94
Second World War, 12, 27, 28, 161
segregation, 50, 52, 82, 110
self-employment, 12, 29, 62, 77, 105
settled status, 62
Settled Travellers, 79
sex
  outside marriage, 13, 28, 119, 120
  sex education, 105
  sexual health, 93
  taboos, 99
  underage, 57, 59, 87
  virginity, 54, 57, 99, 119, 120, 125
sexual abuse, 85, 146
shame, 10, 99, 135, 138, 167
Shaw, M, 48
Shelta, 72, 80
Show People, 19, 21
singing, 4, 57, 59, 73, 77, 83
Sinti Roma, 48
slavery, 6, 49, 60, 66

Slovakia, 53, 55, 56
smoking, 57, 94, 95
social housing, 8, 52, 59, 67, 75, 151, 158
social media, 12, 67, 80, 95, 101, 108, 131, 145, 147, 161, 172, *see also* Facebook
social services, 28, 35
Solas Anois (Gaelic – Comfort Now), 140
soldiers, 44
solidarity, 63
special education, 53, 109
special educational needs, 104
St Boswells Horse Fair, 32
statelessness, 160
statistics
  accommodation types, 16
  age demographics, 91
  criminal justice system, 146
  domestic abuse, 137
  Irish Travellers, 71, 85
  Roma, 47
  UK GRT, 4, 9
stereotyping
  Children's Services, 35
  education, 108
  employment, 53
  hate crime, 147
  Irish Travellers, 74, 80
  media, 38
  police, 135
  prejudice, 17
  racist, 157
  Roma, 63
sterilisation, forced, 6, 48, 49
stigma, 93, 98, 101, 137, 151, 157, 165, 166–8
suicide, 16, 39, 82, 85, 91, 99–101, 123, 157
superstitions, 128, 177

taboo, 84, 99
taxes, 12, 51, 132
terminology, 3, 10, 47, 49

theft, 132, 146
tin-smithing, 72
traditional values, 27, 54, 141
trafficking, 59, 66
trans people, 173
Traveller Mediation Service, 144
Traveller Movement, the, 9, 80, 131, 135, 146, 149, 155
Traveller Times, 15
trespassing laws, 7, 8, 9, 73, 100, 156
trust, 27, 58, 61, 69, 77, 93, 95, 131, 135, 144, 152, 162

unauthorised sites, 8, 13, 156
unemployment, 53, 68, 76, 93, 100, 111, 112
United Nations Convention on the Rights of the Child (UNCRC), 159

values, 27, 34, 41, 54, 141
victims of crime, 131, 136, 147, 149, 156
violence, 134, 143, 144, 146, 151, 167, *see also* domestic violence
virginity, 54, 57, 99, 119, 120, 125

Walsh, Mikey, 165
Warde, M, 173
water, 51, 89, 92
Watson, D, 76, 80, 94
weddings, 86, 122, 125, 161
welfare benefits, 12, 62, 65, 68, 77, 152
Welsh Travellers and Romany, 19
white privilege, 38
winter, 8, 22, 154
women
   assumed promiscuity of, 13
   attitudes to education, 106
   clothing, 27, 54, 63, 69, 124, 141
   crime, 146
   domestic work, 5
   girls' education, 54
   lesbians, 169
   life expectancy, 91, 94
   mourning rituals, 122
   prone to trafficking, 59
   religion, 117
   roles and expectations of, 39, 44, 53, 57, 61, 138, 141, 165, 169
   taboo subjects, 84
   women's health services, 94, 101
   young motherhood, 94
wood, 177
work ethic, 12, 27, 28, 161

xenophobia, 48

younger generation
   age of adulthood, 79
   attitudes to marriage, 120
   discrimination, 158–9
   drugs, 44, 91, 93, 133
   GRT identity, 30
   health, 91, 101
   Irish Travellers, 78
   matchmaking, 87
   Roma, 65, 67
   understanding of history, 31, 34, 82
youth offending teams, 40
youth workers, 56
Youthreach, 111–13

zero-hour contracts, 62